Imperial Germany 1850–19

The German empire was founded in triumph in 1871 and crashed in disaster at the end of the First World War. The main themes of *Imperial Germany* are domestic political developments and their foreign policy context, but it also offers a balanced guide to the economic, social and cultural background of the period. It examines the process of German unification from the aftermath of the 1848 revolutions to its completion with the Franco-Prussian war of 1870. It explores the tensions that arose within an empire formed through war and against the prevailing liberal spirit of the age.

The book makes recent debates raised by German scholarship accessible to English-speaking readers and summarizes significant controversies and competing interpretations surrounding imperial German history. This important study analyses questions such as:

- How damaging was the discrepancy between political backwardness and economic progress in Imperial Germany?
- To what extent was Bismarck's Second Reich the forerunner of Hitler's Third?
- How far was the aggressive foreign policy of Wilhelmine Germany the result of domestic tensions?

Chronologically structured, this textbook is an ideal source for undergraduates and for those teaching the subject at all levels. It is also indispensable background reading for anyone studying more specific aspects of German history.

Edgar Feuchtwanger has written widely on modern German history and is the author of *Prussia: Myth and Reality* (1972) and *From Weimar to Hitler: Germany 1918–33* (2nd edition 1995) and the editor of *Upheaval and Continuity: A Century of German History* (1973). He has published biographies of Gladstone and Disraeli and taught German and British history at the University of Southampton.

Imperial Germany 1850–1918

Edgar Feuchtwanger

London and New York

First published 2001
by Routledge
11 New Fetter Lane, London EC4P 4EE

Simultaneously published in the USA and Canada
by Routledge
29 West 35th Street, New York, NY 10001

Routledge is an imprint of the Taylor & Francis Group

© 2001 Edgar J. Feuchtwanger

Typeset in Goudy Old Style by
BOOK NOW Ltd
Printed and bound in Great Britain by
MPG Books Ltd, Bodmin

British Library Cataloguing in Publication Data
A catalogue record for this book is available from the British Library

Library of Congress Cataloging in Publication Data
Feuchtwanger, E. J.
   Imperial Germany, 1850–1918 / Edgar Feuchtwanger.
      p.   cm.
   Includes bibliographical references and index.
      1. Germany–History–1848–1870. 2. Germany–History–1871–1918. 3.
   Germany–Social conditions–1871–1918. 4. Germany–Foreign relations–1871–1918. 5.
   Germany–Economic conditions–1888–1918. 6. Imperialism. I. Title.

   DD220.F48 2001
   943.08–dc21   00–046016

ISBN 0-415-20788-6 (hbk)
ISBN 0-415-20789-4 (pbk)

Contents

Chronology

1848	March: uprisings in many German states, including Austria and Prussia
	May: Frankfurt parliament opens
	September: Malmö armistice between Prussia and Denmark
	October: Vienna retaken by imperial troops
	December: Prussian national assembly dissolved; constitution imposed

1848 March: uprisings in many German states, including Austria and
  Prussia
  May: Frankfurt parliament opens
  September: Malmö armistice between Prussia and Denmark
  October: Vienna retaken by imperial troops
  December: Prussian national assembly dissolved; constitution
  imposed

1849 April: Frederick William IV rejects German imperial crown
  May: Erfurt Union signed
  June: German national parliament dispersed

1850 March: Erfurt parliament meets
  September: Schwarzenberg reopens Diet of the German Confederation
  in Frankfurt
  November: Punctation of Olmütz

1853 Zollverein renewed for twelve years without Austria

1854–6 Crimean War

1858 November: 'New Era' begins in Prussia

1859 May to July: France and Piedmont at war with Austria

1860 Prussian constitutional conflict over army budget

1861 June: German Progressive Party publishes its programme

1862 September: Bismarck becomes Prussian prime minister

1863 February: Alvensleben convention between Prussia and Russia to
  repress Polish rising

August: Austria calls meeting of German princes in Frankfurt; King of
    Prussia refuses to attend

November: death of Danish king precipitates Schleswig-Holstein crisis

1864   January: Prussia and Austria go to war against Denmark

April: Düppel fortifications taken by Prussian troops

October: Denmark surrenders Schleswig-Holstein to Austria and
    Prussia

1865   August: Gastein convention between Austria and Prussia

1866   June: war between Austria and Prussia

July: Prussian victory at Sadowa

September: Indemnity Bill passed by Prussian Landtag

1867   February: first elections to the Reichstag of the North German
    Confederation

March: Luxembourg crisis

1868   February/March: strong showing by South German particularists in
    Zollvereinparliament elections

1870   July: Ems telegram and outbreak of Franco-Prussian war

September: German victory at Sedan

1871   January: proclamation of German empire at Versailles

December: pulpit paragraph marks aggravation of Kulturkampf

1872   December: law reforming local government in East Elbian provinces of
    Prussia passed by appointing additional peers

1873   May: laws strengthen state supervision of Catholic Church; collapse of
    Vienna stock exchange marks beginning of slump

1875   April: 'war in sight' crisis

May: foundation of united socialist party at Gotha congress

June: articles 'Era Bleichröder-Delbrück-Camphausen' attack Bismarck

1877   June: Bismarck's Kissingen memorandum on German foreign policy

1878   October: anti-socialist law passed

1879   July: law introducing protective tariffs passed

1880   Secession of left wing from National Liberal party

July: Prussian Landtag passes law permitting discretionary revision of Kulturkampf laws

1881 January: introduction of accident insurance proposals marks beginning of Bismarck's social policies

1883 June: health insurance law passed

1884 February: National Liberal secessionists join Progressives
March: German protectorate over Angra Pequena declared
May: Heidelberg programme of National Liberal party

1887 February: cartel elections

1888 March: death of William I
March–June: 99-day reign of Frederick III
June: accession of William II

1889 Mass strikes of miners in the Ruhr

1890 March: Bismarck dismissed; Caprivi becomes chancellor; Reinsurance Treaty with Russia not renewed

1891 March: death of Windthorst
Caprivi's trade treaties lowering tariffs; Pan-German League founded; SPD adopts Erfurt programme

1892 December: Tivoli programme of the Conservative party

1893 February: Agrarian League (*Bund der Landwirte*) founded

1894 October: Hohenlohe-Schillingsfürst succeeds Caprivi as chancellor

1896 January: Kaiser sends Kruger telegram

1897 June: Bülow becomes state secretary for foreign affairs; Tirpitz becomes state secretary of the Navy Office

1898 July: death of Bismarck; First Navy Law

1899 November: 'penal servitude' law (*Zuchthausvorlage*) fails in Reichstag

1900 October: Bülow succeeds Hohenlohe as chancellor

1902 December: new tariff law, raising duties, passed

1903   Dresden congress of SPD rejects Bernstein's revisionism

1905   March: Kaiser lands at Tangiers; first Morocco crisis
      July: Björkö meeting of Kaiser and Tsar

1906   January: Algeciras conference
      December: Bülow bloc formed

1907   February: Hottentot elections

1908   October: Austria declares Bosnia annexed
      November: crisis over Kaiser's *Daily Telegraph* interview

1909   July: Bethmann Hollweg succeeds Bülow as chancellor

1910   March: Left liberals come together in Progressive Party (*Fortschrittliche Volkspartei*); Berlin demonstration against Prussian three-tier law
      May: Bethmann Hollweg abandons law to reform Prussian franchise

1911   July: German gunboat *Panther* arrives at Agadir

1912   January: SPD emerges from elections as largest party in Reichstag
      December: Kaiser holds 'war council'

1913   August: death of Bebel
      November: Zabern incident

1914   28 June: Archduke Ferdinand assassinated at Sarajevo
      5 July: German 'blank cheque' issued
      1 August: Germany and Russia at war
      27–30 August: Battle of Tannenberg
      September: Battle of the Marne; Falkenhayn replaces Moltke as Chief of the German General Staff

1915   May–September: German-Austrian offensive in Galicia inflicts heavy manpower and territorial losses on Russia
      July: annexationist programme by German intellectuals

1916   February: Battle of Verdun begins
      July: British Somme offensive
      August: Hindenburg and Ludendorff form 3OHL
      December: Auxiliary Labour Law permits conscription of men between 17 and 60

1917   February: unrestricted submarine warfare

April: USA enters war; USPD splits from majority SPD
July: Bethmann Hollweg resigns; peace resolution passed by Reichstag
November: Bolshevik revolution

1918   January: strikes in Berlin and other centres
           March: treaty of Brest Litovsk; Ludendorff offensive on Western front
           8 August: black day of German army after British attack near Amiens
           29 September: Ludendorff demands immediate armistice
           3 October: first note by Prince Max of Baden's government to President
               Wilson
           26 October: Ludendorff dismissed; Groener succeeds him as
               Quartermaster General
           29 October: mutinies begin in the German navy
           7 November: Bavarian monarchy falls
           9 November: Prince Max hands power to Friedrich Ebert; Kaiser's
               abdication announced

Introduction

Imperial Germany, or the Second Reich as it is often called, lasted barely half a century. Such an episode, going from spectacular rise and to disastrous fall, but with antecedents and after-effects that stretch much further, poses opportunities as well as problems for the historian. Both spring from the fact that initial success and eventual failure have to be accounted for, and that therefore themes and judgements are more insistently called for than they would be when covering a more indeterminate time-span.

In the case of Imperial Germany, historians, mostly German historians, who are closest to the subject and therefore set the tone, have adopted almost diametrically opposed attitudes, ranging from triumphalism to the severest condemnation. In the nineteenth century the national-liberal school of German historians did much to arouse the spirit of German nationalism and to popularize the notion that unification of Germany by Prussia lay in the logic of history. They celebrated the formation of the German empire of 1871 as the almost inevitable and glorious culmination of German history. This approach became virtually impossible after 1945. Much of German historiography, particularly since the 1960s, veered to the opposite extreme, seeing in the Second Reich a deeply flawed structure and the precursor to the catastrophic, morally and materially destructive, Third Reich. Two books in particular were seminal in putting forward a more negative perspective on the Reich founded in 1871. Fritz Fischer's *Germany's Aims in the First World War*, the English title of a book published in German in 1961, showed that before and after 1914 the view was widely held in Germany that it was the country's destiny to strive for hegemony in Europe and for world power beyond. This attitude was a major cause of war in 1914. In 1973 Hans-Ulrich Wehler's *The German Empire 1871–1918* put the stress on the political backwardness prevailing in Germany's domestic affairs. The ruling élites tried to preserve their control by diverting the resulting tensions into an expansionist foreign policy.

More recently, particularly since the reunification of Germany in 1990, the pendulum has swung back a little. Some German historians have been accused of trying to restore the image of the Second and even of the Third Reich in order to help revive German national pride. However that may be, it remains difficult to discuss Bismarck entirely without reference to Hitler and to examine the imperial period without becoming aware of the early roots of National Socialism. It may be the duty of the historian to understand rather than to sit in judgement and to avoid what has been called the vast condescension of posterity, yet the causal links between Imperial Germany and the catastrophes of the twentieth century are too close to be sidestepped. It is, however, precisely these questions, which arise in untangling the story of the Second Reich, that give the subject coherence and interest and make it essential to an understanding of what happened afterwards.

It is therefore useful to set out at the beginning some of the themes and problems thrown up by the history of Imperial Germany. The creation of the Second Reich is first of all a political phenomenon. Its establishment was the result of political events and not the consequence of inescapable geographical, ethnic or economic facts. German-speaking Central Europe had no clear geographical boundaries and large numbers of ethnic Germans, above all those living under the Habsburgs, were left outside the empire of 1871. A history of Imperial Germany has therefore to give pride of place to political developments, however much these depended on social, economic and ideological factors. It has to explain why unification came about through Prussia and to the exclusion of Austria.

Foreign policy in the broadest sense of the word is an essential theme in the story of the Second Reich. It was one of the merits of Bismarck's rule after 1871, autocratic as it was particularly in matters of foreign policy, that he did not seek to attach the ethnic Germans scattered all over Europe to the Reich he had created. After his fall strong currents of opinion arose, influencing official policy, which wanted to make the Reich the focus of loyalty for all Germans. This was pan-Germanism and in the Wilhelmine period after 1890 it gave rise to the fateful quest for *Weltpolitik*, the idea that Germany had a mission, power-political and even cultural, to become a leading power on a world-wide scale. The importance of the international context in both the formation and the subsequent development of Imperial Germany led the traditional nationalist school of German historiography to assert what they called 'the primacy of foreign policy'. It is the theory that it is the international environment in which a nation is placed that largely shapes its domestic constitution. If Germany was therefore a country with a strong state, in which the military held a prominent place, this was, so nationalist German historians argued, because German nationhood had to be won against a hostile world and, once established, had to be defended against the potential enemies surrounding it. The generation of German historians who came to the fore after 1945 and became so critical of Imperial Germany sometimes substituted 'the primacy of domestic politics' for 'the primacy of foreign policy'. Now it was argued that *Weltpolitik* was essentially a device by which the ruling élites of imperial Germany, particularly during the Wilhelmine period, endeavoured to perpetuate their rule. It was a diversion strategy, a form of social imperialism, by which domestic tensions, particularly the rise of the Social Democratic party, which made Germany well-nigh ungovernable under the existing semi-authoritarian system, were diverted into an ambitious foreign policy with a wide popular appeal. The critics of the 'primacy of foreign policy' theory point out that it was used to justify autocratic, illiberal and anti-democratic tendencies.

In practice neither foreign nor domestic policy has primacy and in the establishment and development of Imperial Germany they were always inter-dependent. If in this book domestic politics occupies more space than foreign policy, it is because its subject is Germany and not Europe or the international system as a whole. Moreover, much of what went on in Imperial Germany also occurred in other advanced European countries or in North America. What has to be explained is why and to what extent Germany was different. Everywhere in nineteenth- and early twentieth-century Europe, nationalism had become a secular religion, imperialism was regarded as manifest destiny, and cruder and more extreme by-products, such as social Darwinism, racism and anti-Semitism, were to be found. It is debatable whether in Germany these phenomena were more strident, extreme and influential than elsewhere. What was peculiar to Germany was that the processes of nation-building, industrialization, urbanization and many other features of modernization were compressed into so short a period of time that they became more or less simultaneous. Therefore there were exceptional problems and stresses. In many countries the growth of a numerous class of industrial workers, the proletariat, led to the rise of socialist parties and trade unions, but in Germany political socialism grew in importance before trade unionism and confronted middle-class liberalism before the latter had a chance fully to assert itself. Middle-class liberals felt challenged by the threat from the proletariat before liberalism had completely triumphed, which it never did. This explains much about the rightward turn of liberals as well as about the illiberalism of the increasingly numerous white-collar workers.

Such reflections have given rise to the theory of the German *Sonderweg*. It originated in the desire to find an explanation for the rise of Hitler and the Third Reich and the consequent descent into barbarism of a nation long regarded as highly civilized. Its central thesis is that the German bourgeoisie was much weaker than those in the major countries of Western Europe and never managed to make a successful revolution, while the one it did make in 1848 failed. Instead there was a revolution from above, largely directed by one man, Bismarck, and accomplished by Prussian force of arms. Imperial Germany was permanently set in its ways by the charismatic rule of its founder, which stunted the forces of self-government and perpetuated the rule of the Prussian military monarchy and the pre-industrial élites surrounding it. This configuration was further reinforced by Bismarck's conservative turn of 1879 (see p. 70), so that the German political system remained archaic, almost feudal, while society and economy modernized rapidly. Politics and society were therefore seriously out of phase.

The reader will find much of this picture recalled in the pages of this book. Nevertheless the Sonderweg thesis in its essence is not what structures these pages. The complexities of the real world always refuse to be subsumed in the simplicities of an overarching theory, though theory helps to make the complexities comprehensible. The weakness of the German bourgeoisie, the starting point of the Sonderweg thesis, is hardly borne out by the events of 1848 or the process of unification. There was no conclusive defeat in 1848 and, as Bismarck always recognized, the liberal German middle classes played an essential role in the establishment of the Second Reich. The Prussian military monarchy survived, because under Bismarck's guidance it allied itself with the German national-liberal movement. After 1870 the chancellor was as much the prisoner of the liberals as they were the followers he manipulated. His leading German biographer, Lothar Gall, used the analogy of the sorcerer's apprentice to characterize the last twenty years of Bismarck's time in office. The sorcerer's apprentice remembers the magic formula that evokes the flood, but forgets how to call it off.

The operation of the German political system remains crucial to an evaluation of Imperial Germany and it is a topic that figures prominently in these pages. Bismarck's overriding aim in constructing the constitution of the empire was to ensure his own survival in power, but it was not a static system and could not be, as he knew full well. The way it operated at the end was very different from what its originator envisaged at the beginning. The Reichstag based on universal manhood suffrage was meant to be a device for weakening the liberals, who drew sustenance from a restricted franchise. But it opened the way to the rise of a political mass-market and facilitated the growth of the most powerful socialist party in Europe. If the social imperialism of later chancellors, such as Bülow, was intended to distract from domestic divisions and weaken this powerful socialist party, it also cost money, which could only be voted by the Reichstag. Therefore the budgetary powers of the Reichstag became more important than ever. Bismarck toyed from time to time with the idea of removing by a coup d'état the Reichstag he had himself established, and used the threat of a coup as an instrument of policy. Right up to 1914 the idea of curtailing or altogether abolishing the Reichstag had a place in the more feverish calculations of right-wingers. But such a coup never came and might well have precipitated a civil war. The German political situation therefore remained open and unpredictable until war broke out, not irretrievably stuck in an authoritarian groove, as the Sonderweg thesis would have it. It then became apparent that German constitutionalism stood the test of total war much less well than the fully parliamentary systems of the Western countries.

Another aspect of the compromise constitutional settlement of 1871, the system of skirted decisions, as the German historian Wolfgang Mommsen calls it, was the balance between federalism and a unitary structure. The most important part of this federal balance was the relationship between Prussia and the new Reich. Prussia made up roughly two-thirds of the population and area of the Reich and it was the intention of Bismarck and his collaborators to ensure the hegemony of Prussia while saving the faces of the other federal states, particularly the bigger ones like Bavaria, Saxony and Württemberg. It was after all Prussia that had called the Reich into being by the victory of its armies. The Reich would therefore be Greater Prussia, but it soon became something else. As German nationalism developed its muscle first against its alleged internal enemies, Catholics, socialists, Jews, Poles and others, and then turned outwards, to claim its place in the sun, it became the overriding loyalty that legitimized the new state. The old Prussian ethos receded, but some Prussian features were so firmly rooted in the initial structure that they remained until the end. The élites that gathered round Court and monarchy and that occupied the leading positions in the army remained mainly Prussian, while the Prussian element receded only slowly in the bureaucracy. The most important Prussian feature that stayed in place till 1918 was the three-tier electoral law, which gave the mainly East Elbian Conservative party a privileged position in the Prussian Landtag, while virtually excluding the SPD, even when it was the largest party in the Reichstag. The Prussian Conservatives fought a desperate rearguard action to prevent the Reichstag, elected on universal male suffrage, from tampering with their fiscal and political privileges. The three-tier franchise remained their most important bulwark against change until 1918 and the most obvious target of attack for the labour movement.

Because of the survival of Prussian features, but also for many other reasons, the German political culture was very different from that prevailing in fully parliamentary systems, as in Britain or France. What is more, most educated Germans wanted it that way, were proud of their system and contemptuous of the more democratic traditions of the West. They believed in a positive Sonderweg, the Central European way, which differed from the licentious West as much it did from the barbaric East. German *Kultur* would make the world whole. It was more profound, more inward than the superficial civilization of the West, which, in the German view, was corrupted by individual greed and egotism. These were the 'ideas of 1914', when they were an arrogant response to often self-righteous attacks from Germany's enemies, but they were implicit in many German attitudes long before the outbreak of war. Such attitudes sustained a raft of arrangements, political, social, economic, that made Germany very different from other contemporary societies in Western Europe. The Reichstag may have been more powerful in 1914 than it was in 1871 and the idea of removing it less realistic, but the Reichstag parties could not and would not make the breakthrough to fully responsible parliamentary government. This was symptomatic of much else that remained unresolved, and amounted to a degree of political retardation amidst great economic and technological modernity. The belief in the superiority of German inwardness and philosophical profundity led the educated German, the *Bildungsbürger* as he was called, to look down upon politics as a lower-order, inherently flawed form of activity. This encouraged conservative inertia and slowed pragmatic reform.

For all its rampant authoritarianism, Imperial Germany was no dictatorship and harboured its own dissenters and social critics, though it sometimes tried to silence them. In the following pages there are brief glimpses of the cultural scene, where the tensions in this society were often brought to the surface and articulated. The court and the bureaucracy wanted the arts, particularly the visual arts, to fulfil a celebratory function and furnish the images to sustain German grandeur. Yet avant-gardism and experimentation was particularly strongly present in Germany even before 1914 and continued seamlessly into the Weimar Republic. Self-confidence and chauvinism existed side by side with anxiety and alienation, hubris and *Angst* complimented each other. Such an ambivalent picture of Imperial Germany is most likely to come near the truth. The one-dimensional hymn of praise offered by the national-liberal school of German historiography is now entirely unconvincing, but too much concentration on the search for the precursors of National Socialism also distorts the perspective.

Chapters 1–4, covering the period from 1850 to the fall from power of Bismarck in 1890, are structured chronologically. Similarly, Chapters 6–10 cover the period from 1890 to the fall of Imperial Germany in 1918. In between, Chapter 5 is thematically structured and deals with the economic, social, political and cultural position during the reign of William II.

Maps

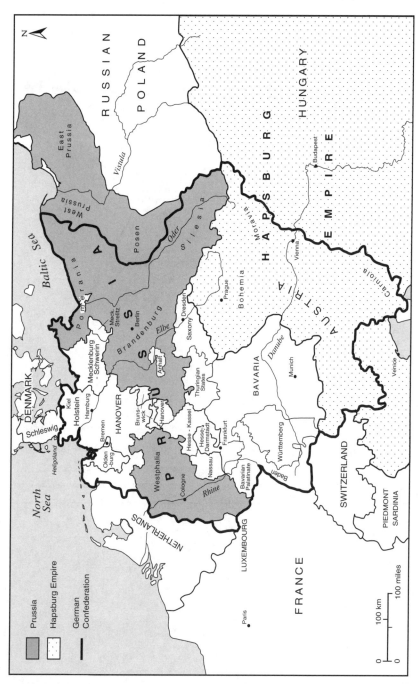

Map 1: The German Confederation in 1815

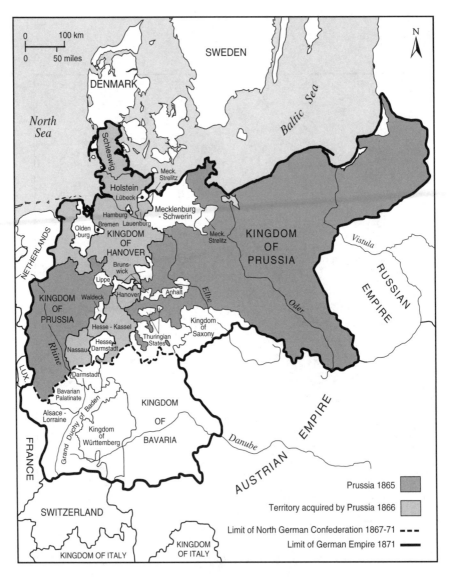

Map 2: The Unification of Germany

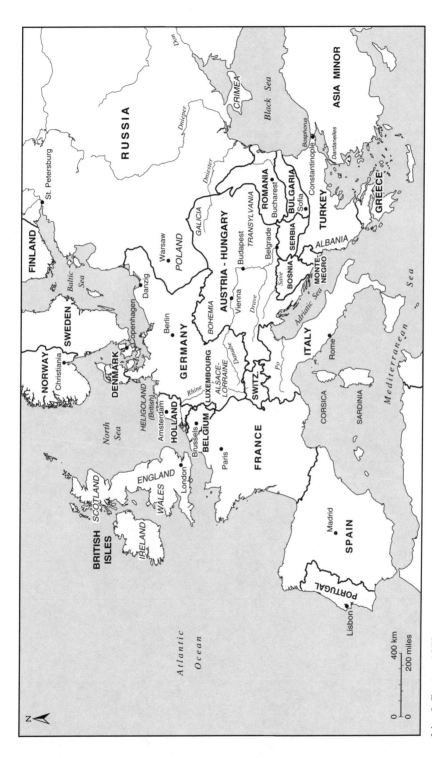

Map 3: Europe: 1878

1 German nationalism between failure and revival 1850–1862

At the beginning of the nineteenth century the first big steps had been taken towards the creation of a modern German national state. The French Revolution and Napoleon had destroyed what remained of the Holy Roman Empire and the number of territorial units that comprised it had been reduced from some 380 to about 40. Napoleon was no less important than Bismarck as a unifier of Germany. At the same time German national consciousness had become a force to be reckoned with. The German Confederation of 1815, which took the place of the Holy Roman Empire, was never likely to satisfy in the long run the aspirations for greater unity in the German-speaking lands of Central Europe. The fact that it became closely associated with the policy of repressing liberalism and nationalism further reduced its chances of survival. The early stages of industrialism created powerful material pressures for greater unity. Nevertheless German unification was not inevitable, nor was the form it would take in any way predetermined.

The obstacles to German unification were hardly less formidable than the pressures towards it. The larger remaining separate states in the German Confederation of 1815 still had a strong life and identity of their own. The loyalty of the masses was still predominantly to their particular state and its ruling dynasty, rather than to the idea of a German nation. This was German particularism with its deep historical roots. The German nation was a cultural rather than a political concept and national consciousness was therefore mainly confined to the articulate élites. Two of the states, Austria in the south and Prussia in the north, were major European powers. Their entrenched rivalry was only temporarily overridden by conservative solidarity in the period between 1815 and 1848. Germany was divided into at least two major religious denominations, Catholic mainly in the south, Lutheran mainly in the north. This religious split also carried with it a profound cultural divide. The elements of division that counterbalanced the pressures for greater unity were therefore great even within Germany, but added to them were the obstacles to German unity on the wider European stage. A united and therefore powerful German state would profoundly affect all other European powers and the relations between them. German nationalists often saw this, the hostility of foreign countries to German unity, as the greatest obstacle to their aspirations. When this unity was eventually achieved it owed much to the window of opportunity that existed in the European power constellation after the Crimean War.

The aftermath of the 1848 revolutions

The uprising in Paris in February 1848 that toppled the throne of Louis Philippe was the fuse that lit the fires of revolution throughout Germany. For years there had been many signs of restlessness in the educated classes, but in the middle 1840s there was added to it acute social misery among the poorer sections of German society. Artisans and craftsmen had for long been under pressure from the beginnings of industrialism. The competition between older and more modern methods of production was particularly evident in the manufacture of textiles. The proverbial hardships experienced by those involved in home handicrafts like weaving were now further aggravated by a general economic downturn. The peasants, still the most numerous class in society, experienced a succession of poor harvests in the years immediately before 1848.

The French revolution of February 1848, the third since 1789, therefore hit Germany at a time when the system established in 1815, usually associated with the name of Metternich, was already badly undermined. When the spark of rebellion spread to the German states, most of their governments saw no alternative to saving themselves by making concessions. This was most conspicuously the case in Vienna and Berlin. In March 1848 Metternich himself had to flee into exile in England, while in Berlin Frederick William IV gave way to the insurrection of his subjects by installing a liberal ministry and allowing the election of a Prussian national assembly. In the area of the German Confederation as a whole preparations went ahead for the election of a national parliament. It met in May 1848 in the St Paul's Church in Frankfurt. The triumph of the revolution was deceptive. The moderate liberals who dominated the Frankfurt parliament had to rely on the existing governments of kings and princes to achieve their dual objective, to unify Germany and to turn it into a constitutional state. For a time they had moral power, but they never had real power. Monarchical government had been only temporarily weakened, for the armies, on which the monarchies had ultimately to rely, continued to obey their commanders. They were recruited from the peasantry, which was as yet scarcely politicized. By the end of the year 1848 the revolution had been crushed by force of arms both in Vienna and in Berlin. The Prussian national assembly was dispersed and a constitution was imposed which left the king in control of the executive government. The Frankfurt parliament was seen to be an emperor without clothes and when its delegates offered the imperial crown of Germany, excluding Austria, *Kleindeutschland*, to Frederick William IV of Prussia in April 1849 it was hardly worth accepting. Against the opposition of the Habsburg empire backed by Russia it would have been dangerous to accept. Within weeks the rump of the Frankfurt parliament was ignominiously dispersed. In the early summer of 1849 there were further radical uprisings, particularly in southwest Germany. The aim of the radicals was to establish, at a late hour, a united republican and democratic German state, the cause which in their eyes the moderates had betrayed. These risings were suppressed by force. The principal objectives of the revolutionary movement of 1848, to replace the German Confederation of 1815 with an externally more unified and internally more progressive framework, had not been achieved.

The last chapter in the catalogue of failure was the attempt to form a union of states around Prussia, loosely linked to Austria, which came to an end with the Treaty (Punctation) of Olmütz of December 1850. This union was an early version of what came about twenty years later, a German Reich without Austria established from above. The attempt to create such a union from below had failed with the refusal of Frederick William IV to accept the imperial crown offered him by the Frankfurt parliament. Frederick William hated revolution and one of the main reasons for his refusal was that he did not wish to wear a crown that to him was tainted by revolution. Yet he was romantically attached to the idea of a more unified German fatherland and would have welcomed something like a revival of the Holy Roman Empire. He naturally wanted to increase the power and influence of Prussia, but he was reluctant to exclude Austria from her traditional German role. He adopted the union project under the influence of Josef Maria von Radowitz, with whom he had formed a close friendship. Radowitz was a Catholic and, although not of Prussian birth, had risen in the Prussian service. This was not unusual, for many who distinguished themselves in the service of Prussia, for example Stein, the great reformer of the Napoleonic age, were not themselves Prussians. Radowitz persuaded the king that some elements of the national as well as of the constitutional aspirations of 1848 needed to be satisfied to achieve a new stability. The union project was to be realized through agreement with the other German rulers, but it was to have a constitution with an elected parliament. The moderate liberals of the Frankfurt parliament, who had offered the German imperial crown to the Prussian king, accepted the union as the best they could obtain in the circumstances and as a way of rescuing something from the wreckage of their hopes. The parliament of the union, elected on the restrictive Prussian three-tier franchise (see p. 10), met in March 1850 in Erfurt.

In the meantime, however, Austria was rapidly recovering her power and was not prepared to forgo her traditional leading position in Germany, which would have been the consequence if the Erfurt union had succeeded. Prince Felix Schwarzenberg was now the effective controller of Austrian policy, having gained the ear of the young Emperor Francis Joseph. He was determined to reassert the position of the Habsburg Empire as a coherent whole, as a great European power as well as the premier German power. Frederick William IV was indecisive and ultimately not prepared for a confrontation with Austria. He was torn between asserting the interests of the Prussian state and restoring the solidarity of the conservative powers that existed before 1848. Radowitz had many enemies, particularly among the Prussian ultra-conservatives, who regarded the union project as revolution in disguise. Austria's time of weakness, when the Prussian union might have had a chance of success, was allowed to pass. It was crucial for the Habsburg empire that it had the support of the Russian Tsar, Nicholas I, in eliminating what remained of the revolution, particularly in Hungary, and in shoring up its German position. Nicholas was suspicious of the Prussian union, again because it smacked too much of revolution. In Germany Schwarzenberg made the re-establishment of the Confederation of 1815 in a more effective form the means of regaining Austria's position as the first power. Bavaria, the largest of the medium states and traditionally close to Austria, had never signed up to the

Prussian union, considering it incompatible with the preservation of her sovereignty. Gradually the other medium and smaller German states abandoned the Erfurt union and rejoined the old Confederation. Only the small North German states surrounded by Prussian territory remained in the Erfurt union.

Matters came to a head in the summer of 1850 over Schleswig-Holstein and Electoral Hesse. The clash between German and Danish nationalism in the two northern duchies bulked large in the events of 1848. When Prussia in September 1848 signed an armistice with Denmark and refused to continue the fight on behalf of the Frankfurt parliament, it was a great blow to the revolutionary cause and the impotence of the parliament was cruelly revealed. After a final flare-up of conflict the two duchies were returned to the Danish crown and their future was settled internationally. In Holstein a regime that owed its origin to the revolution resisted the return of the Danes. The Confederation, obligated by treaty, ordered a federal execution against the Holstein authorities. Prussia objected to this move, Frederick William IV uncharacteristically aligning himself with German national sentiment. In Electoral Hesse the situation came even closer to an armed clash between the two major German powers. The Elector Frederick of Hesse had demanded the intervention of the Confederation against his own parliament, civil service and army, who were resisting his counter-revolutionary policies. Electoral Hesse was still a member of the Erfurt union and Prussia was directly challenged in her vital interests. Her lines of communication to her Rhine provinces lay through Electoral Hesse. In face of Austrian pressure, backed by Russia and most of the smaller German states, Frederick William IV gave way and Radowitz was dropped. The result, Olmütz, was widely seen as a Prussian humiliation, but neither did Austria fully realize her aims. The full restoration of the German Confederation was left to a later conference. The adherence of the Habsburg empire as a whole to the Confederation, the key element in Schwarzenberg's policy, was left in abeyance.

The conflict between Austria and Prussia in Germany was thus left unresolved. It was the problem of deciding between Germany including Austria, *Grossdeutschland*, or Germany without Austria and therefore led by Prussia, *Kleindeutschland*, that was the single most important reason for the failure of the 1848 revolution. The German-speaking areas of the Habsburg Empire could not be integrated with the desired German national state without splitting that empire. By 1849 it was too late to make the other alternative, a Prussian-led Germany without Austria, a reality. The price of excluding Austrian was even then seen to be high and for many, certainly for most German Roman Catholics, too high.

The dilemma between *Grossdeutschland* and *Kleindeutschland* was the most intractable aspect of the double task that faced the men of 1848. They had simultaneously to create a nation and accomplish a transformation of the internal power structure of that potential nation. The difficulties of the internal transformation occasioned equally deep divisions. The majority of the men who came together in the Frankfurt parliament were moderate liberals, who wanted to transform Germany into a constitutional state with the consent of the existing monarchical governments. To do this they needed the popular thrust which in the spring of 1848 frightened the kings and princes into making concessions. Yet the liberals were afraid of these popular forces and were at least as concerned to limit the chaos that might threaten from the streets as they were to limit the powers of the monarchies. The popular revolution soon ebbed and disillusionment with the parliamentary liberals was a factor in this decline of revolutionary fervour. The democrats and republicans who sought to direct the popular wave were themselves not a coherent force. Moderate democrats blamed the extremism of the republicans and socialists on their left for the failures. Everything was vastly complicated by the regional diversity of Germany. The revolutions of 1848 did not succeed anywhere in Europe in permanently setting up democratic republics. The peasantry, still the majority of the population in Germany, had limited interest in change and soon reverted to support for the status quo. Armies, largely made up of peasant recruits, remained loyal to their rulers.

The disasters which overtook Germany in the twentieth century have led many to see in the failure of the 1848 revolution one of the great wrong turnings of history, with a permanently damaging effect. The consequences of failure should certainly not be underestimated. It created a lasting feeling among many Germans that they lacked political talent and contributed to the perception that politics was 'a dirty trade', of which it was better to steer clear. There was, however, not that irrevocable weakening of liberalism which has been too categorically asserted by many subsequent commentators. Liberalism retained the potential to prevail in the future. The German *Bürger* was still convinced that the tide of history favoured him and his way of life and that absolute monarchies and the aristocracies arrayed around them were bound to decline. This conviction survived the disillusionment and self-criticism that followed the collapse of the euphoria of 1848. The revolutions of 1848 had shown that the bourgeoisie was fighting on two fronts: against monarchical absolutism above and against the masses below. By and large the German middle classes were still convinced that in this two-front battle they represented the general good, that they were the 'general estate' transcending narrow class interests. Moreover, the forces of reaction that appeared to have won by 1849 were not simply able to turn the clock back. In most German states, most notably in Prussia, constitutions were left in place after the revolutions. Monarchies were therefore no longer absolute but subject to some legal limitations. Parliaments, however unrepresentative and restricted in their powers, provided an arena for political activity which had not existed before.

In the 1850s German industrialization entered a take-off phase. This greatly restored the self-confidence of the German *Bürgertum*, but it also began to change its composition. The German bourgeoisie had been overwhelmingly a *Bildungs-bürgertum*, an élite based on education. The Frankfurt parliament was sometimes dismissively called an assembly of professors and it was true that professors, teachers, officials, lawyers and journalists made up a large proportion of it. Less than ten per cent of the deputies were businessmen. In the future entrepreneurs and businessmen, *Wirtschaftsbürger*, were to become more prominent among the middle classes. Economic expansion would boost middle-class confidence, but it would also turn the bourgeoisie into a class defined mainly by material interest, rather than an élite of education that could claim to speak for society as a whole.

Even before 1848 there was little left of the old urban patriciate that flourished on the basis of special legal privileges in the small pre-industrial towns of Central Europe. A radical-liberal journalist, August Ludwig von Rochau, drawing the lessons from the failures of 1848, popularized the term *Realpolitik*, that liberals would in future have to pay less attention to ideals than to the material forces that shaped the course of history. The dilemma between spiritual forces and material power is age-old and Rochau, in recommending greater realism in the future, was still confident that liberals, relying more than in the past on their economic self-interest, would prevail. The breathtaking material advance of the 1850s inspired pessimism as well as optimism in Germany, as it had done in Britain a generation earlier, when the 'dark satanic mills' began to impinge on public consciousness. There were doubts, even among liberals, that laissez-faire capitalism and unalloyed individualism had all the answers. There was, after 1848, a greater appreciation among liberals that a flourishing economy required a strong state to promote and control it. The prevailing mood was that in 1848 only a battle, not the war, had been lost.

Nationalism was the other great force which could not be weakened by the failures of 1848. Ever since the Napoleonic era it had gripped the educated classes in Germany. It was the new secular religion of the age and was the driving force of events across the whole of Europe. The economic progress which in the 1850s restored the confidence of the German middle classes also gave a strong boost to nationalism. Only unity beyond that achieved by the Zollverein, the customs union which since 1834 had embraced most of Germany outside the Habsburg empire (see p. 15) would allow the potential of industrialization to be fully realized. Up to 1848 German nationalism had been mainly an ideological force; it now paired with the economic self-interest of Germany's most dynamic class to demand a greater unity.

Economy and society during the restoration

The economic pressures that had helped to generate a revolutionary situation before 1848 were mainly agrarian, poor harvests and high prices, although early industrial developments and their consequences for trades such as weaving were also a factor. The years from 1849 to 1857 saw an upswing in the economic cycle, the early signs of which contributed to the ebbing of the revolutionary tide. The boom was briefly interrupted from 1857 to 1859, and again in 1866, but there was a prolonged slow-down only after 1873, often labelled the great depression. Economic cycles were as yet imperfectly understood phenomena. They were international and indicated that the development of a world-wide, interdependent capitalist market had begun. Britain was still at the centre of this emerging economic system and retained her enormous lead as the first industrial nation, but the area of the German Zollverein, from which Austria was excluded, held by the 1860s a respectable fifth place after Britain, France, the USA and Belgium. The boom of the 1850s was centred, in Germany as elsewhere, on railway building, which in turn stimulated other sectors like coal, iron and steel. The expansion of the railway network made transport and therefore many goods much cheaper and contributed to the growth of major cities. In 1850 the railway network in the area of the German Confederation amounted to 5856 km, by 1860 it had nearly doubled to 11,175 (see Appendix: Table 1). Of this 2967 was in Prussia in 1850, 5762 by 1860. In the area of the German Zollverein iron production rose from 214,560 tons in 1850 to 530,290 tons in 1860, steel production from 196,950 to 426,260 tons. Germany was catching up with the British technological lead in areas such as machine building. Borsig, the largest German manufacturer of locomotives, completed its five hundredth locomotive in 1854, its thousandth in 1858. The extent to which industrialization favoured Prussia as against Austria can be gauged from the estimate that in 1860 the area of the later German Reich had a per capita industrial production of £310 as against £200 in Austria-Hungary, in 1880 sterling prices. In 1869 two-thirds of employment in Austria, excluding Hungary, was still in agriculture, while in the area of the later German Reich it had dropped to just over half (see Appendix: Table 2). In this period of transition from an agrarian to a predominantly industrial economy industrialization and urbanization were concentrated in a few regions, especially those favoured by the local availability of raw materials like coal. The Rhine–Ruhr area was such a region, as was Central Germany divided between Prussian Saxony and the Kingdom of Saxony, while in the Habsburg territories such regions were fewer and less developed. In the Ruhr area the production of coal increased from 1,961,000 tons in 1850 to 11,571,000 tons in 1870, the number employed in coal mining from 12,741 to 50,749, the average number of miners per pit from 64 to 236.

Expansion of economic activity on this scale needs entrepreneurs to organize it, capital to finance it and institutional and legal forms to shape it. Many of the early entrepreneurs were men launching out on their own, who then continued to control the enterprises they built up. Alfred Krupp or August Borsig and their likes ruled like monarchs over the firms that carried their names. But the joint-stock company was becoming increasingly important, though in Prussia the bureaucracy dominated by the old élites of education and birth were suspicious of it. Men like Ludolf Camphausen, David Hansemann and Gustav Mevissen were active as general business leaders in a number of sectors and organized the accumulation of capital through the joint-stock or the commandite principle. Characteristically they were also leaders of moderate liberalism and played important roles in the events of 1848. Hansemann and Mevissen were involved, after overcoming bureaucratic and legal obstacles, in the foundation of joint-stock banks, the Darmstädter Bank and the Berliner Disconto-Gesellschaft, both of which occupied commanding positions in the development of the German economy well into the future.

Although industrialization was the most salient economic transformation of the 1850s, even Prussia remained a predominantly agrarian country. Agriculture itself experienced rising prosperity and productivity, a kind of golden age, which under-pinned the confidence of the traditional agrarian aristocratic élites, especially in East Elbian Prussia. In the quarter century after 1850 German agricultural production rose by 76 per cent. Even before 1848 agriculture had become increasingly market orientated. Feudal restrictions and obligations were abolished and what remained of them after 1848 disappeared in most German states, including Austria, in the 1850s. A class of landless agricultural labourers was created, some of whom migrated into towns and from east to west, providing the cannon fodder for industry. In Prussia's eastern provinces market forces had brought about a considerable turnover in the ownership of estates. A lot of these were heavily mortgaged and only a third of those that changed hands in the thirty years from 1835 passed through inheritance, the others were sold and about six per cent were forcibly auctioned. Many estate owners were therefore from the bourgeoisie, often successful businessmen who, as in Britain, were taking on the lifestyle of the landed gentry. Nevertheless even in 1885 more than two-thirds of the large estates in Prussia's East Elbian provinces, covering between them one-third of the total area, were still in the hands of the nobility. It was of considerable political significance that, up to the time of the depression in the 1870s, the great estate owners of Prussia shared the free trade orientation of the industrial and commercial sector. In southern Germany the situation was rather different. The typical aristocratic landowner did not cultivate his own land, but lived on the income from rents. Small peasant farmers tilled the land. Driven to desperation by poor harvests and low prices, they supplied much of the initial revolutionary impetus in 1848, particularly in south-west Germany.

At the bottom of the social hierarchy the transformations of the post-revolutionary era created the beginnings of an industrial proletariat. Such a proletariat, as opposed to the heterogeneous urban underclasses, was numerically still small in 1848, amounting to perhaps five per cent of the population. Within twenty years this had grown to between twelve and fourteen per cent. It was therefore only in the 1860s that the industrial proletariat, in spite of much internal differentiation, had reached the critical mass that would make it possible to speak of a class conscious of itself and able to make itself felt politically. In the 1840s the 'worker question', which was to become the most urgent social problem of the future, was perceived in Germany as something that had arisen in western Europe, notably Britain, but was only in process of formation in Germany. Questions arising from employment in factories, limitation of hours or the general problem of alienation, were beginning to be debated. In the 1848 revolutions factory workers had played a role in some large cities, notably Vienna, but were not the main driving force. A general ban on combinations was in force in the German Confederation before 1848 and was reimposed afterwards. Trade union organization was therefore difficult, but during the revolution so-called 'workers brotherhoods', a mixture of embryonic union and political party, appeared. In the 1850s the growth of the industrial proletariat raised the question to what extent it should seek its emancipation within the liberal economic order and in collaboration with liberals, or whether it should challenge the market economy from a collectivist or socialist perspective. The latter alternative prevailed, but this did not become clear until the 1860s. The crowding of workers and their families into inadequate housing in the proletarian ghettoes of large cities separated them spatially from the middle classes and was an element in fostering a separate political consciousness.

The diverse groups forming the artisan classes were numerically still more important than industrial workers. In a census of 1861 they made up more than fifteen per cent of the population. In the past they had been protected by guild regulations and they were put under pressure by the spread of the market economy. Many of them, masters and apprentices, had fought on the barricades in 1848/49. To a limited extent the restoration of guild regulations and restriction of access to artisan trades was offered in many German states, including Prussia, as an economic compensation for the political repression that prevailed in the restoration era. No amount of legislation could hope to hold back the market for long and by 1869 freedom of competition was conclusively enshrined in legislation in what was then the North German Confederation, soon to be expanded into the Reich of 1871. The removal of the remaining vestiges of independent city status, which was completed throughout the German Confederation in the 1850s and 1860s, abolished restrictions on movement and settlement. The privileges of urban citizenship, which had existed in the many independent cities of the Holy Roman Empire and which were confined to the higher echelons of the urban social hierarchy, had mostly disappeared in the post-Napoleonic period. Everybody was now a citizen of the state which they inhabited. This knocked away what had been in the past one of the props of guild regulation and control of competition. In spite of their noisy complaints and calls for protection the artisan classes benefited from industrialization. Some found refuge in the more highly skilled sections of the industrial workforce, for others there were new openings in trades like plumbing or various kinds of repair work. Some declined into the unskilled industrial proletariat. In general the more fortunate artisans became part of the lower middle class, the petit bourgeoisie. There is something in the argument that in Germany, because of the long history of independent cities on the one hand and the slow formation of the national state on the other, these groups tended to be nostalgic, backward-looking, yet status-conscious and socially conservative. It was a mentality that proved receptive to nationalistic, anti-liberal, anti-capitalist, anti-Semitic ideologies in Imperial Germany.

Economically and socially Germany was in the 1850s and 1860s in a state of transition. The growth of industry and urbanization, signals of modernity, were the developments that aroused attention, fascination and fear. Whatever the political setbacks, the rise of the liberal market economy was unstoppable. But Germany was still a predominantly rural and agrarian country. In the newly formed Reich of 1871 three-quarters of the population lived in towns and villages of less than 5000 inhabitants and there were only eight cities with a population of more than 100,000 (see Appendix: Tables 3 and 4).

The politics of restoration

The reconstitution of the German Confederation after Olmütz left the smouldering conflict between Austria and Prussia unresolved. This was the major political-constitutional factor, in addition to the economic transformation, that made it impossible simply to turn the clock back to the pre-revolutionary situation. Before

1848 the status quo in Germany had rested on the collaboration of Austria and Prussia. This solidarity of the two conservative German powers could not be fully restored. Under the aegis of Schwarzenberg, Austrian policy proceeded along three interconnected lines: 1. All vestiges of constitutionalism that had had to be conceded during the revolution were revoked. Austria reverted to an absolutist regime, in which all power rested ultimately with the Emperor. 2. The Habsburg territories were to be reconsolidated into a unitary state, in the administration of which the German element became dominant. 3. This unified empire sought admission as a whole to the German Confederation and to the Zollverein, which would create a seventy million block in Central Europe led by Austria. This programme was bound to be resisted by Prussia, which would have had to be content with a more clearly subordinate role than had been the case before 1848. This underlying divergence between the aims of Austria and Prussia did not preclude a good deal of collaboration between the two countries in the imposition of anti-revolutionary repression through the Confederation and its organs and even in the military defence of the confederate area. Not only the king, but many others in the Prussian ruling class, regarded it as their highest priority to prevent the recrudescence of revolution and considered cooperation with Austria essential to this end.

In Prussia in the meantime the classical German constitutional system had come into existence, which in essence lasted till 1918. German constitutionalism is a kind of halfway house between absolute monarchical rule and fully fledged parliamentarism, in which ministers responsible to parliament exercise power. A parliament representing the people as a whole exists, though it may be elected, as was the case in Prussia, on a very restricted franchise. Such a parliament was clearly an advance on the provincial estates that had existed in Prussia before 1848. The monarch, however, retained full executive power, though he chose to exercise most of his powers through ministers, who could be removed only by him and not by parliament. Their accountability to parliament was a juridical, not a political one. The king retained control of vital areas like the army, in which he was assisted by a military cabinet answerable only to him. Decisions of war and peace were his. Parliament could legislate and vote taxes, but was summoned and dissolved by the king. In such a system there were grey areas. If the constitution was granted or even imposed by the king, he could revoke it and resume absolute power. A coup d'état of this kind was often advocated by conservatives. If parliament refused to vote expenditure, for example for the army, then the king, so Bismarck later argued, had the right and duty to fill the gap, by-passing parliament's budgetary power.

Frederick William IV regarded any constitution as an invasion of his divinely ordained prerogative, but once he had taken the oath to the constitution he had imposed in December 1848 he felt bound by it. This imposition of a constitution was itself part of the increasingly successful counter-revolution in Prussia in the autumn of 1848. The constitution was then further modified, the most important change being the introduction of the three-tier franchise which lasted till 1918 (see Appendix: Table 5). This divided the voters into three classes, each paying the same amount of taxes and electing the same number of electors, who then chose the deputies. In the first election under this law in July 1849 4.7 per cent of voters were entitled to vote in the first class, 12.6 per cent in the second, and 82.7 per cent in the third. The vote was not secret and was indirect, via the electors. This system therefore based voting entirely on income and was in fact a plutocratic franchise. It was open to pressure and manipulation and in the 1850s there were very low turn-outs in the third class, for example only 21.6 per cent in 1852. For a decade it enabled the conservative groups to dominate parliament and after a liberal interlude in the 1860s this was again the case in the imperial period. Until 1918 Prussia thus became a bulwark of conservatism. By conceding the principle of constitutional government and parliamentary representation, but severely restricting it in practice, Prussian conservatism created the conditions for its successful survival in the age of liberalism.

The conservatism that ruled the roost in Prussia in the 1850s was itself divided into different groups and principles, according to the methods by which they sought to master the post-revolutionary situation. There were the legitimists, who would have preferred to do away with the constitution and return to the represen-tation of provincial estates. They had no sympathy for German nationalism, which they saw as inextricably linked to the liberal revolutionary project and as a threat to all thrones. Their German patriotism harked back to the Holy Roman Empire and they preferred Austro-Prussian conservative solidarity to conflict. In domestic Prussian affairs they represented the narrow class interests of the Junkers. Thus the manorial police power was restored, as was the right of estate owners to appoint village officials. The provincial estates were revived. The Upper House provided by the constitution was reformed in such a way that it was mainly representative of the medium and small Junker class. Most of these arrangements remained in place till 1918. The leaders of legitimist conservatism had exercised much influence in stiffening the indecisive king in 1848 and became known as the camarilla. Prominent among the ultra-conservatives were the two Gerlach brothers, Leopold and Ludwig. Leopold was constantly in the king's company in 1849 and became Adjutant-General in 1850. Ludwig was, along with the leading conservative political philosopher F. J. Stahl, leader of the parliamentary conservative faction. The group was associated with the newspaper *Neue Preussische Zeitung*, known as the *Kreuzzeitung*, which began publishing in 1848. It was Leopold von Gerlach who in 1851 recommended Bismarck for appointment to the key post of Prussian envoy to the German Confederation in Frankfurt. Bismarck had first attracted notice as a 32-year-old deputy of extreme conservative views in the United Diet summoned by Frederick William IV in 1847 and was a regular contributor to the *Kreuzzeitung*.

The ultra-conservatives were often in bitter conflict with Otto von Manteuffel, who had become prime minister just before Olmütz and remained in office till 1858. Manteuffel's conservatism was the official, state-bureaucratic variety, whereas the legitimists hated the modern interventionist state and its bureaucratic procedures. Manteuffel and his fellow bureaucrats accepted the imposed consti-tution as the best way of creating stability and preventing a recrudescence of revolution. They believed in a strong state, which would provide some social reforms for the masses, would take due account of the economic interests of the bourgeoisie while checking their political aspirations, and would still regard the Junker nobility as its chief pillar while containing their excessive class egotism. The king was in spirit closer to the ultra-conservatives than to bureaucratic conservatism, but Manteuffel remained in office, for Prussia, with her western provinces in rapid economic transformation, could not be governed according to the ideas of the ultras. By the early 1850s a new, more liberal conservative grouping emerged, known from its newspaper as the *Wochenblattpartei*. One of its leaders was Moritz August von Bethmann Hollweg, member of a patrician family from Frankfurt and the grandfather of Germany's chancellor at the outbreak of the first world war. This group of diplomats and high officials, chiefs without Indians, did not believe that it was possible to turn the clock back and to rely on sheer repression. They had mostly supported the union policy aborted by Olmütz, in their eyes a shameful capitulation, and looked forward to a kleindeutsch solution for the sake of Prussia and of German national fulfilment. The Wochenblatt group was supported by the Prince of Prussia, the king's brother and heir, the future Emperor William I. He had played a leading role in the military suppression of the revolution and had to go into exile in England. His English exile had changed his ideas, as had his wife's influence. She, Augusta, was a grand-daughter of the Grand Duke of Weimar, whose chief minister had been Goethe. Later, as Queen and Empress, she became an inveterate enemy of Bismarck.

The anti-revolutionary restoration regimes throughout Germany sought to use religion and the churches to fight liberalism down to its intellectual roots. In Prussia Frederick William IV had always had a strongly theocratic vision of monarchy and it was part of his office to be the supreme bishop of the united Protestant churches. The members of the conservative court party were committed to a similar view and it was central to the political theories of their court philosopher F. J. Stahl. The minister responsible for church affairs and education was Karl Otto von Raumer, a cousin of the Gerlachs. Under his aegis and that of the Supreme Council of the Protestant Churches the training, appointment and discipline of parish priests was closely supervised. In the prevailing Lutheran orthodoxy liberalism and revolution were mortal sins, the work of the devil. A tight grip was exercised on religious education and particularly on the elementary school system. Guidelines issued in 1854, known as the Stiehl regulation, after the official in charge of elementary education, rejected what it called one-sided training of the intellect and declared the main objective of elementary education to be the inculcation of piety and patriotism. In spite of its illiberalism the Prussian school system was very effective in eliminating illiteracy.

In Austria the relationship between the state and the Catholic Church was renegotiated. In the eighteenth century considerable restrictions had been placed on the church and on the control exercised by the papacy over episcopal appointments under the enlightened Emperor Joseph II. Most of this was now undone, for example the state gave up its right to ultimate consent in the appointment of bishops. The coping stone of this new relationship between church and state in Austria was the Concordat of 1855. It included provisions by which publications conflicting with the teachings of the church could be suppressed or professors teaching false doctrine be disciplined. Similar concordats were concluded between Rome and a number of smaller German states, like Württemberg, Baden and Hesse-Darmstadt. Well before 1848 the Roman Catholic Church had become more ultramontane in its fight against the liberalizing and secularizing tendencies of the age. This had led to great conflicts, among which the clash between the Prussian state and the Archbishop of Cologne in 1837 was the most notorious. It also produced an upsurge of popular Catholic piety, pilgrimages, miracles, Marian cults and so on. These manifestations continued in the 1850s and the concordats were attempts by various German governments to remove a source of conflict with forces which in other respects reinforced the anti-revolutionary, anti-liberal post-1848 settlement. It proved counterproductive, for it strengthened the feeling of liberals that theirs was a fight against superstition and obscurantism. It also reinforced the Protestant–Catholic divide, which was closely bound up with the kleindeutsch–grossdeutsch problem.

There was throughout Germany a great deal of repression in the 1850s. As before 1848, the German Confederation became an instrument of this repression and it was a matter on which the Austrian and Prussian governments had little difficulty in achieving a limited collaboration. In August 1851, not long after its reconstitution, the Confederation decided to keep under observation institutions and conditions in the separate states which might threaten public order and security. A committee was set up which examined the constitutions, electoral and press laws in member states and could order changes. Simultaneously the basic civil rights established by the Frankfurt constitution were suspended. In 1854 the Confederate Diet promulgated restrictive press and association laws. It was a policy similar to that pursued after 1815, for example in the Carlsbad Decrees of 1819. In liberal eyes this made it unlikely that the Confederation could ever function as a suitable instrument for closer German union. The ability of the Confederation to translate its policies into executive action was, however, limited in the 1850s by the Austro-Prussian rivalry. The years of revolution had seen a great upsurge of published material and a widening of readership and this could not be undone. Editors and journalists learnt how to get round the censor. A weekly called *Gartenlaube* (*Garden Bower*) was started in 1853 and attracted a wide popular readership, eventually, by the 1870s, reaching an edition of 400,000. It offered entertainment, household hints, scientific and medical information at a popular level, but below the surface it kept alive secular liberal expectations and anti-authoritarian attitudes. Many of its contributors were ex-revolutionaries of 1848.

In Prussia there was press censorship, electoral manipulation and pressure on officials and judges to conform to the conservative policies of the government. The Berlin police chief Hinckeldey became a byword for police rule, with its attendant system of spies and informers, which kept even the king and his circle in their sights. There was a populist dimension to Hinckeldey, for he showed concern for the welfare of the poor in Berlin. South German states had a more liberal tradition and mostly had constitutions before 1848. They now tended to conform to the general repressive spirit. In Bavaria, for example, always determined to maintain her independent position as the largest of the medium states, a measure of the freedoms gained in 1848 was preserved till 1852, when the ministry of von der Pfordten was reconstructed on a more conservative basis. Von der Pfordten was a principal protagonist of a German reconstruction on a tripartite basis, the two major powers and the smaller powers as the third element. The position in Electoral Hesse, which had provided the occasion for the final confrontation between Austria and Prussia before Olmütz, represented repression in an extreme form. Another example of reaction occurred in the two grand duchies of Mecklenburg, where estates going back to 1755 were revived. All attempts to give Mecklenburg a constitution failed until 1918. At the opposite end of the scale Baden became the liberal showpiece (*Musterländle* in the local dialect) after the accession of the Grand Duke Frederick I in 1852. He was the son-in-law of the Prince of Prussia and his influence became therefore significant when the latter ascended the Prussian throne. In general, liberals in the 1850s regarded the atmosphere in small states like Hesse-Darmstadt as stifling and were prepared to accept even Prussian military discipline in preference to it.

The economic struggle between Austria and Prussia

For the future of German central Europe the economic rivalry between Austria and Prussia was of crucial importance. The German Zollverein had been founded in 1834 and Austria was not part of it. Metternich had been well aware that this presented a long-term threat to Austria's position in Germany. Austria's recovery after the upheavals of 1848 had created a second chance which Schwarzenberg wanted to exploit with his proposal that the Habsburg empire as a whole should become part of the German Confederation, creating a seventy million block in central Europe. Prussia's resistance to this scheme, as well as reservations among the medium states, had permitted no more than a revival of the Confederation of 1815, within roughly its original boundaries. To make the exclusion of the non-German Habsburg lands more palatable the Prussians agreed to the exclusion, as had been the case in 1815, of their own provinces of East and West Prussia, which had been briefly included after the 1848 revolution. Prussia could thus, like Austria, claim to be a European great power, apart from her status as a German power. This still left open the question of the Zollverein and its future shape. Bruck, the Austrian finance minister, put forward plans for a wider customs union, including all the Habsburg lands, on the basis of a high protective tariff. This would have suited the economically more backward Habsburg empire, while also boosting the German-speaking entrepreneurial class within it. It would have fitted in with Schwarzenberg's promotion of administrative unity under a German-speaking aegis in the Austrian empire. It was attractive to the southern German states, who were reluctant to see Austria excluded from Germany and were also relatively backward in economic development.

When these Schwarzenberg-Bruck proposals first appeared Prussia was still committed to the Erfurt union. Prussian policy set itself to delay the Austrian proposals, without appearing to go too openly against grossdeutsch sentiment. In the negotiations after Olmütz about the reconstitution of the German Confederation, the Prussians again managed to avoid any immediate steps that would have ensnared them in the Austrian proposals. It was a significant event when in September 1851 Prussia managed to gain the adhesion of Hanover to the Zollverein. Hanover had previously been part of another association, the *Steuerverein*, which also included Oldenburg and the small principality of Schaumburg-Lippe. Because of its strategic situation between the eastern and western regions of Prussia the inclusion of Hanover in the Zollverein enabled Prussia to control the flow of trade to the North Sea ports. In the subsequent jockeying for position the southern and middle German states found that they could not afford to go against the Prussian dominated Zollverein, whatever their political inclinations. Saxony, for example, traditionally Austrian orientated, but now one of Germany's most advanced industrial regions, could not afford exclusion from the Prussian economic area.

In April 1852 Schwarzenberg suddenly died and the position of chief minister was left vacant. Under the neo-absolutist regime the Emperor himself became the ultimate coordinator of policy. The Schwarzenberg–Bruck plans of creating a central European block were pursued with less energy. The European scene was changing, with Louis Napoleon crowning himself Emperor in December 1852. There were fears that this might portend the beginning of another Napoleonic upheaval. Austria might be threatened by the new Napoleon's interest in Italian unity. The Austrians were therefore prepared to end the economic confrontation with Prussia. In 1853 they concluded a trade treaty with Prussia for twelve years, to which other Zollverein states soon adhered. It envisaged a review of Austria's relations with the Zollverein by 1860, thus apparently leaving the question of inclusion open, but in practice this meant little. The Zollverein itself was renewed for twelve years from 1 January 1854. The economic battle had been won by Prussia and it was increasingly obvious that in the dawning age of industry politics and economics could not move in opposite directions. If the Schwarzenberg–Bruck plans for a seventy million central European block had been realized the future would have been very different from what it was to be. Nevertheless, the Zollverein did not, from its inception, make the political formation of Kleindeutschland under Prussia inevitable and it was not inevitable now.

The Crimean War and changes in the European power balance

German historians have often attributed much of the failure to achieve unification in 1848 to the reluctance of the major European powers to see the emergence of a strong state in central Europe. The difficulties inherent in the internal German situation may have been the crucial causes of failure, but it cannot be denied that the British and Russian interest in the Schleswig-Holstein question or the Russian support for the revival of the Habsburg empire as an anti-revolutionary bulwark played an important role in the unfolding of events in the years of revolution. The changes brought about in European power relationships by the Crimean War undoubtedly created an environment that proved to be more favourable to the achievement of German unity.

The Crimean War was fought over the future of the Ottoman empire and the Russian drive to profit from its weakness by territorial acquisitions in the Balkans. The ultimate prize for Russia would have been control of the Dardanelles, giving her access to the Mediterranean. This was an outcome that Britain, and to a lesser extent France, were determined to prevent. The interests of Germany as a whole were not directly involved, but those of the Habsburg empire were. It became a consistent feature of the European power game that there was a potential clash between the Russian pan-Slav and the Austrian–German drive in the Balkans. The diplomatic moves surrounding the Crimean War showed clearly that Prussia was a more German power than Austria and that Prussia's security interests were more closely aligned with those of the German Confederation than were Austria's.

In both Austria and Prussia opinion was divided about the policy to be pursued in the Near Eastern crisis. In both countries there were conservative factions who saw the preservation of anti-revolutionary solidarity as the highest priority and this pointed to an alliance with, certainly not against, Russia. To square conservative solidarity with the power-political requirements of the two countries was not easy, particularly not for Austria. Austro-Russian rivalry in the Balkans was counter-balanced by the fear that Napoleon III's sympathy for Italian nationalism was a threat to the Austrian position in the Appenine peninsula. The compromises over commercial policy and the Zollverein had not removed the underlying rivalry between the two major German powers and alignment with either side in the Crimean War would profoundly affect that rivalry. Buol, the Austrian foreign minister, wanted to use the occasion to force Russia out of the Balkans and extend Austrian domination in that region. At the same time he sought to extract from the Western powers a guarantee for the Austrian position in Italy. In Germany the Viennese policy-makers attempted to line up the Confederation, including Prussia, behind Austria. This powerful central European block might act as an arbiter between Russia and the West at the appropriate time, or, if it became necessary, throw its weight against Russia.

In Prussia the Wochenblatt liberal-conservative group wanted an alliance with the West, in return for which there would be a guarantee of Prussian integrity against any possible French designs on the Rhine. They saw an opportunity in the Near Eastern conflict of realizing their hope of a kleindeutsch union under Prussia and of exacting revenge for Olmütz. The Western powers were asked to refrain from interfering with any moves to turn the German Confederation into a defence union headed by Prussia. There was, however, little disposition in London or Paris to make concessions to the Prussians at the expense of the Austrians, who were regarded as the more desirable allies. Initially official Prussian policy veered towards a Western orientation, but the king was not in the last resort prepared to countenance any steps that would compromise Prussian neutrality or align his country against Russia. The Austrians appeared to score a major success when they got the Prussians to sign, in April 1854, an open alliance for the defence of the Confederation, essentially the continuation of a secret one that had existed since 1851, to which the other members of the Confederation in due course adhered. The fear that this alliance might drag his country into a war with Russia frightened Frederick William, a fear that was exploited by the conservative camarilla. The pro-Western war minister Bonin and the anglophile Prussian ambassador in London, Bunsen, were dismissed. A major domestic crisis ensued, for the Prince of Prussia took the side of the dismissed minister and was accused of insubordination by his brother. William's anglophile wife was already preparing the ground with Queen Victoria for a second English exile. The quarrel between the royal brothers was patched up, Bismarck, still envoy at Frankfurt, acting as an intermediary.

It was at this point that Bismarck began to play a role of some importance. He had supported Olmütz as a reasonable compromise between the two German powers in the interests of anti-revolutionary stability. At Frankfurt he became increasingly convinced that Austria and Prussia were depriving each other of the air to breathe in Germany, as he put it. He left no stone unturned, even in petty matters of protocol, to assert Prussian equality in the Confederation against any attempt to enhance the Austrian status. In the chamber of the Diet only the Austrian envoy customarily smoked, but Bismarck ostentatiously asked him for a light. When the Near Eastern imbroglio started he was at one with his friends the Gerlachs in opposing the Western alignment sought by the Wochenblatt party. But after the signature of the defensive agreement with Austria in April 1854 he concentrated his efforts on thwarting Austrian attempts to use the agreement to lend strength to its moves against Russia in the Balkans. Prussia, he wrote to Leopold von Gerlach in August 1854, should not be reduced 'to the role of supplier of money and recruits . . . while being deprived of any finger in the pie'.

This was exactly the feeling among the lesser German states, who did not want to incur any risks on behalf of Habsburg aggrandisement in a region of little interest to them. It was more important to them to resist possible French expansion on the Rhine. Austria was able to secure a Russian withdrawal from the Danube principalities and in December 1854 signed an alliance with the Western powers. In Frankfurt Bismarck found himself in the unaccustomed position of enjoying the support of the smaller states in the maintenance of neutrality. He scored a major success in isolating the Austrians, when in February 1855 the German Confederation refused to order mobilization to support Austria in possible hostilities with Russia. In the end Austria never entered the war, for not only disagreements among her leaders but also the sorry state of her finances did not allow it. The heavy indebtedness of the Habsburg state was its Achilles heel, frustrating its efforts to play a leading role here, there and everywhere.

On the face of it their indecisive stance in the Crimean War did not enhance the prestige of either major German power. Prussia in particular looked weak and her status as the least of the European great powers seemed to have been confirmed. She was only belatedly invited to the peace negotiations in 1856, at the request of Austria; the German Confederation did not become a party to the final settlement. The real loser, however, was Austria. Schwarzenberg had predicted after Olmütz, which Russia had helped her to secure, that Austria would astonish the world by her ingratitude. Her anti-Russian stance during the Crimean War finally shattered the solidarity of the conservative powers that had dominated the course of events since 1815. This removed a major obstacle to the revision of the status quo in Germany in favour of Prussia. Events surrounding the war had also shown how tenuous the arrangements for a common defence of the German Confederation were. Only just below the surface of the Austro-German defensive alliance there was hostility between the two powers. Buol privately mused that if the war became general and Prussia sided with Russia, Austria with the West, then 'we will take Silesia, Saxony will be restored, let France take the Rhine – we do not care whether it is German or French'. Bismarck, not at this stage a major actor, talked of fighting 'a good war with Austria, to boot her out of Germany'. Not surprisingly there was a strong feeling among many Germans that the Confederation in its existing form was totally inadequate as a framework for the nation.

The New Era in Prussia

In October 1857 Frederick William IV became incapacitated, from a stroke or a nervous illness. His brother William took over temporarily. All those like Manteuffel and the Gerlachs, whose power and influence depended on the king, strove desperately to put off a permanent regency, but a year later it could no longer be avoided and William assumed the full powers of the monarchy. A more liberal ministry was installed. The regent took an oath to the constitution, even though his brother did not want him to. Fresh elections to the lower chamber of the Prussian Landtag were held, which reduced the conservatives from about 200 to 60, while the liberals rose from 60 to about 210. Electoral participation in the third class rose from 12.7 in 1855 to 18.5 per cent; in the first class it rose from 39.6 to 50.2 per cent. In addressing his new ministers William put forward a programme which contained the famous passage 'In Germany Prussia must make moral conquests, through wise legislation, by raising all moral elements, and by taking up elements of unity, such as is the customs union, which will, however, have to be reformed. . ..' It looked like a new beginning, a 'New Era', and liberals everywhere took heart. William had shown some sympathy with the more liberal Wochenblatt group, some of whose members now became ministers, and with kleindeutsch aspirations. He was, however, above all, a military man who had fired on the revolutionaries of 1848 and been reviled for it. Nothing was more important to him than the unfettered control over the army that fell to him as Prussia's ruler. Moreover, he was already sixty-one years of age, a man of the *ancien régime*, and his survival for another thirty years, a longevity unusual for the nineteenth century, was to have a major influence on the course of events. In the 'moral conquests' speech he had also spoken of the need for a healthy, strong, conservative basis for the state, the need to improve the army and warned against 'the stereotypical phrase, that the government must allow itself to be driven on and on to develop liberal ideas, which would otherwise make their way anyhow'. It was a minor by-product of the apparently liberalizing personnel changes that the Prussian envoy to the Confederation in Frankfurt, Bismarck, was promoted to the Prussian embassy in St Petersburg. It was in fact a relegation.

The Italian war of 1859

When the New Era had hardly begun a fresh international crisis was already in the making. Napoleon III had met Cavour, the Piedmontese prime minister, and had made a secret agreement to help Piedmont to drive Austria out of Italy and then hand the conquered Austrian provinces of Lombardy and Venetia over to an enlarged North Italian kingdom. The war between France and Piedmont against the Habsburg empire which broke out in April 1859 had even greater implications for Germany than the Crimean War and stirred and divided opinion much more deeply. One can distinguish three main positions, which cut across party lines. There were those who wished to see Prussia use the opportunity to drive Austria out of Germany and unify Kleindeutschland. Then there were those, a majority, who wanted to support Austria against France, which, since the Napoleonic era and the wars of liberation that ended it, was widely regarded as the national enemy. In between these two camps there was a smaller group who wanted Prussia to help Austria against a French hegemony in Europe, but to extract kleindeutsch unity as a price for this support. Some of the radicals of 1848 took the first position, but so did many of the moderate conservatives of the Wochenblatt group.

Bismarck, from his 'cold storage on the Neva', sent endless letters and memoranda to his friends and superiors, including the regent himself, urging exploitation of the situation at the expense of Austria. 'The present situation' he wrote to the regent's adjutant in his colourful way, 'can mean the jackpot for us, if we allow Austria's war with France to take its toll, and then start with all our armies on the road south, carrying our border posts with us in our canisters, and hammering them into the ground again either on Lake Constance or wherever the Protestant religion ceases to be the majority . . ..' The pro-Austrian position was taken by most Catholics and supporters of Grossdeutschland, by legitimists like the Gerlachs, but also by moderate liberals of 1848 who had become disillusioned with Prussia and her reactionary ways. If you saw Napoleon III as the most sinister, because most effective, of counter-revolutionaries, as Karl Marx did, then you also supported Austria.

It was hardly surprising that the Italian Risorgimento appeared ambivalent to German patriots. It evoked widespread sympathy and admiration and was an obvious model and encouragement for the German national movement. If Italians could do it, then so could Germans, and they might find a leader as charismatic and skilful as Cavour. On the other hand the threat to Austria's Italian position was a threat to Germany and there was a great upsurge of feeling to come to the aid of the Austrian brothers. A defeat for Austria would be a step towards a French hegemony in Europe. The Rhine must be defended on the Po.

Such sentiments were strongest in south and central Germany and among Catholics, but were not absent in Prussia and among Protestants. In spite of this the Prussian regent and his foreign minister Schleinitz were determined to remain neutral. Their calculation was that Austria was the militarily weaker party and would sooner or later face defeat in Italy, but that Prussian intervention should be left to the moment when she could act as arbiter between the warring parties. She would then appear as the saviour of Germany on the Rhine and Austria on the Po. At Frankfurt Prussia refused to acknowledge that an immediate threat to the Confederation existed. Prussia's aim was that an eventual full mobilization of the forces of the German Confederation should take place under Prussian command. Austria would have to pay for help by having at last to recognize Prussian equality in the Confederation and her supremacy at least north of the Main. These Prussian objectives came close to achievement. Austria suffered the expected military defeats, but after the biggest, Solferino on 24 June 1859, France and Austria suddenly made peace. The two emperors met on the battlefield and signed the preliminary peace of Villafranca. Austria preferred to give up most of her Italian position rather than let Prussia take first place in Germany. Napoleon III felt the threat from Prussia on the Rhine and did not want to lose control of the situation. Only Lombardy was handed over to the new North Italian kingdom, Venetia remaining for the time being in Austrian hands. Napoleon got his reward for his help through the transfer of Savoy and Nice to France.

Again, as after the Crimean War, neither Austria nor Prussia came well out of the Italian conflict. The Habsburg empire had suffered a severe defeat which called in question its future as a multi-national state. The neo-absolutist system had failed, the non-German nationalities were restive, the war had further weakened the public finances and the chances of a reorganization of Germany along grossdeutsch lines were much reduced, just when Austria's German position mattered more than ever to the Habsburg empire. But Prussia had again been hesitant, was accused of treason to the German cause, and many kleindeutsch liberals, whose hope had risen in the 'New Era', felt disillusioned.

Failure and indecision made the demand for a new beginning in German affairs only more insistent. Italy stirred emotions in Germany more deeply than the Crimea and proved a great stimulus to national feeling. Song and gymnastic festivals with a nationalist flavour proliferated. The year 1859 was the centenary of Schiller's birth and he was celebrated as a great national popular poet and prophet of freedom. There was a burgeoning of national organizations, political and economic, forming links across state boundaries. The *Nationalverein* was founded in 1859, bringing together liberals and democrats, whose aim was to revive the project of forming Kleindeutschland under Prussian leadership that had foundered ten years earlier. The *Società Nazionale*, which had provided a focus for the Italian Risorgimento, was the model. Subscriptions were so high that membership was confined to men of substance, eventually some 25,000, but they formed an élite network that was also active in other organizations, such as the *Kongress deutscher Volkswirte* (Congress of German Economists), with a free trading programme. Historians played a specially important role in stimulating sentiment in favour of Kleindeutschland under Prussian leadership. They put forward the idea that Germany, unlike her western neighbours England and France, had failed to develop a national state, because her energies were diverted in the Middle Ages to universal aims, such as the conflict between the Holy Roman Emperors and the papacy. They claimed that in more recent centuries, after the Reformation sparked by a German, Martin Luther, Protestant Prussia had emerged with the mission to create a German national state. This way of looking at German history, called national-liberal, became very influential. The liberal national movement had thus survived the winter of repression and could now base itself on a broad politically conscious public. The activists were mainly middle-class, but the national cause had a wider popular resonance. It was a factor that governments had to take into account, but the power to act remained with the princes and their governments. The greater preoccupation of the liberal movement with economic questions showed that, compared with their outlook ten years earlier, they were now more focused on real social forces than ideas, but how to assert their influence on the governments that still possessed the power to act remained an unresolved question.

The Austrian defeat in Italy had not ended the hopes of a grossdeutsch solution to the German problem. Many Germans felt sympathetic as well as guilty towards the Habsburg state and bitter and disappointed towards Berlin. Grossdeutsch sentiment was more diffuse and plans less precise than the way forward envisaged by those who still looked to Prussia. Grossdeutschland would inevitably be less cohesive than Kleindeutschland. It would look more like the existing confederation than a federal state. It was just this that made it attractive to those who had a stake in the survival of the separate states and who distrusted Prussian militarism and discipline. A Germany without Austria was for many a second-best and not only for Catholics an almost intolerable mutilation. By 1862 the many differences amongst the adherents of the grossdeutsch ideal had at least been sufficiently overcome to lead to the foundation of a counterpiece to the *Nationalverein*, the *Reformverein*, but it never acquired the unity and influence of the former.

The Austrian government, if it was to make any progress in the German question, needed to make far-reaching internal changes. These were in any case required to meet the demands of the separate nationalities, especially the Hungarians, and to cope with the perennial problem of financial viability. Changes in personnel had already taken place before the Italian war started. Buol was replaced as foreign minister by Rechberg, who was more inclined towards cooperation with Berlin in German affairs. Soon others particularly associated with the reactionary regime, for example the interior minister Bach, went. In October 1860 a constitution was promulgated which strengthened the *Reichsrat*, the federal organ for the whole empire. It was to be composed of deputies from the Landtage of the component states, which were themselves still chosen on the estate principle. The October constitution failed to satisfy aroused expectations, the nationalities, especially the Hungarians, regarding their interests inadequately represented, while German liberals wanted a tighter and more efficient system of centralization. In December 1860 Anton von Schmerling, a grossdeutsch moderate liberal, entered the Austrian government and was one its directing figures until 1865. He had been a minister in the government set up by the Frankfurt parliament under the Archduke John. In February a further constitutional edict created a more powerful central parliamentary body, made up of two chambers. It still lacked many features of a genuine constitutional regime, such as a bill of rights, and it still did not fully meet the Hungarian desire to be recognized as an equal nation. The foundations had been laid, however, for further liberalization and the Habsburg empire was now a constitutional state. In the early 1860s it might well look to liberals more attractive than Prussia, which was sliding back into repression as a result of its constitutional conflict. It was this conflict over the organization of the army and over the military budget in Prussia which now became crucial for the future evolution of German affairs.

The Prussian constitutional conflict

Disillusionment had overtaken the New Era in Prussia, in domestic as well as foreign affairs. The Italian war and its international repercussions had shown beyond doubt that an adequate army was vital for Prussia, but it was the organization and recruitment of the army that swiftly brought the Prussian liberals and the monarchy on to a collision course. In the Napoleonic era the Prussian army reformers, Scharnhorst and Boyen prominent among them, had attempted to turn the Prussian army into a citizen army. The success of the French revolutionary armies had shown that an effective fighting force could only be built if the ordinary soldier identified with the state he was defending. A system of conscription was established, under which the citizen had to serve for three years in the regular army, followed by two years in the reserve. He then had an obligation to serve fourteen years in the militia (*Landwehr*). The first seven years, the so-called first levy, would in case of mobilization, fight with the army, the second levy would carry out behind-the-line duties. It was generally agreed that this system was by the 1850s in need of reform and the Italian war had made change seem urgent. Since 1815 the population had increased from eleven to eighteen million, but the annual intake of recruits had remained fixed at 40,000, so that only a third of those liable to serve were actually called up, creating a serious injustice. In practice the period of service varied between two and three years, the militia was filled up with recruits who had received only a few weeks' training and their officers were not professionals. Before he became regent Prince William had often argued for change, but there was never the occasion or the resources to implement reforms. In 1854 he had acquired as an adviser Major Albrecht von Roon, who produced for him, after he became regent, a memorandum demanding a larger annual intake, a three-year term of service, and the virtual abolition of the militia. This was political dynamite. Liberals knew that the professional army had quashed the revolution in 1848, while they regarded the militia as a citizen army. This was precisely why the regent and Roon, beyond criticizing the militia's technical competence, distrusted its political reliability. Against this, the army of the line had an officer corps that was still overwhelmingly drawn from the aristocracy and saw itself as the guardians of monarchy and order against revolution. Battle was joined when Roon replaced the more conciliatory Bonin as minister of war in December 1859.

Roon's proposals would have raised the annual intake of recruits from 40,000 to 63,000, still well short of universal service, and the peace-time strength of the army from 150,000 to 220,000. After a three-year term of service there would be a five-year service in the reserve. All that would have been left of the militia would be the second levy, available for fortress and home service. The officer corps of the militia would be professionalized. The cost of the scheme would require a 25 per cent rise in taxation. Compromise on these proposals with the liberal majority in the Landtag would have been possible. The liberals were aware of the need for reform, while some of the generals would have been content with a two-year term of service. As the conflict sharpened, the regent and his military advisers lost interest in compromise and were determined to dispute the right of parliament to have any say over military affairs. William was prepared for some liberal–conservative compromise with the acceptance of the Constitution, but he was adamant that the monarch must have unfettered control over the army. To the ultras it became a choice between a royal army, as the Prussian army always had been, and a parliamentary army. If such intransigence produced another revolution followed by another coup d'état, it would have a cleansing effect. Prussia would emerge strengthened from the morass into which liberalism was dragging it. Among those who held this kind of apocalyptic view of the conflict was Edwin von Manteuffel, the chief of the king's military cabinet. The existence of such a post shows the extent to which there was a military monarchy in Prussia. Even the limited juridical responsibility of the war minister to the Landtag could be by-passed. In essence this situation did not change until 1918.

Roon's proposals were presented to the chamber of deputies in 1860 in the form of a military law incorporating the army reorganization and a finance law. When the chamber rejected the military law, the government took the line that the reorganization did not require legislation and could be carried out under the royal powers of command. The financial problem was solved by a compromise, under which the chamber voted the necessary moneys on a provisional basis. The Old Liberal majority in the chamber was prepared to go a long way to meet the regent and his ministers. Since the beginning of the New Era their motto had been 'don't push'. For all the regained self-confidence of the middle classes their representatives did not want to raise the question of power prematurely, because they were only too well aware that power still rested with the monarchy and its agents. When William became king on the death of his brother in January 1861 he wanted to receive the traditional oath of allegiance from the estates, which would have been incompatible with the constitution. Instead he was persuaded to have himself solemnly crowned in Königsberg, but on 18 January 1861, the 160th anniversary of the crowning of the Elector Frederick as the first Hohenzollern king in the same city. The new regiments, formed under the reorganization which had not been legally enacted, received colours and emblems. The conflict with the chamber was aggravated when the king refused to recognize as temporary another provisional financial vote in June 1861. The government's deliberate defiance of liberal sentiment weakened the Old Liberals, prepared to seek an accommodation at almost any price.

In June 1861 the German Progressive party was founded, through which a number of prominent democrats from 1848, who had so far kept a low profile, re-entered active politics. As was the case with all German political parties, its structure was loose and its programme general, but it at least attempted to be a more cohesive force than the older liberal groups. In December 1861 there were elections for a new chamber, in which the Progressive party obtained 104 out of

352 seats. The various groups of Old Liberals and of the liberal centre were reduced from 195 to 91 seats. The Conservatives mustered only 14 seats. When this new chamber refused to lengthen the term of service beyond two years and to vote any more provisional funds for the reorganization of the army, the king dissolved it once more. The ensuing elections, in May 1862, further strengthened those prepared to defy the government. The Progressives now obtained nearly forty per cent of the seats, there was a further sharp decline of the moderate liberals and even the Catholics, who had supported the king's military plans, found their number nearly halved. Significantly, electoral participation had risen from a low of 16.1 per cent in 1855 to 34.3 per cent and even in the third class it was now over thirty per cent. A dangerous stalemate had been reached.

Bismarck becomes prime minister

The clash between king and parliament came to a head in September 1862, when the chamber debated the budget for the coming year. Even within the government, by now composed only of Conservative ministers, there were voices calling for compromise and briefly these included Roon, the author of the military reorganiz-ation plans. The king, however, refused to budge and threatened abdication. His son and heir, Frederick William, was married to the eldest child of Queen Victoria and, under the influence of his wife, was sympathetic to liberalism. The royal couple envisaged that eventually Prussia and Germany would adopt something similar to the English parliamentary system. But at this moment the son persuaded his father that he should not abdicate and that he should see the crisis through. Even Frederick William was sufficiently wedded to the idea of the Prussian military monarchy not to wish to inherit it at a moment when its power would have been reduced under threat. The Crown Prince could not have known that his father would live another quarter of a century and that his own chance would never come again. The king was, however, also unwilling to subject the country to the trial, perhaps revolution and civil war, that advocates of a coup d'état like Manteuffel had in mind as a way out of the crisis. Bismarck was the man who was offered to the king as the minister who would brazen out the conflict with the chamber without making any compromises diminishing the royal prerogatives. It was not the first time that a ministerial appointment for Bismarck was in the offing. He had been earlier in the year transferred from St Petersburg to Paris, so that he should be nearer at hand in just such an eventuality.

Bismarck was born in 1815. On his father's side he came from a long line of aristocratic landowners, Junkers, in the March of Brandenburg, who, besides running their estates, had served the Prussian monarchy, usually in the army. On his mother's side he came from a family of civil servants, who had been in high places in the Prussian state and close to the royal family. He was well educated and had a brilliant command of language, which might have turned his talents to literature. His ability to write and speak became a vital weapon for him as a politician. He could not settle down to the civil service career for which he was by family background intended. He had an imperious temper, was conscious of his own exceptional ability and found subordination and routine unbearable. He wanted to make his own music or none, as he put it. Between the ages of twenty-four and thirty-two he lived the life of a country squire, administering part of the family estates. He learnt a good deal about agriculture and the economics of running a business, but the life of a country Junker could hardly satisfy a man of his ambition and ability. He read widely in German, French and English, but not in a disciplined way. He had a penetrating mind, but entirely pragmatic and practical, not given to philosophical speculation. In the saddle and on the hunting field he was something of a daredevil and known as 'the wild Junker'. In the aristocratic circles in which he moved there was a strong religious movement, an 'awakening', slightly comparable to the evangelical revival in the Church of England at the same period. Bismarck had a kind of conversion and for the rest of his life he needed the consolations of personal religion in his many moments of stress. He knew that even the most powerful of men, such as he became, were in the hands of destiny. For someone as convinced as Bismarck that he knew best, religion provided the ultimate confirmation that, whatever he did, he was walking with divine destiny. There was otherwise little Christian charity about him, for he pursued anyone who crossed him with relentless, often petty, hatred. Bismarck's conversion was also connected with his marriage to Johanna von Puttkamer, from a leading Pomeranian 'awakened' aristocratic family. She provided him, in the way of nineteenth-century wives, with a firm, quiet base for his stormy and high-flying existence.

In the revolution of 1848 Bismarck acquired the reputation of an extreme reactionary. 'Only to be used when bayonets rule without restraint' was the marginal comment by Frederick William IV against Bismarck's name. But he made so much of a name for himself as a speaker and journalist that he netted the highly significant and sensitive post as Prussian envoy to the German Diet in Frankfurt. He thus entered the diplomatic service right at the top, at the age of 36, having refused to work his way up the hierarchy in his youth. He soon moved away from the legitimist conservatism of his mentors, the Gerlachs, a journey that can be traced in the massive output from his pen, in the form of letters and memoranda, during his Frankfurt years. He acquired that ruthlessly realistic vision that became his hallmark, uninhibited by any preconceptions of ideology, principle or sentiment. In correspondence with his old friend Leopold von Gerlach he argued that the possibility of an alliance with France must be allowed to play a part in Prussian diplomacy. You could not play chess, he said, unless all the sixty-four fields of the board were open to you. For a legitimist like Gerlach the regime of Napoleon III was revolutionary and out of bounds.

When Bismarck began to be talked about as a possible minister, he had in many eyes the reputation of a sinister and ruthless opportunist. For this reason, and also because of pressure from his more liberal queen, the Prussian king hesitated long before calling upon him. As the weeks passed after his transfer to Paris in the summer of 1862, Bismarck had almost given up hope and wrote to his wife that they might after all spend the rest of their lives managing their estates. He was still greedy for power, but only under conditions that would give him more than a toe-hold upon it. He also knew that matters were unlikely to come to the crunch again in Berlin until September, when the chamber was due to reassemble. At the end of July 1862 he went on leave, knowing that it might not be possible to get in touch with him for days on end, but arranging pick-up points for mail and telegrams. While in Biarritz he fell in love with Princess Catharina Orlov, the twenty-two-year-old wife of the Russian ambassador in Brussels. It was a real love affair, romantic yet unconsummated, not untypical for those days. It is unlikely that, even as he gave himself unreservedly to the dalliance with Catharina, he ever lost sight of the fact that his great moment in Berlin might yet come and that he must not miss his chance. His return to Berlin was arranged well before the famous telegram reached him that Roon sent under a prearranged name, 'Periculum in mora. Dépêchez-vous.' It was sent on 18 September, the day after the crown council at which Roon had joined those advising compromise and the king had threatened abdication. It was an extreme situation, and Roon, more in panic than in hope, saw in Bismarck a last chance of avoiding unacceptable alternatives. It was, however, just the kind of situation that Bismarck had always hoped to exploit and for which he was determined to be available. Much of this story, and of subsequent famous events, became known to the world, and especially to the German public, through the reminiscences Bismarck published after his fall from power in 1890. His purpose then was to portray himself as the man of principle who had selflessly ridden to the rescue of the Hohenzollern monarchy, which now, through its unworthy heir William II, had ungratefully dismissed him. Bismarck was always his own best propagandist and maker of his own myth.

On the afternoon of 22 September Bismarck had his interview with the king, as a result of which William decided not to abdicate and to appoint Bismarck prime minister (*Ministerpräsident*) and foreign minister. Again the only account we have is Bismarck's own in his reminiscences written thirty years later, but in this case it is likely to be substantially correct. The king knew that in the isolated position into which he had manoeuvred himself it would be difficult for him to find any man of repute and ability to take on the position as his chief minister. Bismarck, in correct appreciation of the king's psychology, offered himself as the faithful liegeman, who would do the royal bidding even against his own better judgment and whatever the consequences. He would rather perish with him than abandon him to a parliamentary regime. He thereby avoided being tied to any specific course or programme. The king had already drafted a memorandum on that subject, but simply tore it up. Bismarck knew only too well that he would need all the flexibility he could get in the very difficult situation that awaited him.

Subsequent German and European history was overshadowed by Bismarck's personality. Its course led eventually to the great disasters of the twentieth century and the empire that Bismarck established outlived him by only twenty years. This naturally raises the question whether his accession to power prevented other more benign outcomes. It can be argued that if in September 1862 William I had abdicated and been succeeded by his son Prussia and Germany might have developed in a more liberal direction. Such counterfactual historical speculation can never be conclusive. As it was Bismarck had to adapt much more radically to the emerging industrial, urban society than he, the Junker and liegeman of a largely unreconstructed monarchy, initially anticipated. His own handiwork, the united Germany under Prussia, created a framework that greatly speeded up the socio-economic transformation of society. In the later phases of his long period in power, Bismarck increasingly became a prisoner of these developments and had to react to them without being able to control them. On the other hand, the sensational success of his policies up to 1870 undoubtedly prolonged the lease of life of political structures that at the time of his accession were already considered outdated by the majority of the articulate classes. The political framework was increasingly out of phase with the social and economic state of society and Bismarck, by clinging to power for so long, allowed this situation to ossify. No real solution was found before 1914 and the collapse of the Bismarckian empire, with all its dire consequences, cannot be solely blamed on the Iron Chancellor's successors. The style and methods of the founder cannot escape blame.

2   The wars of unification 1862–1870

The beginnings of the Bismarck regime in Prussia

The domestic political situation in Prussia that awaited Bismarck and that was indeed the reason for his appointment was intractable. The new prime minister could not give way to the chamber on the military budget without reneging on his promise to the king, on whom he was wholly dependent for his continuance in office. An obvious way out was to make progress in foreign affairs, to offer a way forward on the big pending questions of greater unity in Germany. On this Bismarck might find some common ground with the Liberals. They were almost to a man supporters of a kleindeutsch solution and were disillusioned with the lack of progress made by Bismarck's predecessors. Appearing before the budget commission of the chamber on 30 September the new prime minister made it clear that he was unyielding on the constitutional conflict and was prepared if necessary to govern and tax without a budget voted by the chamber, but otherwise he sought to sound conciliatory. The 'appalling frankness', which was sometimes Bismarck's way of talking, was, however, hardly likely to find favour with the deputies and many of his remarks were considered offensive. The passage which hit the headlines and has clung to Bismarck ever since was:

> Germany does not look to Prussia's liberalism, but to her power; Bavaria, Württemberg, Baden may indulge their liberalism, but they cannot play the role of Prussia; Prussia must gather her strength and preserve it for the favourable moment, which has already been missed several times; Prussia's borders according to the treaties of Vienna are not conducive to the healthy existence of the state; the great questions of the time will not be decided by speeches and majority resolutions – that was the great mistake of 1848 and 1849 – but by iron and blood.

'Iron and blood' has reverberated through history, linked to Bismarck. The phrase caused a storm of indignation throughout Germany. The historian Treitschke, already a passionate advocate of a Prussian solution for Germany and later one of the chief apostles of the new German nationalism, was disgusted. He wrote to a friend: 'You know how passionately I love Prussia; but when I hear a shallow Junker, like this Bismarck, boast of the iron and blood, with which he will subjugate Germany, the baseness is only exceeded by the ridiculousness of it.' Bismarck had meant to show that there was surely common ground between him and the deputies about Prussian aims in Germany and that these could only be achieved with a strong army, but his remark badly misfired. He was on a steep learning curve and he began to realize how hard his task would prove to be.

The sense of hopelessness which the Prussian constitutional conflict had spread among kleindeutsch liberals was thus aggravated by Bismarck's arrival in power. The Austrians with their limited constitutional reforms were now ahead in the game of appealing to German public opinion. Since the Italian war a number of plans to reform the German Confederation, in its military, juridical or general legislative aspect, had been under discussion, but they had always come to grief on the underlying differences between Austria and Prussia. Reforms suggested by the medium states, led by the Saxon minister Beust, had foundered on the lack of unity even among these states. Another reform plan was promoted by the Austrians in 1862 and found some support among the medium states. An assembly of delegates elected from the parliaments of the member states was to be established at Frankfurt and participate in the promulgation of federal laws. Prussia opposed these proposals when they were tabled in the Frankfurt Diet in August 1862. On the other hand the initiative rested with Prussia in the field of the Zollverein. In 1860 international free trade had received a powerful boost with the conclusion of a treaty between Britain and France, the Cobden treaty. The adhesion of the Zollverein to this system was almost inevitable and was completed in August 1862, when the Prussian government signed a treaty. The Prussians tried to persuade the other member states of the Zollverein to add their signatures. For Austria this created another barrier to inclusion in the Zollverein, for Austrian industry could not compete in so large an area of free trade. The Austrians had tried to block the negotiations with France, in which they were supported by Bavaria and Württemberg.

This was the situation in German affairs as Bismarck found it on coming to office. It was an essential part of his statecraft to build up alternative courses of action for himself and only decide which of these to take at the appropriate moment. The Austrian–Prussian rivalry had preoccupied him since he went to Frankfurt in 1851 and it would now fall to him to resolve it one way or another. One way would be to divide Germany along the line of the river Main, with Prussia supreme to the north and Austria to the south. In December 1862 Bismarck had a number of meetings with the Austrian envoy in Berlin, Count Károlyi, in which, with that appalling frankness characteristic of him, he proposed such a division. Prussia would, in return for a reduction of Austria's German position, support the vital interests of the Habsburg state in Italy and the Balkans. Austria should, he recommended, shift her centre of gravity further east. If no such agreement could be reached, it would be war, 'nous croiserons les bajonettes'. He rejected once more the Austrian proposal to establish an assembly of delegates from member parliaments at Frankfurt. He frightened Károlyi with the spectre of nationalism in suggesting a national German parliament elected by the people, something the multinational Habsburg state could never agree to. He raised this spectre from time to time in the ensuing years and eventually made it real, in a fashion, with the Reichstag of the German empire elected by universal suffrage. To another envoy, especially sent by Vienna to achieve some understanding with the new Prussian prime minister, Bismarck declared that if Vienna gave up the assembly of delegates he would give up all flirtation with the devil of German nationalism: 'This kind of emotional sentimental policy is totally alien to me; I have no time at all for German nationality; I would as soon make war against the Kings of Bavaria or Hanover than against France.'

Not only was Bismarck adept at keeping alternative options open, he was also a master at muddying the waters and concealing his intentions. He knew that an agreement with Austria to divide Germany was always unlikely and that ultimately force would have to decide the issue. In the meantime he continued the previous government's policy of blocking the Austrian proposal of a delegate assembly. He scored his first major foreign policy success, when under threat of Prussia's departure from the Confederation, the Austrian plan was voted down. On the Zollverein and the free trade treaty with France, Bismarck's government stuck to the line that all members of the custom union had to sign the free trade treaty or else face exclusion. It kept this issue separate from the renewal of the Zollverein, which was due in 1865, with Austria still proposing her adherence. The final outcome, after many tortuous negotiations stretching from 1863 to 1865, was that Austria remained excluded, while all the other previous members accepted the free trade treaty. Even Saxony, whose foreign minister, Beust, was the most committed defender of Austria in German politics, could not afford to go against the Prussian economic ascendancy. In the great political events of those years Bismarck skilfully used Prussia's economic advantage over Austria to further his objectives.

It was, however, on the political front that the fortunes of the Bismarck government reached a low point in 1863, at home and abroad. All the prime minister's attempts to come to some understanding, open or covert, with the Liberal opposition were treated with contempt. There was total lack of trust and he himself later said that people spat at the mention of his name. He insisted that if there was no agreement between government and parliament on the budget the government was still entitled to govern and tax. It was the so-called 'gap theory' of the constitution, namely that the king had a duty and right to carry on the government even when he and parliament were deadlocked. The theory attacked the most fundamental conviction of the Liberals, that the rule of law should prevail over the naked exercise of power. Bismarck was driven to adopt ever more dictatorial and repressive methods. There was curtailment of the freedom of the press and a decree of June 1863 gave the government wide discretion to suppress newspapers. Most of the press was liberal and had become more stridently hostile since Bismarck's assumption of power. Direct pressure was applied to deputies holding official positions, of whom there were many, for the growing importance of the economic bourgeoisie was still not reflected in the composition of the liberal parliamentary groups. Officials could be threatened with dismissal and other forms of harassment. The Crown Prince publicly dissociated himself from the repressive measures of the

Bismarck government, raising hopes throughout Germany that the days of this regime were numbered. The repression failed to reduce the strength of the Liberal opposition. When the chamber was again dissolved in September 1863, even direct electoral pressure achieved little. The Progressives got no less than 40 per cent of the seats, though there was some increase in the number of Conservative deputies. What made the Progressive success less impressive and revealed the slender popular base of liberalism was the low electoral participation, only 27 per cent in the third class. In his dealings with the chamber Bismarck was deliberately confrontational, for, given his unpopularity and lack of success, he was also under threat from the ultras, still influential in the circles around the king, whose confidence was vital for his continued retention of office. Bismarck had moved a long way from legitimist conservatism and he saw no future in the kind of coup d'état some ultras were still flirting with.

He himself was toying with another kind of coup d'état, which might well arouse suspicion in the king's circle. The threat of a nationally elected parliament, with which he had frightened the Austrians, was not an empty one. He thought that in Prussia a wide extension of the franchise, possibly universal manhood suffrage, might well undermine the Liberal parliamentary predominance, which emerged from the plutocratic three-tier franchise. In pursuit of such ideas Bismarck had, in the summer of 1863, some remarkable conversations with Ferdinand Lassalle, leader of the recently founded General German Workers Association. Lassalle, at one time an associate of Marx, had put forward a programme of establishing a socialist society on a national basis. It would require the workers to cut loose from the Liberal tutelage and would be brought about through the use of universal suffrage. Lassalle is as much as Marx the founding father of German socialism, but at this stage he had minimal support and carried little clout. He and Bismarck talked, because they found each other fascinating, but that the Prussian prime minister should devote time to such an exploration was a measure of his desperation. One of the Latin tags that Bismarck liked to quote was 'If I cannot win with the gods I will call in the devil.' This is what he was thinking of when he was courting German nationalism, the masses, universal suffrage. It was this that has made commentators describe his method of ruling as 'charismatic' and 'Bonapartist'. He sought to maintain traditional power structures by modern methods, the manipulation of public opinion through press and parliament. Whatever gloss he later put on his conduct at this time, he was plainly often simply floundering. There was, however, also weakness in the Liberal opposition. If the Liberals had really felt strong enough to to confront the Bismarck government, they should have promoted a tax boycott. As long as the government could continue to raise taxes which had not been duly sanctioned by parliament, the ancient weapon of parliaments against absolute government 'no taxation without representation' had no force in Prussia. The Prussian Liberals, conscious of their narrow popular base and fearful of revolutionary upheaval, felt unable to mount a tax boycott. Bismarck could rest secure in the knowledge that behind all the Liberal sound and fury there was little real power.

Nevertheless there was nothing in the course of German and European events in

1863 that made Bismarck's survival any more probable. At the beginning of the year the Polish rebellion dominated European diplomacy and politics. Bismarck immediately decided to make common cause with those in the Tsarist government determined to suppress the rebellion. His emissary to St Petersburg, General Alvensleben, negotiated a convention which allowed troops of both countries to cross their respective frontiers in the pursuit of rebels. In his reminiscences Bismarck claimed that this agreement, highly unpopular at the time with liberal sentiment throughout Germany and Europe, ensured the goodwill of the Russian government during his later moves in the cause of German reunification. It certainly banished the possibility of a Franco-Russian alliance which might have restricted Prussia's room for diplomatic manoeuvre. Bismarck also feared that if the Polish rebellion spread it would cause a dangerous situation in those of Prussia's eastern provinces with a large Polish population. It did nothing to make Prussia under the Bismarck government more attractive to the German liberal-national movement.

In the summer of 1863 the Austrian government undertook its most determined initiative to date to capture for itself the tide of closer German union. The object of the Confederation should in future be not merely German security but German welfare, that is to say economic and social subjects like the Zollverein. A Federal Directory of Five should form the executive organ, there should be an assembly of the member princes and an indirectly elected assembly of three hundred delegates, as well as a federal court and a council to deal with foreign treaties. In a clever diplomatic manoeuvre the Austrians invited the twenty-five German ruling princes to Frankfurt, at a fortnight's notice, to adopt the plan. Bismarck in his reminiscences called it a surprise attack and he had the utmost difficulty in dissuading his king from attending the Congress of Princes. During a difficult interview the king was said to have burst into tears, while his prime minister, on emerging from the royal chamber, gave vent to his feelings by smashing a wash basin. The Austrians could not have seriously believed that Prussia would accept such a plan, but they may have hoped to persuade the medium states to adhere, leaving Prussia isolated. In fact the princes assembled at Frankfurt made their agreement dependent on Prussia's adherence and all the pomp and circumstance of the congress was in vain. It was a negative success for Bismarck. He had again put forward the counterproposal of a directly elected federal assembly, to put the Austrians on the spot, but coming from him, the quasi-dictator of Prussia, it was not taken seriously. But the recrudescence of the vexed question of Schleswig-Holstein was about to change his image in the eyes of a growing number of his compatriots.

The Schleswig-Holstein crisis

The Schleswig-Holstein question was proverbially complicated, but the underlying reality was the clash between German and Danish nationalism, which had already played so significant a role in 1848. Holstein was a wholly German duchy and part of the German Confederation. In North Schleswig there was a sizeable Danish population and Schleswig lay outside the German Confederation. The King of

Denmark was also Duke of Holstein, and in this capacity represented at Frankfurt, and Duke of Schleswig. In the post-revolutionary settlement of 1852 the great powers had guaranteed the integrity of the Danish monarchy on the basis of the equality of its three component areas. The Danish aim was to consolidate the whole monarchy in one constitutional structure, if necessary by recognizing the separate status of Holstein, while wholly incorporating Schleswig. This incorporation was naturally anathema to German national feeling. The separation of the two duchies was also unacceptable, running counter to a centuries-old tradition of remaining 'undivided', and could be construed as contrary to the 1852 settlement. Matters came to a head when in the autumn of 1863 Denmark adopted a new constitution applying both to Denmark and Schleswig. Immediately afterwards the Danish king died without an heir and Prince Christian of Sonderburg-Glücksburg came to the Danish throne. He was the father of Princess Alexandra who had just married the Prince of Wales, a factor which increased Danish confidence in British support. In Germany Christian was known as the Protocol Prince, because the London protocol of 1852 had recognized him as the heir to the Danish throne. On the grounds that other parts of this protocol had been violated by the new Danish constitution, Duke Frederick of Augustenburg, whose father had in 1852 surrendered his claim to the succession in the duchies for himself, now claimed to be the rightful Duke of Schleswig-Holstein. This claim was enthusiastically supported by the German national movement.

Fervent propagandist of his own cause that he was, Bismarck recalled in his memoirs that he had told his king that all his Hohenzollern forebears had extended the Prussian territory and that this crisis was his chance to do the same. At this remark the Crown Prince had thrown his hands up into the air, as if doubting Bismarck's sanity. It is, however, unlikely that the eventual annexation of the two duchies by Prussia was the result of a deep-laid and cunningly executed plan by Bismarck, but he undoubtedly had a clear notion of what he must seek to avoid. High on his list of undesirable outcomes was the creation of yet another genuinely independent medium-size German state right on Prussia's doorstep. The upsurge of feeling in Germany in favour of the Augustenburg duke had explosive and potentially revolutionary implications and could not be allowed to get out of control. The Confederate Diet must not be allowed to use the occasion to enhance its standing. Great care had to be taken that Prussia should not become isolated among the Great Powers by fighting the cause of German nationalism when it was not in its own interest. Almost the greatest danger to Bismarck came from within his own camp. The king was sorely tempted to espouse the Augustenburg cause, thereby recovering the popularity for Prussia in Germany that Bismarck had lost. Among those trying to persuade the king to follow that course was the Prussian ambassador in Paris, Count von der Goltz, who might have displaced Bismarck. In a letter warning him that as a mere envoy it was not his business to put forward policies different from those of the government he represented Bismarck wrote: 'The question is, are we a great power or simply another state of the Confederation . . . ruled by professors, petty magistrates and small-town gossips.' Von der Goltz became a rival whom Bismarck pursued with bitter and undying hatred.

It has always been regarded as Bismarck's masterstroke in the Schleswig-Holstein crisis that he managed to drag Austria in Prussia's wake. The two major German powers had, after all, only just emerged from a collision over the Austrian plan to reform the Confederation, scuppered by Prussia's refusal to support it. It is, however, not difficult to see why there was a sigh of relief in Vienna when the Prussian prime minister refused to endorse the Augustenburg cause. The spectre of nationalism in full cry, aroused by the confrontation with Danish aspirations, was simply too dangerous for the Austrian multinational empire to play with. It was equally dangerous for Vienna to allow international settlements such as the London protocol of 1852 to be set aside without due cause. This would have been the case if the Augustenburg claim to both duchies had succeeded. The Austrians had other worries, particularly what further damage Napoleon III might inflict on them in Italy. Rechberg, the Austrian foreign minister, had always been somewhat sceptical that the German policy pursued by some of his colleagues would achieve much for Vienna. He was therefore glad when Bismarck showed no sign of wishing to steal a march on Austria by making common cause with the German national movement. It looked as if Bismarck was a genuine conservative, as he had shown himself to be with his reactionary domestic policies, and would do nothing to unleash the tiger of revolutionary nationalism. But cooperation with Prussia carried great risks for the Austrians. It alienated them from the German national movement, just when they were in greater favour with German liberals than the reactionary Hohenzollern state. The smaller German states had usually followed Austria rather than Prussia, but it was these states that most favoured the Augustenburg solution. Under the leadership of the Bavarian von der Pfordten, the envoy of his country at Frankfurt, it looked for a moment as if a tripartite settlement of the German question had another chance. The motives of the smaller German states in supporting Augustenburg were somewhat different from those of German nationalists. By recruiting a significant new member to their number they hoped greatly to strengthen the voice of medium-sized German states against both major powers. The most obvious difficulty for the Austrians in the Schleswig-Holstein crisis was that the area of conflict was a long way from Vienna, but not far from Berlin.

Bismarck had thus plenty of material upon which to exercise his diplomatic skills, but one cannot fail to admire the almost superhuman dexterity with which he exploited the infinite complexities and endless twists and turns of the situation. To the Austrians he held out vistas of support for regaining their Italian territories without ever definitely committing himself. He reassured the great powers, especially the British, that the integrity of the Danish monarchy would be preserved by strict adherence to the London protocol, until Danish inability to retreat from the constitution they had promulgated undermined the legality of the protocol. He exploited the differences between the great powers to prevent the international conference convened to negotiate a settlement from reaching any definite result. In the Frankfurt Diet the legal niceties of the situation were exploited so as to frustrate all efforts, by von der Pfordten and others, to establish an independent Schleswig-Holstein state.

When it became clear in November 1863 that the new Danish king Christian IX would stand by the constitution promulgated by his predecessor the crisis moved into high gear. Support for the Augustenburg duke, implying annexation of Schleswig to the German Confederation, swept through Germany and reached a climax in a meeting of nearly five hundred parliamentarians from all over the country on 21 December 1863. A permanent committee of thirty-six was established to support the Augustenburg cause. Austria and Prussia asked the confederate states to suppress this committee as revolutionary. They based their case not on the Augustenburg claim, but on the Danish violation of the 1852 protocol and demanded that the Danes withdraw the constitution. When the Danes refused, Prussian and Austrian troops moved into Schleswig in January 1864, shoving aside the Saxon and Hanoverian troops that had earlier occupied Holstein on behalf of the Confederation. The initial performance of the Prussian troops was mediocre. To reassure London and St Petersburg, Bismarck claimed that, in view of the popular pressure for Augustenburg, simple inaction was not an option. Both Britain and Russia feared that Napoleon III would exploit the situation to further French championship of national movements.

Before the international conference could meet, which Russell, the British foreign secretary, proposed in February 1864, Bismarck ensured that there would be a decisive military victory against the Danes, the storming of the Düppel fortifications in Jutland on 18 April. He also wanted it to weaken domestic opposition. The Austrians were carried along in these operations without securing a definite commitment that they would get compensations if it came to the annexation of the duchies by Prussia. In the meantime the London conference went on its cumbersome way, made more difficult by Bismarck's personal absence from the negotiations. The Prussian prime minister, already in a strong position as a result of the Düppel victory, allowed various hares to run to frustrate any positive outcome. The Russians were strung along by some Prussian support for the Duke of Oldenburg, a close relative of the Russian royal family, as a claimant to the duchies. When the Austrians reverted to supporting the Augustenburg claims during the conference, Bismarck appeared to go along with them, but he gradually let the cat out of the bag that Prussian annexation might after all be the final outcome. He made sure that the Augustenburg solution did not materialize. In a three-hour interview with the unfortunate Duke Frederick of Augustenburg on 1 June 1864 he imposed conditions for allowing the duke to take up his rule in the duchies which would have reduced him to a Prussian puppet. When the duke refused to accept most of these conditions, Bismarck persuaded his own king that the Augustenburger had been unreasonable. Although British public opinion was on the whole on the side of Denmark, Britain could do little to support the Danes without a continental ally. When the conference ended without result on 25 June 1864, the war between Denmark and Prussia and Austria was resumed. Danish resistance quickly collapsed. The duchies were ceded to the two victorious German powers.

The victory over Denmark aroused much enthusiasm in Prussia and throughout Germany. It was the first ray of light for the embattled Bismarck government on its home ground. For the Liberal majority in the Prussian Landtag it posed an irresolvable dilemma. In January 1864, when the military operations against Denmark were beginning, they had refused to grant a war loan to a government that had been levying taxes without parliamentary sanction. Bismarck had taunted them in his most confrontational style. Now he had been proved right and had healed an injury to the German body politic festering since 1848. A number of influential Liberals, including the historians of national liberalism, Droysen, Sybel and Treitschke, began, with varying degrees of reluctance, to support the annexation of the duchies by Prussia. Theodor Mommsen, the famous historian of the Roman empire, also took that line, although he remained a courageous opponent of Bismarck. In the country at large the wider public was becoming tired of the Liberal stance against the monarchy and was impressed by the performance of the army. In Germany outside Prussia there was still strong support for Augustenburg and disgust at the way Prussia and Austria had set aside the ruler who clearly enjoyed the loyalty of the Schleswig-Holsteiners. The impression spread that Prussian liberalism was a paper tiger, unable and unwilling to resist the repressive Bismarck regime. Even though Prussia remained without moral conquests in Germany, her successful exercise of power was gaining respect. Austria was squandering much of the moral capital she had accumulated in the previous few years.

Revival of conflict between Austria and Prussia

Immediately after the end of the Danish war Rechberg, the Austrian foreign minister, and Bismarck met at Schönbrunn to decide what to do with the two duchies ceded to them. They drafted a convention under which in return for the eventual absorption of Schleswig-Holstein into Prussia, Austria would be assisted in regaining her Italian territories. When this draft was put to their respective rulers, Francis Joseph and William, they refused to endorse it. For them it was too risky and William was not yet ready to set aside the Augustenburg claims quite so brusquely. It is uncertain whether Bismarck expected the Schönbrunn convention to have much of a future, or whether he saw it mainly as a tactical device. If the convention had stood, it would have meant that the division of Germany into an Austrian South and a Prussian North, sketched by Bismarck soon after coming to power to the Austrian ambassador in Berlin, would have been realized. It would have meant that at some time Austria and Prussia might have to fight France side by side. It would have implied a settlement of the German question by old-fashioned diplomatic bargaining, rather than with regard to public opinion. The solidarity of the two conservative German powers, characteristic for the period from 1815 to 1848, would have been restored. Bismarck probably did not seriously believe that the clock could be turned back in this way, but if the Schönbrunn convention did not prove a viable way forward then he was likely to be driven into a closer relationship with the German national movement, something that might weaken the Prussian monarchical regime to which he was committed. He would have been the first to admit that in such large questions he was not a free agent.

Besides the Latin tag about pacting with the devil if all else fails, there was another he liked to quote, 'One can only ride a wave, not make it.' Even the riding was hazardous enough.

Almost immediately events occurred that made a continued cooperative relationship between Vienna and Berlin difficult. The negotiations about the renewal of the Zollverein treaty, due to expire in 1865, were about to be concluded and, as mentioned earlier (see p. 15), the exclusion of Austria was about to be confirmed. Bismarck would have liked to soften the blow by a face-saving formula, for he knew that Rechberg, who was useful to him, might be forced to resign. Delbrück, an influential official in the Prussian finance ministry and a strong free trader, insisted that for technical reasons no promise should be made this time about future negotiations with Austria over relations with the Zollverein. Bismarck, on holiday at the time, gave in and Rechberg's resignation soon followed. Schmerling, the prime minister, and Biegeleben, the secretary for German affairs in the Austrian foreign office, both proponents of a more actively anti-Prussian policy, regained influence in Vienna. Throughout 1865 there was smouldering conflict about the future of Schleswig-Holstein, under temporary joint administration by Austria and Prussia. Austria reverted to a policy of pushing the Augustenburg claims, if only as a bargaining counter. The Bismarck government used every conceivable device to weaken the Augustenburg position in the duchies, while giving a fair wind to the movement for annexation to Prussia. In the rest of Germany and in the Frankfurt Diet there was still much support for Augustenburg, but also some for the Oldenburg claimant. In February Bismarck had, after much delay, set out some of the conditions under which Prussia would refrain from annexing the duchies. They amounted to a virtual military control of key bases and of the armed forces of Schleswig-Holstein by Prussia and the building of a canal under Prussian control across the isthmus. These conditions were unacceptable to Vienna. On 6 April 1865, the Diet passed a motion, moved by the middle states, that the administration of the duchies should be handed over to the Augustenburg duke. Austria indicated that she was prepared to accept provided Prussia did so, but Prussia refused.

War between Austria and Prussia over Schleswig-Holstein was in the air. Such a war would blow the Confederation to pieces and decide the future of Germany. Bismarck was, however, in spite of his 'iron and blood' reputation, not the man to engage in war unnecessarily or prematurely. At a Prussian Crown Council on 29 May 1865 the king, now fully converted to annexation, accepted that war was now an option, but Bismarck wanted no immediate decision. His prevarication throughout the year 1865 has puzzled historians but there were a number of reasons for it. There was still the ultra party at court, contemplating a coup d'état and talking of an 'domestic Düppel', and its chief protagonist Manteuffel was always prone to interfere in Bismarck's subtle scheming and trying to undermine his position with the king. By August 1865 the prime minister managed to get him appointed governor of Schleswig and thereby removed from Berlin. At the same time there was still no accommodation with the Liberals in the Landtag and the rigid attitude of the king made it difficult for Bismarck to make concessions over the military budget. He taunted the Liberals mercilessly, for instance when they refused funds for a naval base at Kiel, something that all German nationalists had always wanted and that fuelled the argument for annexation in Prussia. Like the false mother in Solomon's judgment, they would rather kill the child, he said. But he left doors open for patching up the constitutional conflict, if it could be done on his own terms. A war with Austria, a German civil war, could only achieve Prussia's broader objectives in Germany if it found support in public opinion. The Landtag's continued refusal to vote adequate funds made it advisable to secure the financial position of the government beyond doubt and may have been another reason for caution in seeking a showdown with Austria. Bismarck's position as the increasingly indispensable minister rested precisely on the fact that only he could successfully defy the Liberals without resorting to the ultra solution of a coup d'état, but war remained a high risk for him. Years later in retirement he referred to those days as a time when he was 'almost as close to the gallows as to the throne'. Even after the successful war with Denmark Bismarck's dismissal and replacement by a more liberal ministry was still widely predicted.

Last but not least there was the international situation. At the May Crown Council Bismarck had painted a fairly favourable picture, with Russia unlikely to intervene in an Austrian–Prussian conflict, Britain hardly deserving a mention and France probably neutral. The new Italian kingdom was a possible ally. But Napoleon III remained unpredictable and restless. For the survival of his regime he needed successes and his Mexican adventure had failed to provide them. In his contacts with French diplomats Bismarck hinted at all manner of advantages that France might reap if she remained neutral in a future Austro-Prussian conflict. It was characteristic of Bismarck's exceptional skill that he was able to keep all the component elements of an infinitely complex situation in a kind of mental suspension, until they would gel to his advantage. It was fortunate for him that the key figures on the Austrian side, no doubt men of lesser ability than himself, had an even more difficult hand to play. Mensdorff, who replaced Rechberg as foreign minister in October 1864, was more suspicious of Prussia and inclined to put more weight behind the Augustenburg claims. The constitutional reforms, centred round a strengthened *Reichsrat* and initiated in 1861, ran into the sand and by 1865 Francis Joseph decided to suspend them and negotiate directly with the Hungarians, who had always boycotted the Reichsrat. This led to the resignation of Schmerling, whose attempts to mobilize the grossdeutsch movement behind Austria had never found much favour with the emperor. It is, to say the least, doubtful, if the Austrians would have fared better if they had more resolutely backed the Augustenburg claims and aligned themselves more consistently with the middle German states. Any flirtation with kleindeutsch national liberalism was difficult for the Habsburg empire and even a grossdeutsch solution might be a threat to its integrity. It proved impossible to resolve relations with the Zollverein to Austria's satisfaction. Financial near-insolvency and heavy indebtedness ruled out war as anything but a last resort. Fear of revolution, fear of Napoleon and renewed attack in Italy, all severely restricted the Austrian room for manoeuvre.

It was therefore not surprising that Austria and Prussia sought to continue their alliance, even if conflict over the future of Schleswig-Holstein brought them to the brink of war in the summer of 1865. The Prussians largely held the initiative in this confrontation and no doubt Bismarck could have turned up the heat until it reached flashpoint. It was probably because there was still so much that was precarious and incalculable in his situation that he preferred not to go over the brink. He offered few concessions and made the most of the many dilemmas that confronted the Austrians. It was precisely these dilemmas that persuaded Francis Joseph and his advisers to give another chance to cooperation with Prussia. Bismarck, reviled throughout Germany as the reactionary Junker, still appeared to be a better partner for Vienna than a more liberal Prussian government that might have replaced him. The result was the Gastein convention signed in Salzburg in August 1865. The two duchies remained juridically under the joint sovereignty of the two powers, but administratively they were divided, Holstein going to Austria and Schleswig to Prussia. Prussia obtained special rights in Holstein, which fell only slightly short of those that Bismarck had demanded in February. The Austrians paid a heavy price for this agreement, for it further undermined the grossdeutsch cause. Prussia had at least a strategic stake in the duchies, which could not be disputed, but Austria appeared to have gratuitously offended against justice and the right of self-determination. In the negotiations at Gastein the division of the duchies was talked of as legally permanent, but this would have aroused even greater indignation throughout Germany. The Austrians therefore suggested that the settlement should be regarded as provisional and Bismarck readily agreed. It looked like a concession, but it would in fact enable him to aggravate the confrontation with Austria in the duchies at any time of his choosing. If the Austrian leaders still thought of Bismarck as a conservative and guardian of the status quo, they fundamentally misjudged him. In Prussia there was little doubt that Bismarck had scored another triumph and after Gastein the title of count was conferred upon him by the king.

There was also a widespread feeling that the Gastein convention had only postponed a further clash between the two big German powers. Bismarck continued to prepare for a war that he had always regarded as likely. In retrospect and crowned by success he made it look as if he had held all the threads in his hands and pulled them with consummate skill and foresight. In fact the situation was full of uncertainties, his own position remained precarious and the risks were high. On paper the Habsburg empire was still a much larger power than Prussia and when war broke out in the summer of 1866 even the Berlin stock exchange expected an Austrian victory. To move towards war within the foreseeable future was, however, probably the only way in which Bismarck could be sure of remaining in power at all. An important point in the renewed deterioration of Austro-Prussian relations was reached when in January 1866 a pro-Augustenburg demonstration at Altona, in Austrian-controlled Holstein, provoked sharp Prussian protests. Both sides were trying to make themselves look the aggrieved party in the court of public opinion. They were squaring up to what was an old-style cabinet war not sparked by any popular enthusiasm, yet they could no longer ignore the public.

Not the least of Bismarck's problems was again the king, who would need a lot of convincing before finally embarking upon an unpopular fratricidal war. With the king 'he was like a watchmaker who had to rewind the clock every morning'. On 28 February 1866 there was a Prussian Crown Council, consisting of the inner circle of Prussian civil and military decision-makers under the chairmanship of the king. Bismarck's rivals, von der Goltz and Manteuffel were present. Bismarck embarked upon a long historical disquisition, in which he claimed that Prussia was the only viable political creation to emerge from the ruins of the Holy Roman Empire and that Austria had always jealously frustrated Prussia's justified ambition to take the lead in Germany. He was trying to set at rest the conservative fears of his listeners that in contemplating war they were in fact sanctioning a revolutionary enterprise. Only the Crown Prince spoke decisively against war, but this did not mean that there would be no further backsliding by the king. There were many others around him, including the queen and the Crown Prince and Princess, who abhorred a war and the Austrians encouraged them to shake the king's resolve. A definite decision taken by the Crown Council was to seek an alliance with Italy. The military chiefs led by Helmuth von Moltke, the chief of the Prussian General Staff, considered an Italian attack on Austria an essential condition for a Prussian victory. The secret alliance with Italy was concluded on 8 April and envisaged the annexation by Italy of Venetia at the end of a victorious war. The alliance was limited to three months, thus virtually setting a time limit by which Prussia was bound to detonate a war. Bismarck had also worked hard and skilfully to ensure the neutrality of Napoleon III. He had visited him soon after the signing of the Gastein convention, which, with the two German powers riding roughshod over the right of national self-determination, had caused disquiet in France. In subsequent months he held out prospects of territorial gain for France, without ever committing himself, but the French emperor also left his future course open. Bismarck could with greater certainty rely on the non-interference of Russia and Britain in an Austro-Prussian war. Everywhere he sowed confusion whether his real intentions were conservative or whether, for the sake of Prussian aggrandizement and his own survival, he was prepared to ally with himself with the forces of radical change. The Austrian leadership deluded themselves right up to the brink of war that Bismarck was a better safeguard for the status quo than any liberal ministry that might succeed him in Berlin.

Bismarck's first major move to expand the conflict with Austria over Schleswig-Holstein into an attempt to resolve the situation in Germany in Prussia's favour was a plan, tabled on 9 April 1866 in the Frankfurt Diet, to summon a national parliament elected by universal suffrage. The idea to undercut the Liberal majority that always emerged from the Prussian three-tier electoral law by appealing to the masses below had long figured in Bismarck's calculations and had surfaced in his talks with Lassalle. Now it was a bold bid for the support of the German national movement which Austria would find it impossible to match. The Liberals in Prussia and elsewhere in Germany were unimpressed and, coming from such a quarter, it was thought to be a ridiculous gesture. A Berlin comic journal said it might have to cease publication because it could not think of a better joke. But by this time the organized Liberal movement such as the *Nationalverein* was already seriously weakened by years of disillusionment over the Prussian constitutional conflict and the cynical disregard of popular feeling in Schleswig-Holstein. Bismarck was clearly appealing to a wider public and was even trying to make his proposal palatable to the middle states, by pointing to the conservative potential of a wide suffrage. At the same time he could threaten, when it suited him, to unleash a national revolutionary movement.

As war became inevitable both Austria and Prussia sought to rally support in the German Confederation and wherever else they could find it. Bismarck tried to mobilize nationalist discontent in the Habsburg empire by encouraging the formation of Hungarian, Serb and Rumanian legions that would mount diversionary attacks against the Austrians, an indication how far he was now prepared to go to encourage revolution. Vienna concluded a last-minute secret treaty with France, by which Paris undertook to remain neutral and to work for the neutrality of Italy, though for this it was already too late. In return for this Austria would cede Venetia to France, to be passed on to Italy under appropriate conditions. After an Austrian victory there would be compensations for the Habsburg empire, but not to the detriment of France; there might be an independent state on the Rhine formed from the Prussian provinces, though this was only a verbal understanding. Napoleon III thus assured both sides of his neutrality and was clearly calculating that after a long and exhausting war he would step in as arbiter and secure gains for his country. Like most others he expected an Austrian victory and the Austrians had made more concrete concessions to him than the Prussians. For all his skilful manouevrings Bismarck had, however, failed to secure much advantage. The German liberal movement was as hostile as ever. When an assassination attempt on him in early May failed there was scant sympathy and more regret that he survived. When the war started, all the bigger states, Bavaria, Saxony, Hanover, Württemberg and even Baden, often the champion of a kleindeutsch solution, were on the side of Austria and only the small states, that were virtual enclaves in Prussian territory, were on the side of Prussia. Everything therefore depended on the outcome of the war.

The war of 1866

Although smaller in sheer size, Prussia had a more advanced military potential. After the victory at Sadowa, known in Germany as Königgrätz, it was common parlance to attribute it to the Prussian schoolmaster. The ordinary Prussian soldier was well educated in comparison with others, but he was also well equipped. The Prussian needle gun could be fired from a recumbent position, and although shorter in reach, could fire seven shots in a minute, as opposed to two in older types. Moltke had created a general staff through which he could impose a strategic plan. He used modern developments like railways and the telegraph, the importance of which had already been demonstrated in the American civil war, to make his plan effective. The Austrian army was more old-fashioned and cumbersome, requiring a long mobilization period that had already had an adverse effect on their pre-war diplomacy. The German states allied to Austria did not adopt a common strategy. Three Prussian armies were according to Moltke's plan to converge on the Austrian army massing in Bohemia, but to unite only on the battlefield. The third army, commanded by the Crown Prince, arrived only just in time. The Prussian victory was not complete, for the bulk of the Austrian army escaped, but the speed of it was decisive. Those who, like Napoleon III, had based their calculations on a long-drawn-out war were confounded. Bismarck who, when the outcome hung in the balance, had declared that he would seek death on the battlefield rather than face the gallows in Berlin, was vindicated. It was one of the decisive battles of history. The fate of Germany, with consequences that dominated the twentieth century, was decided on the battlefield, by the Prussian military monarchy, by 'iron and blood'. This was to have enormous consequences, not merely on the power, but also on the outlook and political constitution of the future German Reich.

Bismarck still had a hard fight to secure the full benefits of the victory. A swift settlement with Austria was required to avoid outside intervention, especially from France. The Austrians had been victorious against the Italians and provided they were excluded from Germany, it was not in the Prussian interest to see them humiliated or further weakened. Bismarck had a difficult task, pushing him to the edge of nervous collapse, to impose this point of view on the king and the other Prussian leaders. They would have liked a victorious march on Vienna and the exaction of tribute and territory. The Prussian king had been present at the battle of Sadowa, had encouraged his troops and wanted the fruits of victory according to traditional notions of war. Bismarck got his way and with French mediation the preliminary peace of Nikolsburg was signed on 26 July 1866, followed by a full peace treaty four weeks later. Behind the French role as mediator there was a scarcely concealed threat of intervention and a demand for compensation. Austria recognized the end of the German Confederation and her total exclusion from Germany. The only concession she secured in Germany was that the territorial integrity of her long-standing ally Saxony was guaranteed by Prussia. In return there were no territorial cessions by Austria except Venetia. Bismarck later represented it that it was entirely due to his far-seeing magnanimity that no other territorial losses were imposed on the Habsburg empire, but it may well have owed something to French pressure. Both Austria and France had to agree to give Prussia a free hand to make territorial changes and annexations in northern Germany, including Schleswig-Holstein. The only explicit concession that Napoleon III secured was that the South German states were left independent and would not be included in a North German Confederation. The idea that they should form a South German Confederation was soon dropped and they concluded defensive treaties with Prussia, which remained secret until March 1867. Although they had to pay Prussia indemnities, they did not have to cede any substantial territory. In Germany Prussia completely annexed Hanover, Electoral Hesse, Nassau and the City of Frankfurt, thereby creating a continuous territory from west of the Rhine to East Prussia. The King of Hanover, the Elector of Hesse and the Duke of Nassau were dispossessed, an offence against the principle of legitimacy, to which Bismarck secured the agreement of his king only with difficulty. The dethroned rulers received some monetary and other compensations. The King of Hanover continued to resist and therefore his compensation was never implemented. As a result the Prussian government had at its disposal a so-called Guelph fund, secret money which Bismarck later use for various manipulatory purposes. The City of Frankfurt, which resented Prussian rule and the threat it posed to its commercial and financial importance, had heavy fines imposed upon it. Its mayor committed suicide. The question of French territorial compensation was left vague and the events of 1866 were soon seen in France as a defeat. The slogan 'revenge for Sadowa' began to circulate.

The events of 1866 amounted to a revolution. The Pope, Pius IX, greeted the news with the exclamation 'the world has collapsed'. Commentators and biographers down to the present have called Bismarck 'the white revolutionary'. The decisive step towards the creation of a powerful German state in Central Europe had been taken. It had not been done from below, as the culmination of a movement combining nationalism with liberalism, which had been the expectation almost since the beginning of the century. It had been done from above, by the Prussian military monarchy and its army. Power relations in Europe could never be the same again, but the transformation inside Germany was equally far-reaching. Even after the successful war against Denmark the resolve of the liberals in Prussia had been weakened, but most of them were still sticking to their principles. On the day of Sadowa, 3 July 1866, and before the news of the victory reached Berlin, elections to the Landtag had taken place in Prussia. For the first time since the New Era there were heavy liberal losses. The Progressive Party declined from 141 seats in 1863 to 83; the Conservatives rose from 35 to 136 (see Appendix: Table 6). Many liberals now revised their opinion of Bismarck drastically. A leading legal scholar, Rudolf von Ihering had only just written that 'never has a war been unleashed with such shamelessness, such gruesome frivolity . . . One's innermost feelings are revolted by such an outrage against all principles of justice and morality.' Now he bowed down before 'the genius of this Bismarck, who has delivered a masterpiece of political combination and energy scarcely equalled in history . . .' Most liberals, in and out of Prussia, were similarly elated, seeing providence at work, and greeting the end of an Austrian role in Germany as the end of a time that had been a hangover from the Middle Ages. Under Prussia and the Hohenzollerns the modern age would begin. Many Catholics, South Germans and followers of the grossdeutsch ideal were deeply downcast.

Domestic consequences of the war of 1866

The general expectation after the victories of the Prussian armies was that the Bismarck government would now realize what had seemed to be its aim since 1862. An absolute monarchy governing without much, if anything, in the way of constitutional restraints would be formalized. When at the beginning of August the speech from the throne opening the newly elected Landtag announced a step that looked almost like the opposite, it was like a bombshell. The government announced the introduction of an indemnity law, to regularize in retrospect the expenditure which had been incurred without parliamentary sanction since 1862.

It did not mean that the government declared itself to be in the wrong or admitted that the 'gap theory'on which it had acted was illegal. It meant, however, that in the hour of his triumph Bismarck indicated to the Liberal opposition that he was prepared to end the conflict with them. He knew that he could not govern against an important section of the population for ever. They had rejected the olive branch he had offered on his accession to office and at intervals since then. Now they would find rejection much more difficult, for by taking a big step towards German unity he had realized much of what they had always wanted. At the least, the indemnity offer would split the Liberals into those who accepted it and those who persisted in opposition. It also split the Conservatives. Principled legitimists like Bismarck's old friend Ludwig von Gerlach had already parted company with him before Sadowa. Now others who were expecting the victory to be followed by an 'internal Königgrätz' were deeply disappointed. They were confirmed in their suspicions that Bismarck was not really one of them, though for the moment they had no alternative but to vote for the indemnity law in the Landtag. The party landscape in Prussia was thus radically transformed, just when the country was on the threshold of the new North German Confederation, of which it would form the major part. Bismarck did not impose the indemnity law on the reluctant king and his entourage merely because he realized that there was no future in going back to absolutism, or because he had would continue to need the support of the German national movement. By creating alternative centres of power to the monarchy he would strengthen his own hold on power. Even before 1866 he had often found himself at the point of intersection between the court party composed of men like Manteuffel, dreaming of overturning the constitution by a coup d'état, and the Liberal opposition in the Landtag. Now he would institutionalize his pivotal position and make himself more than ever irremovable.

The establishment of the North German Confederation

After the stresses and strains of the war and its aftermath Bismarck went on a prolonged leave of absence from Berlin, something that became a habit with him during the long years of quasi-dictatorial power that lay ahead of him. Detached from the day to day conduct of affairs he sketched the main points of the new constitution that was to operate in Germany for the next fifty years. Much preparatory work had already been done by his assistants, but Bismarck laid down the essence of what he wanted in two drafts, dated 30 October and 19 November 1866. He took little account of constitutional theories and was above all concerned with making the will of the Prussian government, and his own power, prevail in the new set-up. The obvious solution, a federal state built around Prussia, would have aroused too much opposition even in the comparatively minor states that had already acceded to the North German Confederation and would have created a barrier to the future accession of the South German states. Bismarck saw his task as achieving as much centralization as possible, as in a federal state such as the USA, while making it look like a continuation of the German Confederation that had just come to an end. He wanted a parliament elected on universal suffrage, such as he had already proposed earlier in the year and as had figured in the constitution that finally emerged from the Frankfurt parliament in 1849. This seemed to him the best way to connect the people as a whole with the state and much preferable to the existing three-tier Prussian franchise, which favoured the properous middle classes, the mainstay of liberalism. But there was to be no parliamentary government on the English model, for Bismarck's parliament would have no control over the executive. He already envisaged that a federal parliament elected on universal suffrage would be in conflict with Länder parliaments, especially the Prussian Landtag, elected on a restricted franchise, and that these conflicts would limit the power of all these elected assemblies. It was a case of defeating parliamentarism, the fully fledged English version, through parliaments. The central organ in Bismarck's scheme was to be a federal Diet, eventually called the Bundesrat, in which the separate constituent states, or rather their rulers, would be represented by delegates, much like the Frankfurt Diet. The Prussian king would hold the presidency of the Bundesrat and Prussia would have 17 out 43 votes. It was not a majority, but it would require only five of the small enclave states to cast their vote with Prussia to make it a majority. The executive would consist of a chancellor appointed by the president of the Bundesrat, the King of Prussia, but he would be no more than an executant of the business laid down by the Bundesrat. The post was to be held by an official of the Prussian foreign ministry.

When the proposed constitution was discussed in the constituent Reichstag of the North German Confederation elected in February 1867 an important change was made. The chancellor was made responsible to the Parliament of the Federation. By 'responsible' was not meant that he required the confidence of the parliament, as a British prime minister requires the confidence of the House of Commons and has to resign if he loses it. In the German case it meant that the chancellor could be interrogated and asked to give an account of his policies in the Reichstag, but he was neither appointed nor could he be removed by the Reichstag. Even the limited extent to which he was responsible to the Reichstag meant that the chancellor became a much more important figure than was originally envisaged. It also meant that there would be an executive government at the Reich level, initially consisting only of the chancellor, which, rather than the Bundesrat, would become the real centre of power. By the same token the Reichstag would have the potentiality of developing into a really significant forum. It would be in the Reichstag that the representatives of the people as a whole would confront, though not control the executive government of the country, initially the chancellor on his own, later flanked by departmental chiefs subordinate to him, known as Reich State Secretaries. It seems likely that Bismarck saw that the chancellorship in this form was the ideal position for himself, to be held in tandem with the positions of Prussian prime minister and foreign minister which he already held. He may even have suggested this change, known as the Lex Bennigsen, behind the scenes. Bennigsen was the leader of the pro-Bismarck liberals, the National Liberals, but his amendment turned out to have established a quasi-dictatorial chancellorship, rather than the government responsible to parliament, to which the liberals had always aspired.

There were some other points on which Bismarck showed flexibility when the constitutional draft was under discussion in the constituent Reichstag. He had originally envisaged that no-one holding a public office, civil servants, judges, professors, should be eligible for parliament. It was men of this kind who had constituted the core of the liberal opposition that he had fought since 1862. Clearly he did not wish the new parliament to become a real focus of opposition to the executive government headed by himself. On this point Bismarck gave way and public officials continued to form a high proportion of the parliamentary personnel of Imperial Germany. Bismarck did not give way on the principle that there should be no payment of members, because he did not want a class of professional politicians. The effect initially was that representatives of interest groups were slow to come forward, but eventually parliamentary politics in Imperial Germany became professionalized to a considerable extent.

Bismarck was also prepared to make some concessions on the budgetary prerogatives of the Reichstag, the area in which the Prussian constitutional conflict had been played out. In a departure from the original governmental draft the Reichstag was given the right to vote on an annual budget. A fundamental requirement of representative government appeared thus to have been recognized. The military budget, which made up over ninety per cent of the federal budget, was, however, excepted. A fixed sum per soldier, and a fixed number of soldiers in proportion to the population, effectively removed the power of the Reichstag over the military budget, but this arrangement, initially proposed as permanent, was through another compromise to operate until 31 December 1871, then to continue until fixed by further legislation. The indemnity law, which in the Prussian Landtag had recognized the assembly's budgetary powers, did not therefore extend to the military budget. This was now a federal matter, but it was the Prussian king who held supreme command over all the forces of the confederate states. The Prussian military monarchy had resolved the German question by force of arms and retained its exceptional powers over military affairs, the *Kommandogewalt* (power of command). If anything, this military prerogative of the Prussian king, the future German emperor, was even more completely sealed off from political interference than it had been under the Prussian constitution. This position did not substantially change until 1918.

The constituent Reichstag approved the constitution by 230 to 53 votes on 16 April 1867. It had been elected two months earlier on universal male suffrage and reflected the new party landscape created by the revolutionary events of 1866. The National Liberals, those liberals who had accepted the indemnity law and were prepared to cooperate with Bismarck, were the largest party with 80 out of 297 seats. There were now two conservative groups. The larger group, some 60, were mainly the old Prussian Conservatives, who found much to dislike in what had occurred, but had not yet moved into outright opposition to the Bismarck government. The other group, some 40, were now called Free Conservatives, who, as it was often put, supported Bismarck '*sans phrase*'. They were a party of big entrepreneurs and of landowners from outside the Prussian heartlands, for example from Silesia, where some very large landowners were also involved with industrial enterprises and were Catholics. The opposition to the constitution came mainly from those members of the Progressive party who had refused to accept the indemnity law. There were only some twenty of them left, but they were reinforced by representatives from annexed territories like Hanover, from the Poles in the Prussian eastern provinces and from Catholics alienated from the mainly Protestant new Confederation. They formed the nucleus for what was soon to become the Centre party (*Zentrum*), a most significant feature of the German party landscape until 1933.

The big question that historians have raised and answered in different ways is whether those Liberals who had accepted the indemnity law and now the new constitution had sold their soul for a mess of pottage. There are those who argue that the question must not be answered with benefit of hindsight. It was not be foreseen in 1867 that doubts about the liberal vision of progress and enlightenment would spread far beyond Germany. The Prussian Liberals who made their peace with Bismarck, the National Liberals, could feel that much of what they wanted had been achieved. Unity had come before freedom, but freedom could only be achieved in a united country, not in the dwarf states into which Germany had hitherto been divided. Much could still be achieved under the new dispensation and was indeed achieved, especially in the social and economic sphere. A genuinely unified system of law would emerge from the collaboration of the National Liberals with the Bismarck government in the next decade. What were the alternatives? If the liberal movement had remained in rigid opposition history would have by-passed it.

These arguments of the National Liberals and of many contemporary and subsequent commentators were realistic enough. Nevertheless nothing could disguise the fact that the Prussian army had won and that Bismarck had largely imposed his own constitutional solution on the new North German Confederation, soon to become the German empire. The perpetuation of the power of the Prussian military monarchy and thereby of his own power was his objective. He had made it acceptable by some clever window-dressing, perhaps by some concessions that would take him further downstream into a modern industrial urban society than he bargained for. But the expectation that a unified Germany would be a state on the western parliamentary model, with a government responsible to the representatives of the electorate, a state in which a government so constituted would have unequivocal control over all spheres of public policy, including the military, was not fulfilled and was never to be fulfilled before the First World War destroyed the empire. The liberals hoped that there would soon be a time after Bismarck when their visions of the future would be realized, but when the time came it was a quarter of a century on and the situation was very different. Meanwhile Bismarck remained dominant and his only use for parliaments and parties was to reinforce his own dominance.

The North German Confederation and the South

For the German national movement, that had shown itself to be so powerful a force that even Bismarck could not ignore it, the unity of North Germany that was achieved in 1866 was incomplete. Although the treaty of Prague at the end of the war of 1866 had recognized the independence of the South German states Baden, Bavaria and Württemberg, they were already tied to North Germany by major economic and military arrangements. The northern half of the fourth, the Grand Duchy of Hesse-Darmstadt, was part of the North German Confederation. The defensive alliances, already mentioned, were made acceptable to the defeated states by the perceived threat from France. Then there were the economic ties of the Zollverein, which had proved one of the underlying reasons for the ejection of Austria from Germany. The fact that members of the Zollverein had gone to war against each other shows that the customs union was no stepping stone to an inevitable political union, but it was still so strong a necessity for the South German economies that it had to be re-established as soon as the guns were silent. Bismarck himself was well aware how strong the pressures were for the adherence of the Southern states to the Confederation. He was certainly minded to exploit any chance to extend the Confederation south of the Main, provided it could be done on terms that maintained Prussian hegemony and his own power, in the way these had been secured north of the Main. He also knew the obstacles, most obviously the challenge such an extension would pose for France. He was prepared to wait and he made many statements to the effect that the fruit was not ripe for plucking and might not be in his lifetime. He was ambivalent about a closer union with South German Catholics before the North German union was even consolidated. But the course of events, which he had done so much to precipitate, meant that his own future as the greatest of political operators was more than ever bound up with the German national movement.

The first step that offered itself for drawing the bonds closer in internal German affairs was the renegotiation of the Zollverein. Bismarck proposed far-reaching reforms that turned a loose association, in which member states had a veto, into a confederation as close as and analogous in structure to the North German Confederation. There was to be an elected Zollverein parliament, by the addition of representatives from the South German states, elected by universal suffrage to the existing North German Reichstag, increasing its size from 297 to 388. Similarly representatives from the South German states would be added to the North German Bundesrat, but the ability of Prussia to veto proposals in this body was preserved. Bismarck forced these proposals through against considerable opposition in Bavaria and Württemberg. Baden under its liberal Grand Duke had already applied to join the North German Confederation, but Bismarck had blocked this as premature and too provocative for Napoleon III to swallow.

When elections for the South German deputies to the Zollvereinparliament took place in the spring of 1868 Bismarck's hopes of a gradual move towards a closer union were rudely rebuffed. In Bavaria an anti-Prussian Catholic party won 26 out of 48 seats and the pro-Prussian party only 12. In Württemberg a grossdeutsch-democratic party won 11 out of 17 seats. Even in Baden, where the pro-Prussian elements were strongest, the nationalists got only 8 out of 14 seats. These results showed the depth of popular anti-Prussianism in South Germany. For Bavarians and Württembergers Prussia meant 'pay taxes, be a soldier, and keep your mouth shut'. The problem was the economic dependence of the southern states on the enlarged Prussia and on lines of communication through it to the northern seaboard. By 1877 the Zollverein would need to be renegotiated once more and this gave Prussia a kind of stranglehold on the southern states. Bismarck, it was often said, had the thumbscrews on them. Even in the southern states the entrepreneurial classes wanted the completion of unity, but for the moment they were a minority. Plans to form a South German federation were no more successful now than they had been previously and always foundered on the mutual rivalry of these states. Anti-Prussian feeling was counterbalanced by anti-French feeling. The myth of France as the hereditary enemy was well established and the revival of a French hegemony of the Napoleonic type was feared. If the French had wanted to preserve the independence of South Germany they would have needed to refrain from demanding compensations, as they did after Sadowa, that could be inter-preted as an assault on the integrity of the German nation. All these conflicting pressures added up to the fact that there was no inevitability about the extension of political unity south of the Main.

The Zollverein elections and the resurgence of particularism in the South were a setback to the cause of German national unity, but there were also positive developments in the years between 1867 and 1870. In those years the North German Reichstag passed some eighty laws which turned North Germany into a modern state, organized on the principles of free individual citizenship and a liberal market economy. Existing barriers to the free movement of the ordinary citizen, his freedom to marry and to exercise his religion were swept away. Previous restrictions on the right to settle freely in any locality had been linked to the right to claim poor relief. A law of 21 June 1869 removed all restrictions imposed by the old guild regulations on the citizen's right to follow a trade and permitted in principle the formation of trade unions. A law of 3 July 1869 removed previous restrictions on the rights of citizens and their ability to hold public office arising from their religious denomination. A general code of commercial law was promulgated, a supreme commercial court was set up, company, banking and currency legislation was put in place. When the Franco-Prussian war broke out the Reichstag was in process of revising the penal code along lines previously in force in Prussia. After 1871 these North German legal arrangements were extended to the whole Reich and further developed. These achievements were the result of close collaboration between the National Liberal and Free Conservative majority in the Reichstag on the one hand and the Prussian ministries on the other. The key figure was Rudolf von Delbrück, the head of the chancellor's office, who worked with the full blessing of Bismarck. Delbrück was at the same time negotiating a network of trade treaties between the Zollverein area and countries throughout the world based on free trade principles. These in turn had the full support of the National Liberals and their allies in the Reichstag. The leaders of the National Liberals, men like Bennigsen and Lasker, felt themselves justified in believing that their collaboration with Bismarck was achieving enormous results. They were prevented from penetrating into the inner citadel of power, but meanwhile they were helping to transform society in the direction they wanted. This rapid process of modernization in the North German Confederation strengthened the appeal of unification for those classes and groups who were looking forward to a similar transformation in their countries south of the Main.

Future developments depended as much on the general European constellation as on the internal German situation. British and Russian detachment, which had allowed the crisis of 1866 to take its course, could be expected to continue. Count Beust, the former Saxon foreign minister and a long-standing opponent of Prussian aggrandizement, had taken over the conduct of Austrian affairs. He had been forced to resign his position in Saxony as a result of Prussian pressure. The Habsburg empire was, however, in no condition to revise its ejection from Germany. Francis Joseph had been forced into a radical restructuring of his dominions by making the two major components, Austria and Hungary, into equal partners held together by allegiance to a common sovereign. In a symbolic act Francis Joseph was crowned King of Hungary in June 1867. This settlement, which turned both parts of the empire into constitutional states, was known as the *Ausgleich* (balancing act) and turned the Habsburg empire into the dual monarchy. A common foreign and defence policy remained. The dual monarchy could not undo Sadowa, but it could ally with France to prevent further Prussian expansion. In France the impression was widespread that the opportunity opened by the Austro-Prussian war to maintain or strengthen a French hegemonic position in Europe had been missed. Napoleon III's regime was under pressure to show results, but after the failure of its Mexican adventure it was in no condition to go to war. Bismarck, with the North German Confederation still in process of being established in 1867, was not eager to go to war either, though Moltke was quite prepared to risk it.

This was the situation when Napoleon III opened the Luxembourg crisis in March 1867. Luxembourg was part of the German Confederation and the King of Holland was as its Grand Duke represented in the Frankfurt Diet. With the demise of the confederation the future status of the grand duchy was uncertain. It had been a central feature of the compensations demanded by France in the summer of 1866. Bismarck had appeared to agree that France should take over Belgium, as well as the grand duchy by agreement with the King of Holland, but had, once the treaty of Prague was safely concluded, taken an increasingly dilatory line on the matter. Luxembourg was, however not included in the North German Confederation. When Napoleon blundered into the negotiation with the King of Holland over the purchase of Luxembourg, he immediately unleashed a storm of indignation in Germany, which was adroitly exploited by Bismarck. It helped him during the crucial debates in the Constituent Reichstag on the military budget. He used the occasion to reveal the secret defensive treaties made between Prussia and the South German states after the peace of Prague, which in turn unleashed a storm of anti-Prussian feeling in Paris. Under these treaties the military forces of these states were increasingly aligned in internal structure, organization and training with the Prussian army. With neither side prepared to go to the brink, the crisis was settled by an international conference in London. France was allowed an honourable get out by the withdrawal of the Prussian garrison which under Prussian–Dutch treaties occupied the fortress of Luxembourg. The crisis showed that the completion of German unity was unlikely to be possible without a war with France. It became evident that the German national movement was playing an increasingly important role in Bismarck's devious calculations. He was using it as a means to bring pressure to bear on chancelleries all over Europe. On the other hand, Bavaria and Württemberg had in this crisis not been willing unreservedly to commit themselves to war alongside Prussia. The alignment of the South German with the Prussian armed forces met much resistance and in many quarters a militia on the Swiss model would have been preferred. The demands of military service on the Prussian model and high military expenditure were factors feeding the anti-Prussian sentiment in the south.

If Bismarck had hoped to make up for the indecisive outcome of the Luxembourg crisis through his Zollverein reforms he was, as we have seen, to be disappointed. In the years from 1868 there was a feeling that the tide of German unification was receding and that only a great international crisis, most likely a war between Prussia and France, could reactivate it. War was still an instrument of policy for the European cabinet politicians of the age and there were unresolved issues around, other than the German question, that might precipitate it. The eastern question, the future of the Ottoman empire in Europe, was again on the agenda, re-ignited by the Cretan revolt against the Turks; the rivalry between Austria and Russia in the Balkans was active, while Russia was eager to reverse her humiliation in the Crimean war. For Prussia there was the danger of a Franco-Austrian alliance, and the lesser danger of a Franco-Russian alliance. In this parallelogram of forces Bismarck moved with his usual skill, but he could not afford merely to maintain the status quo. He had enhanced the German national movement in the field of forces and given it an institutional base in the Reichstag of the North German Confederation, but the last thing he wanted was for it to make the running. By the end of 1871 the arrangements under which the military budget was kept out of the control of the Reichstag would need to be renegotiated. If the German situation was still stagnant then, there might well be a recrudescence of constitutional conflict. Bismarck was not under an absolute necessity to move forward swiftly, but he must have welcomed any chance of doing so.

Early in 1870 two events illustrated the volatility of the situation. There was yet another attempt to bring Baden, where the pro-Prussian government found itself beleaguered, into the North German Confederation and Bismarck was bringing forward a project to confer the title of emperor on the king of Prussia. When Eduard Lasker, one of the leading National Liberals in the North German Reichstag, put forward a proposal to accept Baden into the North German Confederation, Bismarck repudiated it sharply. He neither wanted parliamentary interference in foreign affairs nor the National Liberals to gain credit for advancing unification. He feared that in Bavaria and Württemberg the anti-Northern forces would be strengthened and that France would be provoked just when a liberal prime minister, Ollivier, had taken office. In Bavaria on the other hand the liberal prime minister, Hohenlohe-Schillingsfürst, had just resigned. He had put forward a number of schemes for closer association between the southern states and the

North German Confederation, but the strong performance of the Catholic, particularist Patriot party in elections in late 1869 forced him out. If the forces of particularism and ultramontane Catholicism were to gain control in Munich, the cause of greater unity would suffer a severe setback. Meanwhile Bismarck had started to test reaction at home and abroad to the possibility of conferring the imperial title on King William, in what form remained to be decided. There were fears again that the reaction in France would raise tensions. The two southern kings, Württemberg and Bavaria, were not in favour, though Ludwig II of Bavaria, the 'mad king', would have been offered some title as deputy emperor. Bismarck left the project on hold.

The war of 1870

The German stalemate was broken in 1870 by the proposal that a Hohenzollern prince should ascend the Spanish throne. Queen Isabella of Spain had been driven into exile by a military-led revolt in September 1868. In the course of 1869 the possibility surfaced that Prince Leopold of Hohenzollern-Sigmaringen might be chosen as the new Spanish king. Hohenzollern-Sigmaringen was the southern, Catholic branch of the dynasty, one of whose members had already ascended the Rumanian throne. Prince Leopold required the consent of King William, as head of the family, for his candidacy. Bismarck clearly saw the potentialities of the proposal for breaking the German stalemate and may well have encouraged it long before it became official. When it did become official in 1870, he did his best to undermine the reluctance of King William to agree to it. He and his agents also worked hard to overcome the scruples of the candidate himself and of his father, the head of the Sigmaringen branch. Several times it looked as if the Hohenzollern candidacy would die a natural death, much to Bismarck's chagrin, but it refused to go away. At vital moments Bismarck retired ill to his country estate at Varzin, given to him by a grateful sovereign and nation, and was unable to transact business. Finally, in June 1870, it looked as if Bismarck had achieved his objective. Prince Leopold and his father accepted the candidacy and King William reluctantly agreed. Before the acceptance would become public the Spanish Cortes would proclaim Prince Leopold king, thereby creating a *fait accompli* which the French government would be unable to change. To French protests Bismarck would maintain the line that it was a dynastic affair and had nothing to do with the Prussian government, but it would still be a boost to Hohenzollern and to German national pride. The intention of creating an accomplished fact miscarried, because owing to a mistake in deciphering dates the Cortes was prorogued before it could carry out the proclamation and the secret of Prince Leopold's acceptance leaked out.

In the meantime the Duc de Gramont had become French foreign minister. Although the liberal premier Ollivier remained, Gramont had much more rigorous ideas about limiting further Prussian advances and old-fashioned views of what French honour and power required. There was in France an on-going conflict between those who wanted to maintain the authoritarian features of the regime and those who saw its future best secured by liberalization. The pressure for reform had come mainly from the educated classes and from the towns. A new more liberal constitution had been confirmed by plebiscite in France in May 1870, but it did not mean a complete turn towards a parliamentary monarchy. This reformed Bonapartist system seemed to enjoy broad popular support, but the political élite, from the emperor down, felt more than ever dependent on public opinion. In this mood Gramont made a bellicose speech in the French parliament on 6 July, declaring that France would not tolerate a return of a two-front menace, as in the days of Charles V. In reply it was the obvious Prussian tactic to maintain that the matter had nothing to with the North German Confederation as a state and was purely a family affair. Signs that Britain and Russia sympathized with the French may well have been factors in persuading Bismarck to pull back from the Hohen-zollern candidature, while retaining as much face as possible. His efforts to diminish any damage to Prussian prestige from this retreat nearly came to grief, because King William disliked subterfuge and was anxious to avoid war. Alone at Ems, taking the waters, while his prime minister was in distant Varzin, he decided to advise Prince Leopold to withdraw his candidature, which the Prince duly did on 12 July. It looked as if Bismarck's plan to use the candidature to boost German national feeling, increase Prussian prestige and at least to produce a shake-up in France had misfired.

But then Gramont and his colleagues, in their anxiety to boost the prestige of the Bonapartist regime and administer a check to Prussian expansionist ambitions, overreached themselves. Benedetti, the French ambassador to Prussia, was instructed to approach the king once more with a demand for something close to an apology and a guarantee that he would never again sanction such a candidature. On 13 July Benedetti more or less waylaid the king as he was on his daily constitutional in the Kurpark at Ems. This was too much for the king and he politely declined to give a guarantee for ever, while later still conveying through an equerry that he consented to Prince Leopold's withdrawal. It may well be that Bismarck, contrary to the graphic account he gave in his reminiscences, antici-pated the reactions of the king, as well as the likelihood that the French would press on in their desire to achieve a palpable success. Otherwise someone as far-sighted as he would hardly have absented himself in Varzin for as long as he did. In fact his absence in Pomerania, without any deciphering facilities, was itself a ploy to give credibility to the position that the Spanish candidature was not an official matter but only a Hohenzollern family affair. The telegraphic report of the proceedings in the Kurpark at Ems to the chancellor, who had at last returned to Berlin on 12 July, gave rise to the famous Ems telegram. This report of the encounter between the king and Benedetti on 13 July, written by the foreign office official accompanying the king, itself omitted the fact that the king had conveyed his consent to Prince Leopold's withdrawal. No doubt William felt guilty about adopting a more conciliatory approach than the stream of telegrams from his chief minister had advised. Bismarck, in the presence of Roon and Moltke, re-edited the despatch received from Ems for publication. The impression was given to the public that the King had strongly rebuffed the ambassador and virtually broken off relations with him, 'deciding not to receive him again' and conveying through an aide-de-camp that 'he had nothing further to say to him'. It was a deliberate ploy to exacerbate the situation, which, with troop movements beginning on both sides, was already hovering on the brink of war. Crowds demanding war were gathering in Paris, Berlin and in other parts of Germany. France declared war on 19 July.

The way the war had broken out produced a very favourable situation for Prussia, both in Germany and internationally. Much of the sympathy which France enjoyed in London, St Petersburg and Vienna at the beginning of the crisis was dissipated. A Franco-Austrian alliance, often talked about, did not exist, and could not come into being in these circumstances. If Austria entered the war on the French side she might be threatened by Russia. Italy's assistance, often under discussion as part of a tripartite Austrian, French and Italian alliance, still encountered the stumbling block of the French troops protecting the papacy. A French project to purchase the Belgian railways in 1869 had caused uneasiness in Britain and Bismarck now fed these fears by publishing the demands for compensation in Belgium made to him by Benedetti after Sadowa. Russia was concerned about Poland, which might be stirred up by Austria if she entered the war on the French side. In the Luxemburg crisis in 1867 it had been uncertain if the southern states would stand by Prussia. Now there was no doubt that public opinion would force their governments to implement the defence treaties with the north.

From this it should not be assumed that Bismarck, for all the support he had given the Hohenzollern candidacy behind the scenes, was necessarily aiming for war. It was always very much part of his political method to produce movement through confrontation. He would then hope to exploit the options which opened up, fully aware that the course of events remained always unpredictable. He may at some stage have hoped that the liberalization of the Bonapartist regime might mean that the incorporation of the South German states might be brought about with French agreement. He was quite prepared for war, and may well have thought that this would be the likeliest solution to the many unresolved problems, probably judging that the military risks were lower than they had been in 1866. War was still an acceptable way of solving international conflicts, in Paris as much as in Berlin. The French were defending their semi-hegemonic position in Europe, but they had been forced on to the offensive. Napoleon III saw it as an integral part of French pre-eminence that his country should be the guardian of the nationality principle. Yet in this case the completion of a German national state created a rival so strong that France's position in Europe was permanently reduced. This underlying conflict of aims was one of the reasons why French policy was so ineffective when faced with the rise of Prussia.

The initial Prussian victories were so swift that there could be for the moment no question of third-party intervention. French mobilization was far less efficient than the Prussian, and even South German contingents were soon effective. The technical efficiency of the Prussian staff work, using modern technology like railways and telegraph, was again demonstrated. The French armies had caught up with the superior rifles that had ensured the Prussian victory in 1866, but the German armies had made further advances in the development of artillery. The French commanders had to give up all hope of mounting an invasion across the

Rhine. By mid-August a German victory seemed likely. The army of Marshal Bazaine was surrounded in Metz. Marshal McMahon's army tried to raise the siege, but was itself pushed up against the Belgian frontier and decisively defeated at Sedan on 2 September 1870. Over a hundred thousand French soldiers were taken prisoner, including Napoleon III. By 4 September revolution had broken out in Paris and a republic was proclaimed. It immediately expressed its readiness to negotiate peace on the basis of withdrawing all objections to German unification, but also of preserving French territorial integrity.

The German demand for the annexation of Alsace and Lorraine now became the great obstacle to ending the war and turned it more than ever into a national war. The annexation is the subject of a great and on-going historical debate. Whereas in 1866 Bismarck had devoted great effort to sparing Austria, this time he fully supported the transfer of territory. He even did something to stimulate the demand for it, which made its appearance in press and public opinion immediately the war started and soon became a flood. Much of the public clamour was based on the proposition that these were German territories that had been taken away in the seventeenth century, when Germany was weak and France powerful. The fact that most of the inhabitants felt themselves to be French and that for many French was their language was brushed aside as a temporary aberration of the current generation, which had been misled. Germany's right to possess these territories on grounds of nationality and historical right was the emotion that swept the general public, but there were also security arguments, especially in South Germany. The possession of fortresses from Metz to Belfort was seen as necessary against the renewal of attack and this view had the backing of the military leaders. Bismarck himself probably believed that French hostility was in any case inevitable, for a proud nation like France would never accept defeat. He did not perhaps realize how profoundly power relationships in Europe would change in the future, with a dynamic, economically powerful Germany arousing apprehension among all her neighbours. It was a far cry from what had been familiar to him all his life, namely Prussia as the least powerful of the great powers of Europe. Whatever he thought of the future, he would have found it difficult, in 1870, to fight against territorial change, as he had successfully done in 1866, and therefore he did not even try. It would have complicated his relations with the generals, the king and public opinion even further.

The demand for Alsace and Lorraine became a major factor in prolonging the war and thus a difficult diplomatic problem for Bismarck. He had succeeded in isolating the conflict but its prolongation created unforeseeable opportunities for intervention. It also sparked bitter disagreements between Bismarck and the military leaders from Moltke down. These had already featured in the previous two wars, particularly in 1866, but they now became vicious. Bismarck's position was ambivalent, for he was the saviour of the Prussian military monarchy, with its uncontrolled power of command, he was proud of the rank of major-general that had been conferred on him and usually appeared in uniform. But to the officers of the general staff, the 'demi-gods', he was 'the civilian in the cuirassier's jacket'. The generals, even the sober Moltke, wanted triumph and annihilation of the enemy, while Bismarck was plagued by nightmares of intervention and a spreading European war leading to revolutionary upheavals. As usual he was weaving a complicated web of negotiations, threats and deceits between the French republican government and what remained of the Bonapartist camp, the imprisoned emperor and the exiled Empress Eugenie. The crude triumphalism of the generals interfered with these designs, but for the moment the generals were the heroes of the hour to the general public, not the civilian prime minister. There was much about this war that was still old-fashioned, for example the presence of kings, princes and prime ministers on the battlefield, with their splendid retinues, or the personal surrender of Napoleon, his meeting with the Prussian king and his departure into an honourable captivity in the splendid castle of Wilhelmshöhe, near Cassel. But as the German armies moved to besiege Paris it took on many aspects of a modern war. There was guerilla fighting behind the German lines, there was a civil war in France culminating in the Paris Commune in March 1871, there was the effort of the newly proclaimed French republic to continue the fight for France's territorial integrity. In a spectacular gesture Leon Gambetta, one of the leaders of the republic, left besieged Paris in a balloon to raise fresh armies against the invader.

In the final months of 1870 Bismarck was in a highly nervous state. He was trying to assert himself against Moltke and the generals. When he demanded a speedy conclusion of the Paris siege by bombarding the city, Moltke raised humanitarian as well as technical objections. Bismarck wrote to his wife that it was 'wafting incense with phrases'. Moltke's plan of starving the city out was hardly more humane. By January 1871, when the French resistance was faltering, the king agreed that the prime minister must be fully informed of the course of military operations and that the chief of staff should not deal with the French authorities without prior consultation. Meanwhile Bismarck was determined to impose his own version of the enlarged Germany, a straightforward extension of the North German Confederation, against the remaining pretensions of particularist rulers as well against the soaring ambitions of popular German nationalism in its hour of triumph.

Last but not least, there was the third front, the battle to fend off all foreign interference in the negotiation of peace. As was usual in cases of major wars, a call went out that that a European congress should be called to mediate and help to find a settlement. Adolphe Thiers, the veteran leader of the French republic, went round the capitals of Europe to enlist support for a peace that would preserve his country's territorial integrity but he returned empty-handed. The Russians were irritated by French republicanism, fearing the further spread of revolution in France and the encouragement this might give to Polish nationalism. They had been subtly encouraged by Bismarck to use the occasion to free themselves from the restrictions on their naval sovereignty in the Black Sea imposed after the Crimean War and this they did in October 1870. After this Bismarck encouraged British efforts to give a veneer of legality to Russia's unilateral action through an international congress. Gladstone, who had become prime minister for the first time in 1868, was shocked by the annexation of Alsace-Lorraine without any consultation with the inhabitants, but even his cabinet did not follow him in his efforts to call for a plebiscite. On the whole, informed as well as wider public opinion in Britain did not feel that the French defeat had damaged British interests. There was still an inclination to believe that the Prussian victories had strengthened the balance of power in Europe, but the treatment of France after her defeat aroused anti-Prussian sentiment. The Austrians knew that they could not now prevent a Prussian Kleindeutschland from coming into being and that their best hope lay in arranging themselves with it. The Italians, from whom France had hoped for help, used the occasion to take over the papal states after the withdrawal of French troops in September 1870. Luck, as well as adroit diplomatic footwork by Bismarck, thus allowed the greatest upheaval in European power relationships since 1815 to take place without any of the powers other than the chief protagonists becoming involved. The consequences in the future were far-reaching.

The creation of the German empire

The completion of the German imperial edifice was a task of great complexity. The German national movement had played an essential role in what had been achieved; Bismarck had used its dynamic to the full, but was determined not to be driven by it. The leaders of the Prussian National Liberals were allowed to play only a supporting part in the negotiations with the southern states. Bismarck did not want to drive the South German rulers and their governments, who clung to what remained of their independence and power, as unwilling partners into the Prussian embrace. The main difficulty lay with Württemberg and Bavaria, particularly the latter. Bismarck made a number of concessions to their self-esteem, which were bitterly criticised by the advocates of national unity, but which in the end amounted to very little. In the Bundesrat, now expanded to 58 representatives, the Prussian 17 votes still gave Prussia, together with the enclave states, a veto over constitutional changes, which could be blocked by 14 votes, but the four southern states together had 16 votes and could also block it. Bavaria and Württemberg retained some reserved rights, such as command of their armies and appointment of officers in peacetime, and their own postal service. Bavaria could send its own diplomats in some cases, notably to the Vatican, and the Bavarians had the chairmanship of a committee of the Bundesrat on foreign affairs. In practice all this turned out to mean very little and was soon not much more than a curiosity.

The symbolic unity of the new national state was as important as its constitutional structure. Bismarck now returned to the project of reviving the imperial title, with its heavy historical overtones. It would be easier for the other German rulers, particularly the three kings, to subordinate themselves to a German emperor than to a Prussian king. The imperial title would be a consolation prize for the German national movement, disappointed by the apparent survival of particularism. It would symbolize a truly national monarchy, not a return to the medieval universal empire. Bismarck's greatest difficulty was again with his own king, who wanted nothing to downgrade his dignity as king of Prussia. Perhaps he had a gut feeling that the new title would bode ill for his dynasty, as indeed it did.

The key to overcoming the king's scruples lay, as with the completion of the constitution, in Bavaria. Bismarck had to bribe the Bavarian king, Ludwig II, to write to his brother king on behalf of the other German princes urging him to take the title of German emperor. The price was annual payments from the secret Guelph fund, which arose from the dispossession of the king of Hanover after 1866. There was even a ten per cent commission to Count Holnstein, the emissary who negotiated secretly on behalf of the Bavarian king. These sordid details only came to light after Kaiser, Reich and all the German dynasties had vanished in 1918. Bismarck had obtained his aim, an empire founded not, as had been proposed in 1849, from below but from above. The enterprise was sealed in the famous ceremony in the Hall of Mirrors at Versailles on 18 January 1871. William I was still unhappy with the title of German Emperor and would have preferred Emperor of Germany. He was not on speaking terms with his prime minister on that day. The Grand Duke of Baden, the most consistent advocate of a united Kleindeutschland among the major rulers, got round the difficulty by calling for cheers for 'Emperor William'. Although the three other kings, Bavaria, Saxony and Württemberg, were absent, the ceremony featured princes, generals and officials in uniform, like Bismarck himself in lieutenant-general's uniform. There was hardly a civilian or parliamentarian in sight. Its venue, Versailles, underlined the rise of the new German Reich over the humiliated body of France.

The short duration of this Reich, its disastrous end in 1918, and the even more catastrophic collapse of the modern German national state in 1945, inevitably suggest that there was something wrong with its initial construction. A critical view of these events finds a fertile starting point in the heavy symbolism of the founding ceremony, deliberately coinciding with the proclamation of a Prussian kingdom exactly 170 years earlier, and the annual anniversary celebrations of this founding ceremony and of the victory at Sedan. The new Reich was born in an atmosphere of rampant triumphalism. A spirit of nationalist arrogance was unleashed which grew as the power of the new Germany became increasingly manifest. A few contemporary observers, like the historian Jakob Burkhardt, saw the dangers. Georg Gottfried Gervinus, a liberal of the 1848 generation, wrote that the recent Prussian wars had revived, on a much bigger scale, the danger of a warlike order that was believed to be dead.

For latter-day critics there is the counterfactual question of what alternatives there were to the establishment of a German national state through force of arms wielded by the semi-absolutist Prussian military monarchy, a revolution from above. The ideological and economic pressures for German unity were sufficiently strong, it could be argued, to have prevailed one way or another. The grossdeutsch solution encountered almost insuperable obstacles, for it would have required an end to the Habsburg empire. Since 1945 there has been something of a rehabilitation of the German Confederation of 1815, for it was compatible with the peace of Europe, while the German empire turned out to be a source of war. It seems, however, very unlikely that the Confederation, which for most of its career was used as a means of repression, could have satisfied German nationalism in an age when a national state seemed the natural aim of all nationalities, particularly the large ones. The economic realities pointed inescapably to Prussian domination. A democratic option was, after the failure of the 1848 revolution, not available and any attempt at a replay of revolution would have been resisted by the majority of German and European governments. It is possible that without Bismarck, or after his death or removal from power, a more liberal regime might have been installed in power. This was clearly the hope of many liberals, but such a regime, without the restraint in international affairs which Bismarck practised after 1870, might even earlier have embarked upon an ambitious foreign policy. Inconclusive as such speculations are bound to be, it is certain that what happened had a dark side to a much greater extent than the bulk of the German population, in their euphoria, realized.

3   Imperial Germany – the liberal phase 1870–1879

Constitution and political structure of the Reich

The first Reichstag of the new empire was elected in March 1871 under an electoral law promulgated in 1869, which remained in force until 1918. There were 382 deputies, raised to 397 in 1873, when Alsace-Lorraine was fully incorporated. They were elected by all men over the age of 25 by secret ballot. If in a constituency no candidate obtained 50 per cent of the vote, there was a second ballot to decide between the two candidates with the highest number of votes. In the first election of 1871 electoral participation was only 51 per cent, but it rose throughout the imperial period, with some setbacks, to nearly 85 per cent in the last election of 1912. The number of second ballots rose over the same period from 45 to 190. This indicates that Bismarck's calculation, that the Reichstag would occupy a some-what limited place in the constitutional system, was not borne out in the long run. Universal suffrage, which he had regarded as a means of containing the liberals, proved a potent engine for politicizing the masses. One aspect of the emerging political mass market was the rise of more coherent parties. The German political parties had hitherto been fluid parliamentary groups without much of a permanent structure in the country. Now this changed gradually, though the speed with which parties adapted to the rise of mass electorates varied. The liberal parties were slowest to adapt and retained longest the reliance on local notabilities to fight elections and this was one reason why they became progressively weaker.

In this, the first Reichstag of the new empire, the future of the German party landscape was foreshadowed. There were now two major liberal parties, two conservative parties, the Catholic Centre, and the socialists, as yet small, but soon to grow. The National Liberals, the group that had accepted the indemnity law in 1866 and had since collaborated with the Bismarck government in creating the basis for a modern market economy, emerged as the largest party, with 30 per cent of the vote and 125 seats. The anti-Bismarckian Liberals, the Progressives, had 46 seats. The pro-Bismarckian Free Conservatives, who often worked closely with the National Liberals, had 37 seats, while the traditional Conservatives, whose support for the government was less reliable, had 57. Shortly before the elections a new Catholic party, the Centre, *Zentrum*, had been formed and it immediately obtained nearly a fifth of the vote and 63 seats. It was not the first Catholic political grouping that had arisen either in Prussia or other parts of Germany, but now a number of factors came together to make such a party much more coherent and more power-ful. There were the perennial concerns about the independence of the Church, its institutions and its role in education. These appeared to be under threat in a number of German states including Prussia. There was the threat to the papacy from the Italian occupation of Rome and the papacy's own riposte to nationalism and liberalism. The first Vatican Council of 1870 and the proclamation of papal infallibility sharpened the conflict with liberalism and caused tensions within Catholicism. In Germany the Catholics were now a minority in a Protestant state. The economic liberal order established in the North German Confederation and now extended to the whole Reich bore hard on those Catholic regions and groups which were tied to an older social order. Economic individualism was opposed by Catholic advocates of social inclusiveness, among whom the best known was Wilhelm von Ketteler, the Bishop of Mainz. Ludwig Windthorst, who soon emerged as the leading figure of the *Zentrum,* was a former Hanoverian minister and a supporter of particularism. When the party was founded it was not hostile to the new empire, merely concerned to protect Catholic interests within it. It was, however, the first major party that could base itself on a definite milieu, or camp, and on a network of associations and organizations through which it could mobilize its voters. The other party clearly arising from a milieu was the Socialdemocratic Party. In this first Reichstag it was still in its infancy and with 3.2 per cent of the vote elected two deputies, one of whom was August Bebel, who became the leader of the party for a generation and the 'Socialist emperor' of Germany. The unification of the two wings of the socialist movement was still to come, but Bebel aroused attention at the opening of the new Reichstag with a speech portraying the Paris Commune as the portent of the future. Bismarck later declared that it was this speech that first alerted him to the peril of socialism.

The role intended for the Reichstag in the complicated constitutional scheme devised by Bismarck was limited. It shared the legislative power with the Bundes-rat. Since the Bundesrat was composed of representatives of the Reich's twenty-five governments, who could only act on instruction from those governments, federalism was thus used to limit parliamentarism. In practice much legislation was prepared in the Prussian ministries, later in the Reich offices which were established to deal with specific functions such as railways, the postal system, finance and so on, which initially had been concentrated in the chancellery. Sometimes, as with the economic legislation of the late 1860s and early 1870s, there was consultation with parliamentary leaders, for example the prominent National Liberals Lasker and Bamberger. When legislation was introduced in the Bundesrat it had usually been agreed with the other governments. The Bundesrat was therefore merely a bureaucratic mechanism, often attended only by officials, which did not even have its own building and met in secret. It never became the seat of executive government, as originally intended and led a somewhat shadowy existence. Its negative blocking function was, however, entrenched in the consti-tution and remained essential. Members of the Reichstag could not be members of the Bundesrat and thus the world of executive government was separated from the parliamentary world, though members of the Bundesrat could speak in the

Reichstag. It was only when the barrier preventing Reichstag deputies from becoming members of the Bundesrat was removed, ten days before the fall of the empire in 1918, that a fully parliamentary system became possible. To begin with, the chancellor himself held the whole system together, though increasingly other members of the bureaucracy, other Prussian ministers or the state secretaries heading the new Reich offices, could represent him in the Bundesrat. The chancellor presided over the Bundesrat; he was the Prussian prime and foreign minister, and the only Reich executive known to the constitution. Although the federal principle embodied in the Bundesrat created another barrier to fully-fledged parliamentarism, as a bureaucratic mechanism it facilitated the advance of the Reich as a unitary state. What was proposed by the bureaucracy, initially mainly Prussian, but then increasingly a Reich bureaucracy, was never blocked by the Bundesrat. The governments of the other states of the federation never on any major issue invoked their voting power in the Bundesrat against the centre. The Reich was no longer a confederation, but a federal state, in which federal law took precedence.

In the spheres reserved to them, above all education, the police and taxation, the governments of the federal states, especially Prussia itself, continued to exercise real power. Since Prussia comprised a good two-thirds of the area and population of the Reich, the existence of the Prussian system of government remained a major factor in the system as a whole. The Prussian Landtag was still elected by the three-tier franchise, had a preponderance of Conservative deputies and even by the twentieth century very few Socialists, when the Socialists were on the way to becoming the largest party in the Reichstag. There was never a Reich minister for war, only a Prussian one. The Prussian king, who was *ex officio* also the emperor, retained his special control over the military, which he exercised through a military cabinet, to which there was later added a naval cabinet. It was only the Prussian king, as emperor, who appointed the federal chancellor, not the other rulers. As the cohesion of the Reich developed, so loyalties increasingly focused on the Reich monarch, the emperor.

In the financial field, however, the Reich remained somewhat underdeveloped. Direct taxes were levied only by the constituent states, the Reich levied indirect taxes, customs and excise. The states made grants to the Reich from the taxes levied by them, calculated on the basis of population only, not on the size of their economies. The German term for these grants was *Matrikularbeträge*, grants calculated on the fixed distribution ratio. As the activities of the Reich increased, not least in the military sphere, it suffered from a lack of taxing power, a problem that was never resolved before 1914. The affluent classes, overrepresented in the Prussian Landtag and to a lesser extent in other state parliaments, were determined to cling to the protection against increased direct and progressive taxation given them by the federal structure.

Nevertheless the Reichstag, and the relations between it and the Reich Chancellor, became the hub of German politics, the place which attracted the attention of the public. This happened much more rapidly than Bismarck intended or foresaw, and is another facet of the growing cohesion of the Reich. No legislation was possible without the Reichstag and legislation was an increasing necessity in any modern state. The practice of handling relations between Reichstag and Reich Chancellor was established during the long years of Bismarck's ascendancy. To obtain what he needed from the Reichstag the chancellor did not rely on a party, but on a shifting combination of parties. To keep these combinations in line he could use the threat of dissolution and fresh elections. Legally the right to dissolve rested with the emperor and the Bundesrat, but neither of them ever resisted the will of Bismarck in this matter. Beyond this Bismarck in his later years occasionally threatened a coup d'état. Since the constitution had been brought into being by agreement between the separate states represented in the Bundesrat, it could be abrogated again, so Bismarck argued, by the same process. This threat was never carried out, but was never entirely absent throughout the duration of the empire.

Bismarck was so overwhelming a figure, his standing with the public as the Reich founder so monumental, that almost unlimited means of manipulation were open to him. This gives some justification to labelling his rule charismatic, Caesarist or Bonapartist. Bismarck's successors found the management of the Reichstag increasingly difficult, but the parties in the Reichstag never reached the point of translating their power into the control of the executive, as they would have done by toppling a chancellor and insisting on the appointment of a successor from their ranks. The parties of Imperial Germany preferred to represent their specific milieus, or camps, rather than enter into the combinations and compromises necessary to control the executive. This was Bismarck's legacy, a hybrid between parliamentary and monarchical government. It has also been called a system of 'skirted decisions', since the choice between fully representative and fully authoritarian government was deliberately not made. It was also a compromise between federalism and a unitary state. As a federation it was lopsided, because of the overwhelming size of Prussia. Initially it looked as if it might be Greater Prussia, though many of those loyal to the old Prussia feared that their country was itself in process of abolition. Soon the new Reich was the overriding reality, but it also exhibited some Prussian characteristics, the addiction to military values and the continued importance of the Prussian aristocracy in the army, in the bureaucracy and in the imperial court.

The Kulturkampf

It remains surprising that one of the predominant themes of the early years of the empire was a bitter clash between the authorities and the Catholic Church. Catholics were a large minority in the new state, over a third of the population, when they were a majority in German-speaking central Europe. A policy of integrating them in the empire would have made sense, the more so since there were many contentious issues between Catholicism, clerical and lay, and other sections of state and society. In some German states there had been something like a Kulturkampf for years. In Baden, with its Liberal government, there was conflict over schools and ecclesiastical appointments, while the Catholic part of the population felt hard pressed by the spread of economic liberalism. In Bavaria, where the ruling establishment consisted mainly of liberal Catholics, there was a similar, but less bitter conflict. In Prussia there had for a generation been much tension and conflict between Rhineland Catholics and the authorities controlled from Berlin. The final demise of grossdeutsch hopes in 1866 had left some Catholics unreconciled, but the majority, including such prominent figures as Bishop Ketteler, accepted the new dispensation. The proclamation of papal infallibility, coinciding with the collapse of the pope's temporal power, brought fresh problems, but almost as much within Catholicism as between Catholics and non-Catholics. In Germany there were many liberal Catholics, who had reservations about papal infallibility, and some pushed their disagreement to schism with Rome. These 'Old Catholics' included Ignaz von Döllinger, a famous theologian and friend of Gladstone's. Many German Protestants saw Döllinger almost as a new Luther and placed exaggerated hopes in him. The foundation of the *Zentrum* in December 1870 was not motivated by a defiance of the new empire, but by a desire to secure Catholic concerns within it. One of these concerns was to secure the position of the Pope himself, now that he was a prisoner. Bismarck, however, refused to give any commitment, when, in February 1871, a delegation led by Ketteler asked on behalf of the Catholics in the Prussian lower house that the emperor should help towards the restoration of the papal states. He replied sharply when in the new Reichstag a month later the demand was repeated. His reaction was equally negative when the Centre party asked for the inclusion in the new constitution of some basic rights already entrenched in the Prussian constitution, but for the specific and limited purpose of protecting Catholic rights in particular.

There has always been puzzlement among historians why Bismarck should then have moved on to a general and bitter conflict with the Church and the Centre party. There was plenty of material for conflict between ultramontane Catholicism and the liberal secular state all over Europe, but without Bismarck's deliberate exacerbation of the clash it would never have become so predominant an issue in the German empire. The Centre party only became a large oppositional force because of the chancellor's offensive. A number of explanations are possible, in addition to the fact that Bismarck always believed in confrontation as a political method. The chancellor had anti-Catholic prejudices, but they did not usually determine his policies. In his early years as prime minister he had accepted Catholic support in the constitutional conflict. The appearance of Catholic particularism in the Zollverein parliament of 1868 had irked him and he had encountered Ludwig Windthorst, the Hanoverian loyalist, who later as Centre party leader became his most formidable domestic opponent. There was an element of paranoia in Bismarck and even in the hour of his greatest triumph dark forebodings gnawed at his peace of mind. The sudden appearance of the Centre party, in which all manner of enemies of the new Reich, Catholic particularists, Poles, Alsace-Lorrainers, seemed to foregather unsettled him. It was a conservative party, representing populations and institutions that were conservative. With its network of associations and clubs, transcending normal divisions of left and right, it mobilized sections of the conservative camp beyond Bismarck's control. Soon traditional Prussian Conservatives, already frightened by the chancellor's revolutionary policies, were driven into further hostility by the apparent secularism of Kulturkampf measures. Bismarck's calculation that a wide franchise would weaken the Liberals, because the conservative masses would support the king's government, was called in question. The chancellor appeared to be dangerously isolated in the embrace of his former enemies, the Liberals, even threatened in his hold on the king. His fears of the Centre party were genuine, if paranoid, but he was also adept at using anti-Catholicism as a means of manipulation. It would tie the National Liberals more closely to him while eventually confronting them with a dilemma between their liberal convictions and their abhorrence of Catholic obscurantism. The technique of putting enemies of the Reich, *Reichsfeinde*, in the pillory as a means of strengthening his own control grew on him and he later used it against the Socialists. His determination to remain personally an independent yet supreme power in the state made such techniques necessary. Nobody could trust him, nobody could rely on him, he could trust and rely on nobody. For all the heroic almost superhuman stature he now acquired among the population at large, he was surrounded by a miasma of distrust. These are possible reasons why he sought a fight which eventually proved unwinnable.

An opening salvo in the fight was the abolition, in June 1871, of the so-called Catholic division in the Prussian Ministry of Culture. This section had arisen out of earlier clashes between the Prussian state and the Catholic Church and it had done good service in minimizing friction. It was now seen as a kind of Catholic Trojan horse, for Bismarck saw in its head a defender of Polish nationalism within the Prussian establishment. The presence of Poles in the Centre party had inflamed the chancellor's hostility to the party. There was also the difficult problem how the state should deal with liberal Catholics holding official positions, for example chairs in universities, who refused to accept the doctrine of papal infallibility. Fears were raised that the Catholic division in the Prussian ministry would enforce an ultramontane loyalty. The abolition of the division earned the applause of Liberals, but was seen as a declaration of war by Catholics. There followed a law for the Reich as a whole, enforcing the so-called pulpit paragraph. Under it priests could be prosecuted for making pronouncements undermining public order. It had originated in Bavaria, but when such measures were applied in Prussia their execution was always more rigorous. Only twelve out of 46 Progressives voted against this flagrant attack on free speech in the Reichstag and only one National Liberal out of 125, the Jew Lasker. It was an early indication how corrosive of liberalism the Kulturkampf would prove to be.

In January 1872 Bismarck cleared the decks for further anti-Catholic measures by appointing a strongly etatist Liberal, Adalbert Falk, as Prussian minister of culture. This appointment enabled Bismarck to step back personally from the conflict when it suited him. After it had all ended in frustration the chancellor blamed Falk, in combination with the prevailing spirit of the times, for taking him further along the anti-Catholic road than he would have chosen. There was little sign of restraint in the first major clash between him and Windthorst on 30 January 1872, when Bismarck declared: 'When I returned from France I could not consider the formation of this party [the Centre] in any other light than as a mobilization of a party against the state.' The formation of a confessional party was 'the most monstrous phenomenon on the political scene'. Windthorst, anti-Prussian, anti-Bismarckian and a most formidable parliamentarian, had only come to the fore in the Centre party because of Bismarck's declaration of war. There followed a school supervision law in the Prussian Landtag, which removed the right of Catholic priests to supervise religious teaching. This produced an alliance between Conservatives and the Centre, which Bismarck sought to weaken by playing upon the alleged anti-national character of the Catholic Church in Germany. In the end the Conservatives grudgingly supported the government. On the other hand the Liberals now had the bit between their teeth and demanded a law against the Jesuits. In the Reichstag they strengthened the government's modest proposals in such a way that the Jesuit order was effectively expelled from Germany. The battle was becoming fiercer, with nuns being prevented from teaching and bishops, who sought to discipline schismatic Catholics, finding themselves without the normal state financial support.

A further aggravation of the conflict was reached in the Prussian May laws of 1873. The state would in future supervise the training of priests and they had to take a 'cultural exam', a measure first introduced in the Baden church–state conflict, to test their fitness for office. Ecclesiastical appointments had to be notified to the state authorities and they could veto them. When bishops and others ignored the notification law and boycotted the cultural exams, the state hit back with financial penalties, closure of seminaries, invalidation of ecclesisatical appointments and imprisonment. An assassination attempt on Bismarck in July 1874, which was blamed on Catholic incitement, intensified the campaign of repression. By 1875 the work of monastic orders in the schools and in care for the sick and elderly had virtually ceased. The pope responded by threatening with excommunication anyone assisting the execution of the anti-church laws. Numbers of priests, Catholic newspaper editors and others were condemned to financial penalties and even imprisonment. Newspapers and meetings were suppressed. For years many bishoprics and parishes remained vacant. It was a by-product of this situation that civil marriage became obligatory throughout the Reich by 1875, something which even the emperor strongly disliked. Some of the Kulturkampf legislation applied to the Reich, but much of the campaign was specific to the states. It was most rigorous in Prussia and Baden, less so in Bavaria, where there was no parliamentary majority for anti-Catholic measures. Among states with a sizeable Catholic population Württemberg was least affected. The Liberals fought the Kulturkampf with passionate conviction, seeing themselves as the defenders of all that was modern and progressive against benighted obscurantism.

The most obvious long-term consequence of the Kulturkampf was the consolidation of the Centre party as a major independent force in the German political system. It became the political spearhead of a Catholic milieu, the separation of which from the Protestant majority was thereby reinforced. Catholics felt themselves to be second-class citizens and this feeling was only gradually mitigated before 1914. The following of the party was very heterogeneous, stretching from

Silesian and Westphalian aristocrats to the artisan class in the Catholic regions of Germany. By its cross-class appeal the Centre, in the localities where it was strong, reduced the voter-potential of parties to the left and to the right. At the Reichstag elections of 1874 the Centre received nearly 28 per cent of the vote and elected 91 deputies, out of 397. For the time being it was the major opposition party, while the National Liberals became more than ever the governmental party.

This situation was reinforced by the further alienation of the Prussian Conservatives from the Bismarck government. In 1872 a new law for the governance of rural districts was promoted in the Prussian Landtag by the National Liberals and their allies. The powers of the Landrat, the government representative in rural areas, was strengthened against that of the estate owners. Elections to the district councils were in future to be conducted on the three-tier electoral law. The Junkers in Prussia's East Elbian provinces felt threatened in their authority. They had never been reconciled to the loss of their police power after 1848 and many aspects of the Kulturkampf alarmed them. For many of them Prussia, rather than the new Reich, was the focus of their loyalties. The rural district reform was voted down in the Upper House of the Prussian Landtag and only passed after the creation of new peers. In the event the reform did not undermine the position of the landowners in Prussia's eastern provinces to anything like the extent they feared. Bismarck for a time in 1873 passed the Prussian premiership to Roon, an arrangement which proved in practice unworkable. The old Prussian Conservative party increasingly disintegrated. Meanwhile the National Liberals and the Free Conservatives in the Reichstag, in co-operation with Delbrück as head of the chancellor's office, proceeded apace with the legislation that turned the whole German Reich into a unified market economy, with a legal system based on the independence of the individual citizen. A unified currency, the mark, was introduced, and in 1875 a central bank, the Reichsbank, was established. The development of commercial law begun during the North German Confederation was carried on. The National Liberals could feel that they were shaping the new Reich in vital respects, but they found themselves in the antechamber of power rather than in the seat of power. The elections to the Prussian Landtag of November 1873 and to the Reichstag of January 1874 formed a high watermark of liberalism. The National Liberals, the Free Conservatives and the Progressives together had 237 out of 397 Reichstag seats. The Conservatives, deprived of their traditional governmental support, had only 22 seats, leaving the Centre with 91 as the real opposition.

Economic boom and bust

Nothing did more to bring about the decline of liberalism than the economic depression which started in 1873. It put an end to a boom which in its final phase was boosted by the euphoria generated by the foundation of the Reich. Railway building was still the most important accelerator of economic activity. Between the years 1870 and 1873 the rail network in the Reich grew by nearly 27 per cent (see Table 1) and the amount of goods traffic by over 70 per cent. Coal production rose by 38 per cent between 1870 and 1873, iron production by 61 per cent and steel production by over 50 per cent. This real growth was further boosted by the optimism and sense of limitless opportunity of what came to be known as the *Gründerzeit*, the foundation era. The stock market index climbed from 96.4 in 1870 to 193.1 in 1872. The French war indemnity of 5 billion francs, an enormous sum by the standards of the time, was always thought to have made a major contribution to this boom, especially as the French managed to pay it off more rapidly than was considered possible. The effect in reinforcing the boom was probably psychological as much as real. There was an inflationary element to the boom, in that the wholesale price index rose by more than 30 per cent, the cost of living index rose by 25 per cent, and the price of iron more than doubled (see Appendix: Table 7). There was a building boom and even after the destruction of the Second World War traces of it can still be found in German cities. The *Gründerstil*, seen particularly in villas and apartment blocks for the well-to-do, was heavy and grandiloquent.

The collapse of the boom started in Austria in May 1873, soon spreading to all the major industrial economies and financial centres, including London and New York. In Berlin the collapse struck in October 1873. In Germany the shares of nearly 450 public companies, which at the end of 1872 had a market value of more than 4.5 billion marks had by the end of 1874 a value of less than 2.5 billion marks. The shares of the three major Berlin banks, Disconto-Gesellschaft, Darmstädter and Handelsgesellschaft, dropped from 335, 216 and 160 to 179, 160 and 120 respectively. There was a massive price collapse of industrial goods like coal, iron and steel: between 1873 and 1875 the index numbers of iron prices fell from 181 to 76, of coal from 116 to 49, of wholesale prices together from 118 to 79. Considerable productive capacities were rendered idle: for example the M.A.N. works in Nuremberg had delivered 4000 wagons to the railways in 1872 and employed 3500 workers; by 1879 they employed only 800 and delivered only a few hundred wagons. Economic historians now discount the concept of a great depression lasting till 1896 and see this downturn more as the collapse of an inflationary boom, which left the secular upwards trend of production and investment fundamentally intact. The social product shrank between 1873 and 1879, but only nominally, because of the fall in prices, and it was then still nominally 40 per cent higher than in 1869. The annual production of iron actually rose from 2.22 to 2.23 million tonnes, that of steel from 1.58 to 1.72 million tonnes, and of coal from 36.39 to 42.03 million tonnes (see Appendix: Table 8). Nevertheless, the effect on wages of the price deflation was severe: for example the income of Krupp workers was halved between 1873 and 1878. Optimism gave way to deep pessimism from the top to the bottom of society. With hindsight, perceptions of economic doom were exaggerated, but at the time they aggravated the effect of the depression. There was a steep rise of social tensions, the political repercussions of which soon became evident. After 1879 there was some recovery again until 1883, then renewed downturns in 1884–7 and 1891–5, but there was very high investment in industrial and house building between 1886 and 1890 and the social product increased by nearly 15 per cent. Overall production did not keep pace with the rise in productivity, which was reflected in lower prices and unemployment in some sectors. But 1873 was not a collapse comparable to 1929, only the beginning of a period of less consistent growth.

Nonetheless the psychological and political consequences of the collapse of 1873 were profound. For the liberal expectations of progress it was never glad, confident morning again. On paper the Liberals were at their zenith in 1874. Without them the chancellor could not obtain the legislation he needed and much of it was of the kind the Liberals wanted. But Bismarck had no intention of admitting them into the inner citadel of power, the *arcanae imperii*, and was uncomfortable even with the extent to which he depended on them. Within the National Liberal party there was a left wing, which for its part wanted to set a limit to compromise with the Bismarck government. Its leader, Eduard Lasker, became almost as much a hate figure for Bismarck as Windthorst. In 1873 Lasker attacked corruption within the government and pointed the finger at men close to the chancellor. One of them was Hermann Wagener, who had in the 1860s tried to organize a popular movement of conservatism, the *Preussische Volksvereine* (Prussian People's Associations), and was later among those who advised Bismarck to pursue a policy of social amelioration. Lasker showed how the tentacles of the corrupt railway king Strousberg and his investment in railway construction in Rumania penetrated deep into the highest echelons of the Prussian establishment. The collapse of the Strousberg empire was among the most sensational manifestations of the economic collapse.

Already the next great parliamentary battle was looming, the settlement of the military budget, which had been renewed for three years in 1871. The left wing of the National Liberals wanted annual control of what was the largest component of the Reich budget. It would be the achievement of a basic requirement of liberalism, for which they had been fighting for the last fifteen years. The generals led by Moltke wanted the *Aeternat*, the permanent fixture of the military budget and therefore its removal from parliamentary control. Bismarck in lengthy and often secret negotiations maintained a position halfway between the extremes. He did not want to surrender to the Reichstag now the control against which he had fought on behalf of the Prussian crown for so many years, but he did not want to reinforce the independence of the military from civilian control either. The compromise was a fixture for seven years, a period which, since the Reichstag had to be re-elected every three years, meant the exclusion of legislative control for at least one whole Reichstag. Although even the National Liberal left voted for it, it was a nearly complete victory for the military monarchy. In other matters not so close to the nerve centres of power, the Liberals could still shape legislation to a greater extent. The press law of 1874 was based on a ministerial draft, which would have imposed penalties on newspapers for publishing attacks on basic institutions of the state and the social order, like military service. The Liberals, National Liberals and Progressives in the Reichstag were sensitive to provisions that might have been turned against them, and managed to draw some of the teeth of the official proposal, but by no means all. The freedom of the press and absence of censorship was the norm, but means of official intimidation and control remained in practice. A few years later a comprehensive ban was imposed on the socialdemocratic press.

The end of the liberal period

The process by which the collaboration between Bismarck and the National Liberals came to an end was long drawn out. Even before the collapse of the boom in 1873 shook a central pillar of liberalism, free trade and free markets, what in Germany was often called Manchesterism, was under attack from many quarters. Official policy, under the guidance of Delbrück, was still driving towards freer trade and the last protective tariffs on iron were removed only on 1 January 1877. In the meantime powerful industrial pressure groups were being organized, which first were concerned to halt the remaining moves towards free trade and then increasingly turned to protection as a means of combating the depression. The most important of these was the Central Association of German Industrialists (*Centralverband deutscher Industrieller*) founded in February 1876. It was a feature of the slump and the collapse of prices that industry was driven to rely increasingly on exports to maintain production. The overall index of export volume in Germany's foreign trade rose from 17.7 in 1873 to 26.1 in 1878 (1913 = 100), a fifty per cent rise. In some sectors the rise was particularly striking, for example exports of iron and steel goods rose between 1876 and 1878 from 807,000 tons to 1.3 million tons. Representatives of the iron and steel industries admitted before a Bundesrat enquiry of 1878 that they were resorting to dumping. The debate over protection and free trade became nationalistic and there was much talk of protecting national labour. To the protectionist voices coming from many sectors of industry were added those of the agrarians, who had hitherto, particularly the bigger landowners of East Elbian Prussia, been firmly in favour of free trade. These bigger, often Junker, landowners were in fact not in the van of the agrarian demand for protection, for they did not feel the threat of overseas competition until the middle 1870s. It is therefore somewhat premature to speak of an alliance of 'iron and rye' in favour of protection. It was rather the smaller agricultural producers in the vicinity of developing industrial and urban areas who initially wanted to see their home markets protected.

The rise of the socialist movement

The pressure for the abandonment of free trade was one element in the big political shift to the right that was finally consummated in 1878/9. Another major factor was the rise of the socialist movement, a consequence both of the industrialization and of the growing social tensions caused by the slump. When Lassalle had founded the General German Workers Association (*Allgemeiner Deutscher Arbeiterverein*, ADAV) it proved to be a significant step in the detachment of the industrial proletariat from the Liberal movement. The completion of this detachment took, however, some time yet and the main reason for this was the fact that the question of national unity, the process of state formation, was still the overwhelming problem. What came to be called the social question, in other words the conflict between proletariat and bourgeoisie, was only just beginning when there was as yet no German state. It was also, as long as the Prussian constitutional conflict remained unresolved, uncertain how far the attainment of a liberal-democratic constitution would progress. Lassalle therefore backed a kleindeutsch solution of the German question, from which he hoped a democratic constitution would in due course arise and enable the workers to make their weight felt. After his early death in a duel in 1864 Lassalle's successors continued the pro-Prussian orientation.

This was what mainly distinguished them from the other branch of the workers' movement founded by August Bebel and Wilhelm Liebknecht. Their Saxon People's Party of 1866 was still a part of the anti-Prussian liberal-democratic movement and became a clearly separate workers' party only in 1869 at Eisenach, the Socialdemocratic Workers' Party (*Sozialdemokratische Arbeiterpartei*, SDAP), also known as the 'Eisenacher'. Liebknecht knew Marx and the Eisenacher affiliated to Marx's First International, founded in London in 1864. Their commitment to Marxism as a doctrine was, however, at this stage tenuous. Another peculiarity of the German workers' movement was that trade unions were less important than the early political parties. It was not until 1869 that, as part of the liberalization legislation of the North German Reichstag, the right of collective bargaining was recognized, though in practice it was still difficult to exercise. What there was of trade unions often arose only in course of actual strikes or under the stimulus of the political workers' movements. Lassalle believed in the iron law of wages and his followers were slower than the Eisenacher to encourage trade union activity. There were also unions still committed to the Liberals and others to the Catholics. The overall effect of all these circumstances was that in Germany there was not, as there was in England as the original industrial country, a trade union movement before there was a political labour movement; nor was there the possibility after 1866 of the political thrust of the working class taking its place in a broadly based liberal party. As Liberals moved closer to the still only semi-constitutional state, so the political representatives of the industrial working class were driven into opposition and in due course into the role of enemies of the state, *Reichsfeinde*.

The founding of the Reich soon made the division between pro and anti-Prussians in the workers' movement academic. Another divisive factor, the cult of Lassalle's personality and then those of his successors, also receded in the early 1870s. At the same time the rapid spread of industrialization and urbanization in the boom years up to 1873 heightened class consciousness. Strike activity rose to a peak of 362 strikes in 1872, some of them on a large scale, though it declined steeply when the slump came. Nearly 125,000 voters supported the socialist parties in 1871, 3.2 per cent of the total vote; by 1874 the number was over 350,000 or 6.8 per cent. The number of deputies remained low, because under the dual ballot system the socialists could never hope to win seats in the run-off ballot, for no other party was prepared to make common cause with them. There was repression, most conspicuously the incarceration of Bebel and Liebknecht for high treason in 1872–3. The logic of events drove Lassalleans and Eisenacher to overcome divisions and in 1875 a united Socialist Workers' Party, effectively what soon became the Socialdemocratic Party of Germany, was founded at Gotha. The Gotha programme was an amalgam of various influences and was heavily criticised by Marx, who in his London exile was out of touch with events in Germany. Lassalle's vision of the working class obtaining power through the institutions of a national state had never fitted well into the Marxist dogma of an international proletarian revolution coming only after the phase of bourgeois dominance and in dialectical opposition to it. The Lassalleans, with their willingness to make a temporary alliance with the reactionary feudalist state against the bourgeoisie, had aroused the suspicions of Marx and Engels. In practice this doctrinal hair-splitting meant little even to the articulate leaders of German labour. For the moment it was enough that there was a party claiming to represent the German working class against economic and political oppression and able to make the most of the one clearly progressive feature of the German political system, universal manhood suffrage. It was a party whose conduct was legal but whose rhetoric was revolutionary. The rest of society, for generations frightened by the spectre of revolution, did not make such fine distinctions and was simply alarmed by the rise of socialism.

Bismarck breaks with the Liberals

Another component of the crisis which eventually produced a change of direction in German politics arose from the federal system of taxation. As the range of state activities increased, in Germany as in other industrializing countries, the income of the Reich, dependent on the contributions from the separate states, became inadequate. Rising military expenditure was another factor. Bismarck would have liked to recast the whole system so that the Reich became the principal taxing authority and the Länder its dependents, rather than the other way round. He was also in favour of indirect taxes, which were less dependent on frequent parliamentary approval. Even before the question of protective tariffs as a source of income for the Reich became acute, he was casting around for other sources of income, the creation of a state tobacco monopoly or the nationalization of the railways. In a big speech he made in the Reichstag on 22 November 1875, after a prolonged absence from Berlin for health reasons, he stated his preference for indirect taxes, but also reaffirmed his absolute opposition to a collegiate cabinet based on parliamentary approval. In his usual sarcastic manner he said that as a parliamentary prime minister he would never be able to get the annual budget ready in time.

As it was, Bismarck was still so central a figure that the resolution of the manifold pressures that were building up depended largely on him. Yet he was also in a dangerously exposed position, plagued by the nightmare that on the death of the emperor, now nearing eighty, his successor might install a 'Gladstone ministry'. The extent to which he was now isolated from his former allies and from his Prussian peer group was highlighted by a series of articles in the summer of 1875 in the *Kreuzzeitung*, the paper with which he was associated at the beginning of his career in 1848. The articles were entitled 'Era Bleichröder–Delbrück–Camphausen'. It was a vicious attack on international, liberal capitalism, fuelled by rapacious, socially irresponsible greed, which, it was alleged, had for years guided official policy in the interests of the personal enrichment of leading figures.

Bleichröder, Bismarck's Jewish banker and personal financial adviser, and through him Bismarck himself, were the main targets: 'Our fellow citizen of Semitic race and Israelite faith has the ear and confidence of the leading German statesman and his ministers.' The distinction between productive capital, mostly that of Prussian landowners, and unproductive capital, mostly that of international Jewish financiers, was to have a long pedigree in Germany, down to Hitler and the Nazis. There was an accusation of personal corruption against the 'Prince-Chancellor', who had been well served by Bleichröder when 'on a small diplomatic salary and with no considerable private fortune' he had to represent his sovereign in St Petersburg, Paris and Frankfurt. For a while Bismarck did not counter-attack, but when he realized early in 1876 that even some of the big Junker landowners were beginning to move towards protection he saw an opportunity to reshape organized conservatism more in his own image. In another big Reichstag speech he hit back hard against the elements behind the *Kreuzzeitung* articles and eventually had them put on a kind of 'proscription' list. They were the traditionalists among the Prussian aristocracy who had since 1866 felt that Bismarck's revolutionary policies were riding roughshod over 'their' Prussia. They had deeply resented the Prussian local government reforms of 1872 and the manner by which they were enacted through a creation of peers. By the summer of 1876, with the chancellor's help, a new conservative party was founded, the German-Conservatives (*Deutsch-Konservative*), still mainly dependent on East Elbian landowners, but also representative of agrarian interests throughout Germany. The German-Conservatives were loyal supporters of the chancellor and their patriotism was focused on the Reich. Bismarck now had another iron in the fire in his endeavour to maintain himself above party and in his game of playing parties off against each other.

But the game was by no means over. In April 1876 Delbrück resigned, preferring to go before he was pushed, but it was probably not at a moment of Bismarck's choosing. The chancellor was still prepared to work with the National Liberals on his own terms and sometimes even the left wing of that party around Lasker supported his policies. This was the case on railway nationalization, which most Liberals saw as a means of strengthening the cohesion of the Reich. Even outside Bavaria, which retained its special rights over railways, there were 14,000 different fare tariffs in Germany. Bismarck was prevented from extending the powers of the new Reich Railway Office by the entrenched strength of federalism, not least in his own camp, the Prussian state ministry. Among those who frustrated Bismarck's railway policy was Camphausen, the Prussian finance minister and convinced adherent of liberal economics, who had been one of those attacked in the *Kreuzzeitung* articles. When the chancellor had warned the Liberals in the Reichstag against risking confrontation with him over their demand for further parliamentarization, he pointed out that the Reich was still too much of a federation and not yet not unified enough for such a trial of strength. The Reichstag elections of January 1877 showed the first shift against the Liberals since the foundation of the Reich (see Appendix: Table 9). The percentage drop was not considerable, from 29.7 to 27.2 per cent, but the number of seats dropped from 155 to 128. The Progressives also lost 14 seats. The refounded Conservatives on the other hand went up from 6.9 to 9.7 per cent and from 22 to 40 seats. The left wing of the National Liberals around Lasker lost their pivotal position, but a major reform of the Reich's finances still required the cooperation of the Liberals.

Bismarck was still mainly concerned to maintain his grip on power in a rapidly changing situation. In March 1877 he tried to remove the head of the Admiralty, Admiral Albrecht von Stosch, a member of the Prussian state ministry, whom he regarded as a possible rival for the chancellorship should the Crown Prince accede to the throne. Instead the incident showed the limit of the support the old emperor was prepared to give his overmighty chancellor. William refused to accept the resignation of Stosch, but when Bismarck then threatened his own resignation the emperor's reported reply was 'never', but there was nothing in writing. The Empress Augusta was in favour of accepting the chancellor's resignation. Bismarck regarded her with deep and abiding hatred and for him she was guilty of high treason. He had for years made much of his fragile health, had been absent from Berlin for prolonged periods and now again demanded and obtained a long period of leave. The chancellor's utter ruthlessness when it was a question of power was again demonstrated, but even those who groaned under 'the chancellor dictatorship' still regarded him as indispensable in foreign affairs. With the crisis in the Balkans turning into war he kept a grip on German diplomacy from the depth of Pomerania. His eldest son Herbert kept an eye on affairs for him in Berlin.

The chancellor, on leave, was not idle in searching for a way forward that would ensure his continued grip on power. He engaged in a prolonged negotiation with Bennigsen, the leader of the National Liberals, which culminated in an offer to the Liberal leader that he should become Bismarck's deputy as chancellor and as Prussian prime minister. Bennigsen demanded that two other leading figures from the left wing of the party should join him. It was virtually certain that Bismarck would reject this demand. Historians have debated whether this was another missed chance by the Liberals. Their problem was that they needed to keep the party united, when there was always the danger of a split between those who were still prepared to go a long way with Bismarck and those who felt that liberal principles had to be more strongly asserted. Many Liberals felt that time was on their side. Bismarck could not last for ever and his growing difficulties would compel him to come to them in any case. The future turned out to be very different. It can also be argued that Bismarck's intention was precisely to strain Liberal unity and to undermine the party. It was certainly part of his usual game of leaving himself alternatives.

When Bismarck returned from leave in February 1878 he gave the first clear indication of a change in economic policy. He had long advocated a tobacco tax or even a state tobacco monopoly as a means of strengthening the revenue of the Reich. A tobacco tax was among a number of tax laws that had been prepared, but Bismarck now declared that he regarded this only as a stepping stone to a tobacco monopoly. Thereupon Camphausen, the Prussian finance minister resigned, and shortly afterwards Achenbach, the trade minister. These two ministers were after Delbrück the most obvious obstacles to a change of policy towards protection. Previously another personal change, the death of Pope Pius IX on 7 February 1878, had also opened new possibilities. His successor, Leo XIII, was much less intransigent and Bismarck had known for a long time that the Kulturkampf had reached a dead end. Even so the composition of the Reichstag would still have made a far-reaching change of economic taxation policy difficult, even if the Centre Party were to end its opposition to the government. Bismarck was far too cautious to anticipate such a change and for the moment his aim may well have been to put the National Liberals under greater pressure to give him firm support on his own terms. He put forward a scheme for creating deputies so that he could devolve at will the duties which fell to him as the sole minister of the Reich. Thus there would be a general deputy or Vice-Chancellor, more or less what he had offered Bennigsen, and the various offices, railways, posts and telegraphs and so on, that were gradually being separated from the office administered by Delbrück until 1876, could also act on behalf of the chancellor. This came close to creating a Reich cabinet, but stopped short of it in not giving it parliamentary responsibility.

Bismarck thus again refused to give way to a demand which the Liberals in the Reichstag had voiced insistently over the years and they in turn watered down the chancellor's scheme. Stalemate seemed to frustrate further development of the Reich both administratively and financially and to prevent vital decisions, particularly in the economic sphere, from being taken. The distribution of power between the Reich and Prussia remained unresolved. The impression of deadlock was reinforced by the appointment of second-rank figures to the position of the resigning Prussian ministers. There was much speculation about the future of Bismarck, while the chancellor himself heightened the atmosphere of crisis by promoting press discussion about a Reichstag dissolution and a coup d'état through which the constitution would be changed. He used his own, entirely exceptional position with the public in a manner that gives substance to accusations of manipulation and Bonapartism. Eduard Lasker, increasingly his most conspicuous antagonist, wrote in his memoirs that Bismarck seemed to be waiting for something to turn up that would enable him, by stirring up popular passions, to recover the initiative.

Something did turn up, two assassination attempts on the emperor, on 11 May and 2 June 1878. Neither had any particular connection with the Socialists, but Bismarck immediately decided, after the first attempt which did not hit the emperor, to put the blame on them. A repressive anti-socialist law was put before the Reichstag, the main purpose of which was to demonstrate to the frightened public that the Liberals were not serious in wishing to suppress subversive agitation. It was badly drafted and the Reichstag Liberals were bound to reject it, if their liberal principles and devotion to the rule of law meant anything. The second attempt wounded the emperor quite seriously, for a man of over eighty. It is said that when the news was brought to Bismarck his first reaction was triumphant – 'now we dissolve the Reichstag and push the Liberals against the wall until they squeak' – before he even asked about the old man's condition. When there was resistance in the Bundesrat, particularly from Baden, to a premature dissolution, Bismarck again used threats of a constitutional coup. An unscrupulous electoral campaign was unleashed, using all the resources of press manipulation at the disposal of the chancellor. The Socialists were portrayed as revolutionaries threatening the established order and the Liberals as their unwitting allies. The many interest groups advocating a change of policy towards protection were very active in the election and tended to outflank the Liberal parties still committed to free trade. They suggested in the minds of the voters that the ideological quarrels of parties were somehow outmoded.

The campaign took place against the background of the Congress of Berlin, which showed Bismarck, at least for a credulous German public, as the arbiter of Europe. The result of the elections was that the National Liberals suffered the loss of a further 29 seats, being reduced to 99 out of 397 (see Appendix: Table 9). Their percentage of the vote had declined from a peak of over 30 per cent in 1871 to 23.1 per cent. The Progressives also suffered a further decline. The Centre on the other hand maintained their percentage of the vote and slightly increased their seats to 94. Both Free Conservatives and German-Conservatives increased their seats, to 57 and 59 respectively. The Socialists lost share of the vote and seats, but the drop in their actual votes was inconsiderable, given the hysteria unleashed against them. Bismarck had hit out against his enemies, personal and political, with an almost irrational fury borne of paranoia. He had succeeded to some extent, but he was still not quite the Bonapartist dictator that some commentators saw in him. Unless he had carried out the threat of a constitutional coup he was still dependent on a Reichstag representing social forces that could not be ignored. The Liberals were, however, the big losers. They had scarcely adjusted to the political mass market of which they were still half afraid. Their faith in the self-healing powers of the market looked irrelevant in face of the economic crisis.

Anti-socialist law and protection

Bismarck's success and the dilemma of the National Liberals were reinforced by the first outcome of the elections, the reintroduction of the anti-socialist law. It was a foregone conclusion that the Progressives and the Socialists themselves would vote against it. The Centre also did, mindful of the persecution they had suffered and were still suffering. There were, however, many Catholics who felt that socialism was for them also a profound menace. It was an agonizing decision for the National Liberals and they managed to modify the law slightly. An amendment by Lasker limited its duration to two and a half years. The National Liberals voted for the anti-socialist law, because the election campaign had shown them the weakness of their position. They feared another dissolution of the Reichstag and an even more ruthless demagogic appeal they could not match. Thus they voted for measures which could in no way be regarded as compatible with liberal principles and the rule of law. The authorities were empowered to prohibit associations, meetings and publications which could further socialist aims and the subversion of the existing order. A so-called 'lesser state of siege' could be proclaimed for specific districts, where all public meetings had to be licensed, police powers and discretion were strengthened and expulsions were made possible.

The major limit to the law, without which it would have been unconstitutional, was that it still enabled the Socialdemocratic party to field candidates in elections and to maintain its parliamentary presence. For a time the Socialists had difficulty in adjusting to the conditions of illegality in which they now had to operate and experienced setbacks, but soon the party resumed its inexorable rise, made almost inevitable by the rapid industrialization and urbanization that was going on. Bismarck had embarked upon another conflict even more unwinnable than that with the Catholic Church. He had, in the debates on the socialist law in the autumn of 1878, indicated that he realized that something more positive was required than mere repression. He had talked vaguely of assuring to the workers a higher participation in the profits of industry and offering them a shortening of hours. But it turned out to be a vain hope that even considerable advances in social policy would be accepted by the workers as a substitute for genuine emancipation.

In 1879 the introduction of tariffs on a range of industrial and agricultural goods followed. In addition to the numerous pressure groups that were now lobbying for protection there was also a cross-party association in the Reichstag, including some National Liberals, pressing for tariffs. There was hard bargaining between the different interests, agricultural and industrial, and it was said that the Reichstag was becoming almost indistinguishable from the Berlin stock exchange. Bismarck had been converted to the need for protection especially for agriculture, for as a landowner he was well aware of the pressure from overseas competition that had now decisively changed the market in agricultural commodities. The desire to use customs duties as a way of strengthening the revenues of the Reich still bulked large in his calculations. If this aim had been achieved, it would also have meant a further reduction in the budgetary powers of both the Reichstag and the separate Länder parliaments. It was still this central question of parliamentary power that produced the main confrontation between Bismarck and his Reichstag opponents of the left of the National Liberal party and the Progressive party. Lasker accused Bismarck of trying to undo the compromise reached in 1866 and of favouring, through imposts on consumption, the owners of property over those without property. The leaders of the Liberal left tried to rally the liberal middle classes against the threat of absolutist government. Bismarck counter-attacked by accusing Lasker of being a member of a political class that 'toils not, neither does it spin', implying that he and his government were better protectors of the rights of property. Bennigsen tried desperately to maintain the unity of his party and pre-serve as much of the budgetary control of the Reichstag as possible, but Bismarck was now clearly out to split the National Liberals and accepted no deal with them.

The tariff law of 1879 could therefore only be passed with the help of the Centre party. There was much about a protectionist policy that appealed to Centre party supporters, not least those from the working class. Bismarck put Windthorst and his party under pressure by negotiating directly with the Vatican about an easing of the Kulturkampf measures. The Centre insisted, however, that the federal element in the taxation system should not be too much weakened. In a widely noticed incident, Windthorst, attending for the first time one of the chancellor's parlia-mentary soirées, was seen in a private discussion with Bismarck. A compromise was negotiated, known as the Franckenstein amendment, the name of the Centre deputy who moved it. The budgetary powers of the parliaments in the separate Länder, and to some extent those of the Reichstag, were preserved by limiting the amount the Reich could retain from tariffs and duties to 130 million marks. The remainder would have to be passed on to the Länder, who in turn had to continue their matricular contributions. Bismarck therefore sacrificed the aim of strengthening the Reich revenues to his determination to block any advance towards parliamentarism. He was still deeply fearful of being replaced by a 'Gladstone ministry' after the accession of the Crown Prince. The tariff law passed on 12 July 1879 with a majority of 100, drawn from Conservatives, Free Conservatives and Centre. It also included 15 National Liberals. There was a further move to the right in the Prussian ministry. The Kulturkampf minister Falk was replaced by the strongly conservative Robert von Puttkamer.

The move towards protectionism and the break between Bismarck and the National Liberals amounts, in the view of many historians, to a refoundation of the Reich. It can also be argued that there was not so much a refoundation as a continuation of the system of 'skirted decisions'. Any hope that fully fledged parliamentary government would develop from the semi-constitutional compromise of 1866 and 1871 was dashed and no such development occurred before 1918. Bismarck played a crucial role, but many developments, the decline of liberalism, the rise of socialism and the pressure for protection, cannot be attributed to him. He used these developments with the one overriding aim, his survival in power. When he previously played the master manipulator in bringing about German unity, there was a forward-looking, creative quality about his manipulation which was now lacking. To keep his system going required increasingly desperate expedients. As for the tariffs, they were not initially very high, though the agricultural ones were steadily raised, with a brief exception in the 1890s. Nevertheless the overall effect was considerable. For agriculture it was not only tariffs but an increasingly rigorous policy of veterinary controls of meat imports that worked for the producer and against the consumer. The cost of living of the German working man was kept higher than it should have been for the benefit of farmers, including the politically privileged Junkers of Prussia. It was bound to aggravate social conflicts serious enough already.

Foreign policy during the first decade of the Reich

The arrival of a unified German Reich profoundly altered power relationships in Europe. In an often quoted speech in the House of Commons in June 1871 Disraeli, then leader of the Conservative opposition, called it a European revolution as great as that of 1789. It could only come about through the defeat of two of the European great powers, Austria-Hungary and France, and through the acquiescence of two others, Britain and Russia. It had therefore to be the prime aim of German policy to ensure that no reversal of what had occurred could be attempted and that the new state of affairs continued to remain acceptable to the other powers. In foreign even more than in domestic affairs all hinged on Bismarck. Even those who were adversaries in domestic politics deferred almost unquestioningly to his supremacy in the conduct of foreign policy and Bismarck sometimes used his control over foreign policy as a tool for the achievement of his domestic aims. There can be no doubt that when Bismarck put it about after 1870 that Germany was a 'saturated' power, he meant what he said. He certainly set his face against anything that might be called pan-Germanism, the incorporation into the Reich of German speakers elsewhere, particularly within the Habsburg empire. Such a programme already figured in some minds and was to become a major factor in the future, but Bismarck would have nothing to do with it. This policy of consolidation did not mean that Bismarck's policy was one of quietude and peace at all costs. This would have been entirely out of character for one who believed as much as he did in the need for conflict and confrontation. Bismarck was quite prepared to threaten war when it suited him, but there was never an occasion after 1870 when he seriously considered carrying out the threat.

The main problem for German foreign policy after 1871 was to prevent hostile coalitions from forming against what was in effect a semi-hegemonic power in the centre of the continent. One method of achieving this was to encourage the other great powers to pursue their interests on the periphery, which would prevent them from coalescing against the central power Germany, while needing the support of that power. Most immediately this balancing act, of making the new Reich attractive as a partner without becoming the tool of another power's interests, showed itself in relations with the two other empires of the continent, Austria and Russia. The Austrians, as we have seen, were still hoping to use the Franco-Prussian war as an occasion to recover the position they had lost in 1866. Beust, the Austrian foreign minister and long-time antagonist of Bismarck, realized that an alliance with France was not possible in July 1870 and soon accepted the changed situation produced by the French defeat. Bismarck's objective in his relations with Austria was to assure the policy-makers in Vienna that he had no intention of encouraging the grossdeutsch sentiments that the Prussian triumph had stimulated in German-speaking areas of the Habsburg dominions. When in the summer of 1871 Emperor William took the waters at Bad Gastein, for the first time since 1865, he was loudly cheered by the crowd. Bismarck's efforts to turn Austria into a reliable ally had to avoid endangering the close understanding with St Petersburg which had been so vital in the wars of German unification. Austro-Russian rivalry in the Balkans was a fundamental fact of life, which even temporary accommodations could not conjure away. It was a bonus for Bismarck when in November 1871 Beust was replaced by Count Andrassy, who had once been a Hungarian revolutionary condemned to death in 1848. Andrassy no longer harboured any ambition to recover Austria's German role.

For the Russians the rise of the Reich meant that whereas they had been in the role of patron of Prussia on its way up they were now confronted by a power in many respects superior to themselves. Here, as in the relationship with Austria, personalities were significant: Gorchakov, the Russian chancellor and foreign minister, was jealous of the world-historical role played by Bismarck, and the French language and culture remained potent among the Russian aristocratic élite. A counter-influence was the fear aroused by the Paris Commune and the dislike of

French republicanism. Tsar Alexander II was William I's nephew and in the German emperor's simple mind the Russian alliance was never to be questioned. Out of these contradictory materials the three-emperor league was eventually constructed in 1873, mainly to the specifications of Bismarck. The ideological element, here conservative solidarity, there revolutionary socialist subversion, was used in the construction, but matters had moved a long way since the Holy Alliance after 1815. The three-emperor league had little substance, mainly because Bismarck did not want to make a choice between Austria and Russia, nor was the threat of revolution as real as it had been earlier in the century.

A major German objective was to keep France isolated, especially as the French recovered much more quickly than anticipated, paid off the war indemnity imposed upon them and thereby brought the German occupation to an end. The republican government of Thiers fell in 1873 and the possibility of a monarchist restoration loomed under his successor Marshal MacMahon. When in March 1875 the French assembly passed a cadre law to improve the strength of the army, Moltke and the German General Staff were alarmed. Bismarck, with the mixture of realism and pessimism characteristic of him, already suffered from nightmares of hostile coalitions, *cauchemar des coalitions*. He saw a possible Austrian–Russian understanding in the Balkans and possibilities of Franco-Russian and Austro-French rapprochements. He decided to teach the French a lesson, show them their isolation, possibly force them into a humiliating climbdown by withdrawing the cadre law. It was the 'war-in-sight' crisis, the title of an article in the *Post*, regarded as a Bismarck mouthpiece. No doubt Bismarck also had domestic motives – it was the height of the Kulturkampf. The fear of ultramontane influences in Vienna and Paris plagued him. The 'war-in-sight' crisis misfired for Bismarck. The British Government took the initiative in offering mediation and it became clear that neither London nor St Petersburg were prepared to accept a further humiliation of France. Bismarck became very irritated with Russia and Gorchakov. It was only after this crisis, when Bismarck had explicitly to give up his attempt to force the French to withdraw the cadre law, that the German chancellor fully adjusted to the changed position that his own earlier triumph had created. France was no longer seen as the disturber of the European peace, but this was how others might easily perceive the new Germany. German policy had to tread a fine line between appearing as a threat to others and being itself under threat as the power in the middle.

It was just at this point that the crisis in the Balkans, which started with the risings in Bosnia-Hercegovina in July 1875, came to Bismarck's assistance. He could now assume with some credibility the role of the pivotal power acting with disinterest as the 'honest broker'. He still had to take great care to avoid being driven into exclusive support for either Russia or Austria. As he put it to the German ambassador in St Petersburg in October 1876:

> It cannot correspond to our interests to see the position of Russia seriously and permanently injured by a coalition of the rest of Europe, if fortune is unfavourable to the Russian arms; but it would affect the interests of Germany just as

deeply, if the Austrian monarchy was so endangered in its position as European power or in its independence, that one of the factors with which we have to reckon in the European balance of Power, threatened to fall for the future.

For a time the evolution of the crisis aided him, for the two empires were acting in unaccustomed accord. The Reichstadt agreement of July 1876 envisaged a division of the spoils between Austria and Russia in case of the anticipated Ottoman defeat by Serbia and Montenegro. But when the Turks won, the Russians were under pressure to act as the protector of the Christian subjects of the sultan. Bismarck was not willing to back them unreservedly as 'mandate holders' for Europe, as this might unleash a general European war, with Britain and Russia on opposing sides. 'Who is Europe?', he asked with his usual cynical realism. In a speech in December 1876 he used the famous phrase that Germany's interests in the Eastern Question were 'not worth the healthy bones of a single Pomeranian musketeer'.

When the Russo-Turkish war started in March 1877 the German balancing act became even more difficult. During his prolonged leave of absence Bismarck wrote what is probably his best-known foreign policy analysis, known as the Kissingen dictation. It highlights the long-term considerations that should guide German foreign policy, but with the pragmatism characteristic of the author it does so with the immediate problems arising from the Balkans crisis very much in mind. Its five main points are that Austrian and Russian interests and rivalries should be deflected eastwards; that Russian defence needs in the Orient and on her coasts should make the German alliance necessary for her; that a state of affairs should be attained satisfactory to both Britain and Russia, so that its maintenance should be in their as much as in the German interest; that Britain's interests in Egypt and the Mediterranean should keep her divided from France; and that relations between Austria and Russia should be such as to deter them from anti-German conspiracies, in which centralizing or clerical elements in Austria might wish to engage.

When Turkey faced defeat at the end of 1877 the threat of general war became once more real, with Britain and Russia on opposite sides, and Austria in the anti-Russian camp. In a debate in the Reichstag on 19 February 1878 Bismarck used the famous phrase that Germany would act as the 'honest broker', but not as either the arbiter or the schoolmaster of Europe. To public opinion at large the Congress of Berlin, which convened on 13 June 1878 under the chairmanship of Bismarck, showed him at the height of his power and prestige. This was useful in the Reichstag elections that were then progress. In Europe the German refusal to demand any territorial aggrandizement looked impressive. In fact the Congress was not quite the German triumph it appeared to be. The ground had been prepared, even before the Congress convened, for a serious curtailment of the Russian gains which had been imposed by the victorious tsarist empire on the Turks in the treaty of San Stefano in March 1878. The principal effect was the drastic reduction in size of the Greater Bulgaria, expected to be a Russian satellite, which had been agreed in the treaty. The Russians blamed Bismarck for what they saw as a defeat, even though he had devoted considerable effort to convincing the Austrians and the British that a Greater Bulgaria would not necessarily be loyal to Russia. It was the insistent demand of Gorchakov that Germany should give Russia the kind of cover that Russia had given to Prussia up to 1871, but policy could not indefinitely be based on gratitude nor could Germany tie herself unconditionally to Russian interests.

The dual alliance

In the aftermath of the Congress, during the meetings of the Commission set up to settle various outstanding issues, relations between Berlin and St Petersburg further deteriorated. The German agrarian tariffs introduced in 1879 became another grievance for the Russians. On 15 August 1879 Alexander II wrote a letter to his uncle, the German emperor, threatening dire consequences if the two nations were roused against each other. It became known as the 'box on the ears' letter. Bismarck had already come to the conclusion that closer ties with Austria were necessary, but he probably hoped that these would force Russia in turn to come back to something like the three-emperor league. An alliance with Austria had broad support in German public opinion and was widely seen as a substitute for the grossdeutsch solution that had been consigned to the dustbin of history in 1866. Bismarck briefly toyed with the idea of a public alliance, ratified by parliaments in both countries, with a customs union thrown in, but Andrassy was not prepared for that. It would, quite apart from other problems, have created difficulties between the German speakers and other nationalities in the Habsburg empire. Bismarck had in any case great difficulty in persuading his sovereign to accept this choice for Austria and against Russia. It was the last time that there was a major clash between the overpowering chancellor and the ageing monarch, with threats of resignation and veiled hints of abdication. The dual alliance, a secret treaty, obliged both countries to assist each other in case of a Russian attack. In case of another power's attack only neutrality was guaranteed, unless that third power was supported by Russia. The dual alliance became the most persistent of European power alignments until the collapse of both parties in 1918 brought it to an end. For Germany it proved ultimately a fatal tie to a weaker partner. This was not to be foreseen in 1879 when the Habsburg empire, although beset by problems, was still a major power. Survival and integrity were even then a vital German interest.

As it was, Bismarck succeeded by 1881 in reviving something like the three emperor league. He was helped in this by the return to power, in 1880, of a Liberal government under Gladstone in Britain. The Gladstonian policy of supporting the self-determination of the Balkan nationalities was suspect in Vienna as well as St Petersburg. A Liberal government with radical support in London even gave impetus to the anti-democratic, anti-revolutionary tide running strongly in the three empires. Three months before the conclusion of the new three-emperor alliance Alexander II was assassinated. The alliance obliged the three powers to remain neutral if one of them was attacked. It meant that territorial gains by both Russia and Austria in the Balkans would be subject to prior agreement and that Germany therefore was given a certain braking capacity on potential Russian–

Austrian conflicts in that area. For Russia it meant that she was protected from the pressure of the Western powers, particularly Britain, that had proved humiliating in 1878, in return for a recognition of Austrian interests in the Balkans. The Russian view that Turkey was obliged to close the Straits to third powers in case of war was accepted, so that a British fleet could not have entered the Black Sea, as was threatened in 1878. Germany had for the time being prevented a Franco-Russian rapprochement. In 1882 the alliance of the three empires was supplemented by the tripartite alliance of Italy, Germany and Austria. The Italians were nervous about a French attack, since the latter had settled, in 1881, in Tunisia. Bismarck had encouraged this diversion of French interest to Africa, away from the recovery of Alsace-Lorraine. The tripartite alliance laid to rest the old enmity between Italy and Austria, but it was limited by an Italian declaration that it was not to involve her in hostilities with Britain.

All these complex arrangements showed Bismarckian diplomatic mastery at its height and for the moment removed the *cauchemar des coalitions*. The durability of these alliance systems was, however, not very great, for they could not remove fundamental conflicts of interest. The Bismarck system of the 1880s consisted of expedients rather than solutions. The three-emperor alliance was limited to three years, though renewed in 1884 for a further three. The need for secrecy showed that powerful influences, such as the pan-Slav orientation in Russia or the pan-German in Germany, would have opposed some of the alignments had they been made public.

4 Bismarck's system in decline 1879–1890

Domestic developments in the 1880s

The turn towards conservatism seen in the socialist law of 1878 and the tariffs of 1879 did not solve any of the underlying problems of a rapidly changing German society, nor did it enable Bismarck to find the docile majority he wanted in the Reichstag. The ideal solution in his mind would have been to do away with the Reichstag altogether. The threats of a constitutional coup which he made more or less openly from time to time were, however, never carried out and perhaps even he did not think they seriously could be. He tried by one means and another to reduce the importance of the Reichstag, curtailment of sessions, of budgetary control and so on. Alternatively he tried to make the parties more amenable and in the case of the Socialists to suppress them. He wanted to end the Kulturkampf, but the process of turning the Centre into a governmental party was to be long drawn out and Bismarck could not rely on Centre party support for the remainder of his time in office. Their support for the tariff law did not extend to other matters and they remained suspicious of the state and of Bismarck's manipulations.

In March 1880 the National Liberal party finally split, something that Bismarck had desired for some time and that his manoeuvres helped to bring about. Prominent figures, such as Lasker and Bamberger, left the parliamentary National Liberal group and the dissidents became known as the Secession. There was an element of desperation in their move, for they had little confidence that there was a large popular constituency to which they could appeal. In the Prussian Landtag elections of 1879 the two Liberal parties, National Liberal and Progressives, had dropped from 232 seats, out of 433, to 142, while the Conservatives had risen from 41 to 110 (see Appendix: Tables 5 and 6). Liberalism was in decline under the three-tier system, which had traditionally favoured it, as much as it was under the universal suffrage of Reichstag elections. Lasker lost his seat in the Prussian Landtag. The Secession was not prepared to accept any more of the retreats Bismarck had forced on the National Liberals. The Secession was, however, not just a gesture of resignation. There was also the hope that, by keeping the liberal flag flying, a new reunion of Progressives, Secessionists and left-wing National Liberals would create a revived Liberal party. Such hopes were to be disappointed for at least the next thirty years.

Thus Bismarck's problem remained that he was without a reliable majority in the

Reichstag and even more than in foreign policy he was driven to expedients which lacked the creative, forward-looking quality that had earlier given him the power to shape events. One way of undercutting the parliamentary parties and depriving them of the air to breathe was, in the chancellor's view, to encourage direct dealings between the government and important groups in society. The growing importance of interest and lobby groups, evident in the pressures for protection, seemed to offer a way of doing this. In September 1880 Bismarck himself took over the Prussian ministry of trade and put forward a proposal to create a Prussian Economic Council. The Council consisted of representatives of experts from industry, trade and agriculture, put forward by chambers of commerce and similar bodies, as well as of a number of royally nominated individuals, including working men. Legislation might be agreed between the Council and the executive. Bismarck would have liked such a council at Reich level, but the Reichstag blocked it. Even the Prussian council met only four times, the last in 1887.

Bismarck's social policy

The social policy, resulting in a system of health insurance in 1883, accident insurance in 1884 and old age and invalidity insurance in 1889 also arose in part from Bismarck's desire to find a way of taking the life out of the parliamentary party system. Nevertheless it was the most remarkable and long-lasting achievement of Bismarck's last decade in office. The growing army of propertyless workers were to be tied directly to the state and the wind was to be taken out of the sails of the socialists. By becoming a pensioner of the state the worker would acquire a conservative mentality and a loyalty to the monarchical state. The roots of social policy were obviously broader than these immediate political motives. The chancellor's views on how to deal with poverty were influenced by his background as a Junker landowner and by a traditional sense of religious obligation. It had long been evident that not only in Germany older methods of relieving poverty, based on a more static, rural way of life, were no longer adequate in an age of industrialization, urbanization and social mobility. In Germany an influential organization of academics, the Association of Social Policy, had been founded in 1872, which advocated an approach to economic problems based more on historical, social and cultural factors than that adopted by the school of strict laissez-faire market economists. The latter referred to those connected with the Social Policy Association contemptuously as pulpit socialists. Men like Gustav Schmoller and Lujo Brentano advocated a social market philosophy of major reforms promoted by the state. It would take the sting out of the growing class war and reduce the potential for revolution. There was in any case in Prussia a long tradition of state intervention in the economy, which also explains the readiness to resort to protective tariffs.

The actual policies adopted in the 1880s could not have been implemented if Bismarck had not pressed them against the resistance they were bound to encounter. Some schemes already existed, particularly in the mining industry. They, and new ones being proposed, in general minimized the burden on employers. Among Bismarck's advisers on social policy were Hermann Wagener, mentioned earlier as the promoter of a movement of social conservatism in Prussia, and Theodor Lohmann, an official who until 1884 helped in the drafting of the insurance laws. Lohmann was, however, concerned to emancipate the worker and to give him the sense of being a full citizen. These were not Bismarck's aims and he and Lohmann eventually parted company over the details of the proposals. In so far as Bismarck's main motive was to undercut the loyalty of the worker to the Socialdemocratic party he entirely failed to achieve his immediate objective. In the longer run the insurance laws undoubtedly contributed towards making or keeping the Socialdemocrats a reformist rather than a revolutionary party. It gave the German worker that stake in his country which made him leap to its defence in 1914.

When the first social policy proposals, accident insurance, were introduced early in 1881 they aroused suspicion among the Reichstag parties. They were seen as an example of the chancellor's dictatorial and manipulatory style of governing, not as a genuine attempt to solve growing social problems. Comparisons were made with the way the Romans bribed the mob by distributions of corn. Bismarck counter-attacked in typically confrontational manner by accusing his opponents, particularly those from the liberal Left, of doctrinaire 'Manchesterism'. It was an accusation that has been echoed by commentators, and contemporary and subsequent historians. It was, however, hardly surprising that the parties were deeply distrustful of the chancellor and his threats to the powers of the Reichstag. Even the Centre party, where there were many to whom the social policy held appeal, found it difficult to accept it from the hands of Bismarck. Accident insurance was, moreover, particularly contentious, as it involved employers' liability and might damage industrial competitiveness. Bismarck was himself an opponent of factory legislation and limitation of hours, because of his reluctance to impose excessive burdens on industrial employers. In fact Germany, while in the van on social insurance, dropped behind other industrial states in this type of protective legislation. Accident insurance encountered so much resistance that it could not be passed into law until 1884. Insurance was organized by industrial branches, something which seemed to accord with Bismarck's desire to enhance corporative institutions, and contributions came entirely from employers, who in return were freed from liability. It was, however, a less state-centred scheme than Bismarck would have liked.

In the meantime the less contentious health insurance scheme was enacted. Voluntary local schemes, which existed on a small scale, were left to continue and to start with catered for an increasing number, until by the early 1890s they were gradually superseded by the official compulsory panels. These were locally elected and soon became bastions of socialdemocratic influence. They turned out to be an important element in fostering a positive attitude towards the state among workers. The number of those insured rose by leaps and bounds: in 1885 it was 4.3 million, 9.2 per cent of the population and 40 per cent of wage earners, by 1917 this had risen to 15.6 million, 23 per cent of the population and virtually all wage earners. The amount of sickness pay was modest and not really sufficient to reduce the risk illness posed for wage earners and their families. The old age and invalidity insurance of 1889 realized Bismarck's intention of making the worker a dependant of the state more fully and was the most innovatory of the schemes. Traditionally poverty was regarded as the inevitable companion of old age. Contributory pensions initially encountered a lot of opposition even among workers. To have to pay for an exceedingly modest pension available only at age seventy, an age not many were likely to reach, seemed a bad bargain.

Changes in party alignments

Remarkable as social policy was as a long-term achievement, it did not solve the problem of government in the 1880s. Bismarck managed to get the second septennial settlement of the military budget through the Reichstag in May 1880, with the support of the National Liberals, but against the votes of the Centre. It was characteristic of the governmental orientation of the National Liberals that they did not criticise Bismarck's foreign policy nor question the military requirements of the state. The second septennial settlement increased the strength of the army and laid down extended exercise periods for the reservists, all of which cost money. The social policy proposals also needed more revenue, but the way Bismarck wanted to raise it, for instance by renewing the proposal of a state tobacco monopoly, would have further reduced the budgetary powers of the Reichstag. It was one more reason why the Liberals and the Centre were so hostile to Bismarck's initial plans for accident insurance.

The Reichstag elections of October 1881 produced a setback for the Bismarck government, in spite of massive official pressure to influence the voters (see Appendix: Table 9). It was part of the turn to the right of 1878/9 that all holders of official positions, down to those holding modest judicial or teaching positions, were constrained to support the government in elections and to use their influence on others for that purpose. At one time there was a liberal element in the Prussian civil service and this was still strong enough to slow the moves towards protectionism until, beginning with the departure of Delbrück in 1876, personnel changes at the top made conservatism and support for the national state the touchstone of recruitment and promotion. The conversion of the Prussian civil servants into unquestioning upholders of conservative loyalty to the state is often associated with Robert von Puttkamer as minister of the interior in the 1880s, but it was inherent in an older tradition of Prussian state service. Loyalty now meant that support for parties that were not governmental, left Liberals, the Centre, most of all Socialdemocrats as declared enemies of the state, was scarcely possible for holders of official positions, however lowly. Yet neither direct electoral pressure nor massive government propaganda could turn the elections of 1881 into a success for Bismarck. The two Conservative parties loyal to the government, German-Conservatives and Free Conservatives lost share of votes and seats, the Progressives more than doubled both votes and seats and the Centre maintained its position well. It was the only election in which the Liberal Secession campaigned as a separate party and it got almost the same number of seats as the remaining National Liberals.

Within the Conservative camp there appeared a new grouping which adopted the label Christian-Social. Its chief figure was the Protestant pastor and Court preacher Adolph Stoecker, a passionately nationalist, monarchist demagogue, who claimed to be able to wean the workers from their socialist delusion. As time went on, highly placed persons like the eldest son of the Crown Prince, the future Wilhelm II, and the influential chief of staff General von Waldersee became supporters of Stoecker and took his claims to offer an antidote to the alarming poison of socialism seriously. Stoecker soon resorted to anti-Semitism to reinforce his demagogic appeal. The crisis of liberalism had reinvigorated and modernized deep-seated and long-standing anti-Jewish prejudices. Treitschke, in the 1860s among Bismarck's liberal opponents, now the most prestigious figure in the national-liberal school of historians, had lent respectability to anti-Semitism in his widely read German history and ended a famous article in the Prussian Yearbooks in 1879 with the cry 'the Jews are our misfortune'. Neither Stoecker or Treitschke embraced the racial form of anti-Semitism, but this was beginning to make a showing in innumerable publications. Jews were becoming the scapegoats for all those groups who saw themselves as losers in the rapidly advancing process of modernization. They were also blamed for the recession and for the fraudulent promotions of the preceding boom. Anti-Semitism was indicative of the way German nationalism was changing. Up to 1871 it was a progressive, broadly anti-establishment ideology; now the new nationalism of the Reich was aggressive, expansionist and exclusive of all minorities. As for Bismarck, whatever Junker anti-Jewish prejudices he may have had in his early days, he made use of Jews in his most confidential, personal service, as in the case of Bleichröder, his banker. But such was his paranoia about being forced out of power that he was prepared to use any means to hang on. He saw Stoecker's potential use as a successful demagogue and would not condemn him, but he did not wish to be seen endorsing vulgar anti-Semitism either.

The outcome of the 1881 Reichstag elections showed that Bismarck's reputation as an almost mythical hero among the mass of the population was not sufficient to underpin his exposed political position. When promoting his accident insurance scheme in the spring of 1881 he had attacked the parties as being motivated only by the most narrow party advantage and by the sole sentiment of 'getting rid of Bismarck', but no amount of cajoling, manipulation and direct pressure had worked. Even the Socialdemocrats all but maintained their position in spite of massive repression. There had been large numbers of expulsions and arrests, hundreds had been forced into exile, large numbers of socialist associations had been prohibited and publications been impounded. In some places, for example Altona, Socialdemocrats were subjected to the lesser state of siege provided in the anti-socialist law, but in South Germany the repression was less severe. Yet the socialist share of the vote fell only marginally further, from 7.6 to 6.1 per cent in a reduced poll, and their seats actually rose from 9 to 12. They were adjusting to the narrow amount of leeway the repressive law left and from now on their rise was inexorable and almost uninterrupted.

Yet Bismarck had also achieved much of his anti-parliamentary, anti-party purpose. Even the large SPD of the future was not able to force a fundamental constitutional change towards fully parliamentary government. The move in that direction which at one time seemed inevitable was in fact halted and the system of 'skirted decisions' was maintained. The gradual suspension of the Kulturkampf and the alleviation of the anti-Catholic laws was mainly achieved by direct negotiations between Berlin and Rome. The Centre party was as it were outflanked and considerable tension arose within the Catholic community and within the Centre party between those prepared to accept Bismarck's concessions and others who remained suspicious of his intentions. Leo XIII favoured the acceptance of concessions while Windthorst tried to maintain the principles and bargaining power of the party in the Reichstag and the Prussian Landtag. Bismarck exploited this situation with his usual tactical ingenuity, though in Windthorst he was up against a formidable parliamentary operator. The relief laws of the early 1880s left the Prussian government firmly in control, but by allowing many priests to return to their parishes lessened the fighting spirit of the Catholic grass roots. Bishops were allowed to return to their sees, but selectively, so that so-called 'state Catholics' were favoured. Among the politicians of the Centre party a gap opened between those drawn to the conservative policies of the chancellor and those who like Windthorst stuck to their principles, particularly on constitutional issues. In the vote on the renewal of the anti-socialist law in 1884 the gap showed up dangerously. Windthorst was determined to maintain the opposition to the law, but 39 Centre deputies still voted for it and 18 stayed away. 26 of the recently united Progressives and Secessionists also voted for it and 13 stayed away. It was a complicated game of poker, for the supporters of the law really wanted it to be defeated, so that a premature dissolution of the Reichstag would follow and an electoral battle, in which the opponents of the law could be pilloried as favouring 'the party of revolution'. Thus was Bismarckian manipulation debasing German politics.

The Liberal Secession was not the prelude to the rise of a large Liberal party engaged in a genuine contest for real power, and in the circles around the Crown Prince there was a mood of resignation. In 1883 Bennigsen, the National Liberal leader, tired of the attempt to keep National Liberalism united and resigned. In 1884 the Secession and the Progressives led by Richter united in the *Freisinnige Vereinigung*, often simply called *Freisinn*. It was not the hoped for large reinvigorated Liberal party, merely what remained of its left wing. When Lasker died on a tour of the United States, Bismarck, with characteristic vindictiveness, refused to pass on to the Reichstag the message of condolence sent by the American Congress. The remaining National Liberals were now led by Johannes Miquel, the Burgomaster of Frankfurt. He was an 1848 revolutionary but had moved steadily to the right. Under his inspiration the National Liberals adopted, in March 1884, the Heidelberg Declaration. It endorsed support for Bismarck in almost all respects, protective tariffs, social insurance, tax reform, a strong army and anti-socialism. A special appeal was made to the farming community, especially the smaller farmer, among whom the party now enjoyed support outside Prussia. Cooperation with the recently merged left liberal parties was renounced. The evolution of the National Liberals towards a governmental party, which had begun in very different circumstances in 1866, was complete. The party now joined the Conservatives and the Free Conservatives as groups on which Bismarck could rely. In the Reichstag elections of 1884, which took place without a premature dissolution, these three groups obtained 157 seats, while the *Freisinn* got only 67, as compared with the 106 seats which had made up the combined total of Progressives and the Secession in the previous elections (see Appendix: Table 9). There was little change in the position of the Centre, but the Socialist proportion of votes rose strongly, from 6.1 to 9.7 per cent, though the dual ballot system meant that the Socialists got only 24 seats. It was still twice as many as in 1881, though in percentage terms the party had hardly advanced since 1877. Bismarck's carrot-and-stick policy was not working, but he could now more effectively use the socialist threat to frighten the bourgeois parties. He still did not have a reliable majority in the Reichstag, but on balance his position was stronger than it had been in 1881. He had less to fear from the ever more imminent change of monarch. His attempt to by-pass or 'dry out' the Reichstag had failed, but he could now hope for an increasingly compliant one.

Foreign and colonial policy in the 1880s

The 1880s were a period of increasing colonial and imperial rivalry between the powers. Bismarck had encouraged some of these rivalries on the periphery in order to divert tensions from the Reich and from Central Europe. There was therefore a compelling reason for Germany herself to refrain from colonial involvements, which would get her sucked into these rivalries and greatly complicate her security problem. This consideration was so fundamental to Bismarck's conduct of foreign policy that it has always been a puzzle for historians why he allowed such colonial commitments to be undertaken in the 1880s.

Some historians emphasize the social–imperialist aspect of Germany's entry into colonialism, namely that German imperialism was above all a diversionary manoeuvre to distract from domestic social tensions. This was certainly a motive for some of the early advocates of German entry into the colonial race and became an important one for later policy makers. For Bismarck it is likely to have been a subordinate consideration, not going much beyond the desire to add to his propaganda appeals in the Reichstag elections of 1884. For him the colonial commitments remained an episode, on which he all but turned his back in his last few years of power. On the whole he was a believer in free trade imperialism and in informal empire, for which the British had set so successful an example. He had turned down out of hand a French offer in 1871 to cede territory in Indochina instead of Alsace-Lorraine. But he could not close his ears to the growing clamour for German participation in the colonial race, particularly once the economic depression and the turn towards protection had provided stronger arguments for it. In 1880 a German firm with interests in Samoa and influence in quarters close to the chancellor asked for state support, when it was threatened with bankruptcy. The Reichstag, where National Liberal free traders were embittered by Bismarck's treatment of them, turned down the Samoa proposals, but with the help of

Bleichröder a private rescue was undertaken. Soon the colonial–imperial idea, that Germany had a mission and must on no account allow herself to be excluded from the division of the world, gained momentum. In 1882 a Colonial Association was founded which had the support of many influential establishment figures.

It was probably immediate diplomatic considerations that persuaded Bismarck in March 1884 to take the decisive first step into colonial empire. It was the declaration of a German protectorate at Angra Pequena insistently demanded by the Bremen trader Adolf Lüderitz. At this point a kind of Franco-German colonial alliance directed against Britain figured in Bismarck's calculations. It was a card he played both in Egypt, where French claims interfered with British control, and along the coast of West Africa. His immediate aim was to distract French attention from Alsace-Lorraine and put Britain under pressure to tie herself more positively to Germany. It was a policy which came to a dead end in 1885, when the government of Jules Ferry fell. French revanchist aspirations were not to be easily distracted, while Britain proved more accommodating in colonial matters, though by no means willing to abandon splendid isolation. Most of what Germany now acquired was done so with British consent, though this was sometimes grudgingly given. The result of the flurry of colonial activity in the 1880s was that Germany acquired widely separated footholds in Africa and South-East Asia. There was South-West Africa, what is now Namibia, in Central Africa there were Togo and the Cameroons, in East Africa it was the area that is Tanzania. In south-east Asia there was the north-eastern corner of New Guinea, various islands to the north of it, known as the Bismarck Archipelago, the Marshall Islands, and an informal presence in Samoa. There was little chance of consolidation and endless opportunity for complications. Bismarck soon reverted to his scepticism about the utility of direct colonial control and rated the ability of German officials as colonial administrators low. When in December 1888 a German Africa explorer visited him he made the often quoted remark: 'Your map of Africa is very fine, but my map of Africa is in Europe. Here is Russia and here . . . is France, and we are in the middle; that is my map of Africa.' But the German craving for world power was not to be so easily distracted. Bismarck had whetted the appetite and among his motives was the quest for ways of stimulating national solidarity behind his continued leadership.

Anti-Polish measures

There were other ways rewarding the groups and parties considered loyal to the Reich and exposing the others, Progressives, Centrists and Socialists, as subversive or at least fellow-travellers of subversion. Tariff levels for agricultural commodities were raised in 1885 and in 1887 and were then up to five times as high as they had been in 1879. This appealed to the Conservatives and to the reconstituted National Liberals and aggravated the tensions between different groups in the Centre Party. Then there was the intensification of anti-Polish measures, something with fatal long-term consequences. Tensions between German and Polish nationalism had been building up at least since 1848, but were at least mitigated as long as the Poles were subjects of the non-national Prussian state, where some respect for the rule of law and civil rights prevailed. They were more difficult to contain within the Reich, based on German nationality. They were greatly aggravated by the Kulturkampf, which bore very hard on the Catholic Poles and their ethnic identity. Bismarck had always regarded Polish national aspirations as a threat to Prussia and his understanding with Tsarist Russia owed much to solidarity against Polish nationalism. His rather old-fashioned view was that the sense of Polish nationality was the preserve of the Polish aristocracy and of the clergy, while the peasants might gradually be converted to the superior German civilization. They might continue to use Polish as a popular language, but they would be educated in a school system using mainly German. Under the School Supervision Law passed in the course of the Kulturkampf in 1872, clerical school supervision was replaced by secular inspection. The teaching of the Polish language was reduced.

This combination of religious and linguistic repression aroused resistance and a national-democratic movement spread among the two million Poles in Prussia's eastern provinces. German public opinion, now highly sensitive to nationalist issues, was in turn aroused by statistical evidence that the Polish population, particularly in the province of Posen, was increasing at the expense of the German, and incidentally also at the expense of the Jews, who, ironically, were culturally and linguistically predisposed towards the Germans. There was an even more marked decline of German landownership compared with the Polish. The Poles had a higher birth rate, but the effect of westward migration in search of industrial employment and better life chances was even stronger. More Germans than Poles migrated, except in Upper Silesia, whose Polish miners sought work in the Ruhr. Aroused German nationalism now demanded positive policies to support Germanism and there is no doubt that Bismarck, in pursuit of his general policy of consolidating the voting blocks supporting him, pandered to these demands. In 1885 over thirty thousand Poles and Jews of non-German nationality were expelled from Prussia, a previously unheard of procedure, the precursor of twentieth-century ethnic cleansing and genocide. A Settlement Law of 1886 channelled large sums of money towards the buying up of Polish land for German resettlement. It had the support of Conservatives, Free Conservatives and National Liberals and had some sympathy even in the Centre. Windthorst tried to do his best for the Poles, but Leo XIII was more interested in appeasing the German chancellor. Bismarck exploited the differing party situations in the Prussian Landtag and the Reichstag and went out of his way, in his most confrontational manner, to dramatize the threat to the future of the Reich from its internal as well as external enemies. Those who were not with him, Progressives, Centrists and Socialists, were the enemy within.

The external threat was becoming more serious again in the mid-1880s and in this Bismarck was not exaggerating. The three-emperor league had been renewed in 1884, but soon a fresh crisis centred on Bulgaria was undermining its substance. Under Prince Alexander of Battenberg that country had not proved the docile Russian satellite that had been anticipated and feared in 1878. In 1885 a rising against the Turks broke out in Eastern Rumelia and the insurgents proclaimed Alexander of Battenberg the ruler of a united Bulgaria. But now St Petersburg did not want what it had been prevented from having at the Congress of Berlin. The Russians withdrew their officers serving in the Bulgarian army and threatened to intervene to restore the country's status as their satellite. In November 1885 the situation was further complicated by a Serb attack on Bulgaria. Belgrade wanted to secure compensation in Macedonia in return for accepting a Greater Bulgaria. Serbia was regarded as an Austrian satellite and the Russians suspected Austrian designs behind the Serb attack. Contrary to expectations the Serbs suffered a severe military defeat at the hands of the Bulgarians and were only saved from complete disaster by the Austrians. There was a temporary compromise, when the Turks consented to Alexander of Battenberg being recognized as governor of East Rumelia, but in August 1886 he was kidnapped and removed by a group of Russian officers. Even thereafter the Bulgars refused to conform to the requirements of the great powers. They elected Ferdinand of Saxe-Coburg-Gotha ruler of a Greater Bulgaria.

There was repeatedly a threat of a European war between Germany's two major allies, in which she, and probably the other major powers, would become involved, something that Bismarck was desperate to avoid. It was still fundamental to the German national interest that Austria-Hungary should survive as a major power. It was equally vital to avoid war with Russia, which could turn into a two-front war against France and Russia. It was a complicating factor that German opinion was pro-Austrian and anti-Russian. Bismarck's policy, in so far it amounted to a refusal to provoke the Russians, was criticized as never before. At a more subordinate level there was economic tension between Russia and Germany, over the rising level of protection keeping Russian grain exports out of the German market, later over the dependence of Russia on the German capital market. In the army Moltke and Waldersee, soon to be his successor, favoured a preventive war against Russia, possibly against France as well. Bismarck thought preventive war far too high a risk and strove, ultimately with success, to maintain his alliance system. It required ever more complicated balancing acts and this was the time when he is often compared to a juggler keeping five balls in the air.

The cartel elections

The domestic political situation and the foreign policy crises were inextricably mixed up, something that Bismarck had always recognized as a fact of life. Interpretations based on the primacy of domestic policy can easily be exaggerated. The crisis in German foreign policy was real enough and not conjured up for domestic reasons, merely exploited for that purpose. It turned out useful for Bismarck's balancing act that revanchist sentiment in France was again on the rise and that it was being spurred on in Paris by the colourful figure of the minister of war, General Boulanger, a man with Bonapartist aspirations. Bismarck played down the Russian threat and played up the French threat. In November he brought forward the demand for a new septennial military budget, based on an increased strength of the army, which would normally not have been due until 1888. His plan was to provoke the opposition parties into blocking his demands and thereby to have a pretext for an early dissolution of the Reichstag. Elections would be fought under the shadow of a foreign threat and on the refusal of some sections of the Reichstag to support preparations against it. They would become a plebiscite for or against the government and this intention succeeded to an ominous extent.

The three pro-Bismarckian parties, Conservatives, Free Conservatives and National Liberals, formed a so-called cartel for the elections held in February 1887, agreeing to support each other on the second ballot. National Liberals and Free Conservatives made considerable advances in the proportion of votes gained on the first ballot, the more striking since electoral participation rose from 62 per cent in 1884 to 77 per cent in 1887. Cooperation on the second ballot meant that the three cartel parties obtained 220 seats, as against 157 in 1884, and now had a majority in the Reichstag (see Appendix: Table 9). The Progressives lost more than half their seats, while the Centre just held its ground. The Socialists got over 10 per cent of the vote, but saw their seats reduced from 24 to 11, because the electoral system was so heavily loaded against them. It looked as if Bismarck was once more on the crest of a wave, but the cohesion of the cartel turned out to be deceptive. Differences of economic interest, between agrarians and exporting industries, divided the cartel parties. Some National Liberals still refused to vote for the second of the 'peace laws', which ended the Kulturkampf. Anti-Catholicism was to them the one remaining badge of their liberalism. Some Conservatives wanted to make common cause with the right wing of the Centre, on social issues and on the independence of the churches, even the Lutheran churches, from the state. Bismarck had the majority he had long sought, but it was not always reliable.

In foreign affairs Bismarck was still able to impose his ideas. His position continued to be that Germany was a saturated power and that the main task was to safeguard her position in Europe, which one may regard as semi-hegemonic. It was to be done, if possible, without incurring the risk of war, though the threat of war was used both in domestic and in foreign policy. It was mainly the French threat that Bismarck used in his manipulation of opinion, though behind it there was the real danger that a Franco-Russian alliance might come into being. The hue and cry over the French threat was allowed to subside again, a process facilitated by the resignation of General Boulanger in May 1887. With regard to Russia Bismarck did not allow himself to be pushed by the hostility of public opinion or the talk of a preventive war. But in accordance with his usual carrot-and-stick tactics and obfuscation of his real intentions, he allowed the Reichsbank, in November 1887, to refuse to accept Russian state bonds as security against loans, the so-called Lombard stop. The growing Russian dependence on the French capital market became a factor in the eventual entente between the two countries, but the interdependence of diplomacy and economics should not be overestimated at this period. Diplomatically it proved impossible to renew the three-emperor league again, but Bismarck counteracted this by the secret Reinsurance Treaty of June 1887. In case of an unprovoked war between Austria and Russia Germany would remain neutral; Russia would remain neutral in a Franco-German war not unleashed by Germany. Germany recognized Russian rights with regard to Bulgaria, East Rumelia and the Straits. These latter provisions were in clear contradiction to the Mediterranean entente, which Bismarck had helped to promote earlier in 1887, and to the renewal of the three-power league between Austria, Italy and Germany. Italy was given support against French expansion in North Africa and the right to have her claims considered in the Balkans, while giving Austria security against an Italian attack should she become embroiled with Russia in the Balkans. In the Mediterranean entente Britain joined Austria and Italy against French imperial aspirations, but above all against Russian expansion at the expense of Turkey and against Russian designs to change the status of the straits. If the Reinsurance Treaty had become public it would have gravely damaged the credibility of German diplomacy.

It is not surprising that many even right inside the German establishment regarded this system as over-complicated and that after the fall of Bismarck they tried to simplify it. For Bismarck it was a continuation of his system of keeping tensions away from the Reich and refusing to shoulder the burden of containing Russia in the Near East. The survival of the Habsburg empire was a vital German interest, but in Bismarck's view there was no need to encourage or underwrite Austrian aims in the Balkans. When in early 1888 the danger of war, mainly over Bulgaria, again seemed real, a further expansion of the German army and its reserves was proposed by Bismarck in the Reichstag. As a warning to Russia, the two-power league of 1879 with Austria was made public. But Bismarck still insisted, in a broad review of his policy, that his policy was one of peace. In a famous sentence he said: 'We Germans fear God, but nothing else in the world; and it is the fear of God that makes us love and preserve peace.' The first part of sentence was echoed innumerable times in Germany in years to come, but the second part was forgotten. In 1889 Bismarck briefly suggested to Salisbury an Anglo-German alliance against French aggression, but it is doubtful if he seriously thought it would be accepted. He was always suspicious of making an alliance with a parliamentary state like Britain, but less averse to the Tory Salisbury than to the Liberal Gladstone. An Anglo-German entente would have been a useful supplement to his security system and he was understandably reluctant to see even any informal understanding disturbed by colonial complications. Ideologically an alliance of the three continental empires was his preferred option, but to the many who were now critical of him even in his conduct of foreign policy his approach looked old-fashioned. Adept as he was in using the press and in manipulating opinion, the hard core of policy-making was for him still a matter between courts, cabinets and diplomats, and of fine tuning a system of checks and balances. War was still an instrument of policy, not to be lightly used, but the raising of mass armies, which his own military budgets of the late 1880s were designed to facilitate, was, along with the effects of industrialization, foreshadowing an age of total war.

The fall of Bismarck

The increasingly out-of-date appearance of the Bismarck regime was highlighted by the rapid transition of the throne through three generations in 1888. On 9 March William I died, aged nearly 91. Frederick III, mortally ill from cancer of the throat ruled only fourteen weeks. On 15 June William II, aged 29, ascended the throne. Bismarck's nightmare of many years, a liberal emperor, dominated by an English wife, installing a Gladstone cabinet, had never become real. It may well always have been a myth, but one with a long afterlife. The decline of liberalism was exploited and aggravated by Bismarck, but it is unlikely that it could have been avoided if Frederick William had come to the throne earlier. Now Bismarck had a new problem, how to make himself indispensable to a young man who was bound to want to be master in his own house and who was seen by many to embody their hopes for the future. It was not yet as clear as it was to become within a few years and as it is to posterity that the young emperor lacked the capacity to fulfil such hopes. He was in fact highly unsuited to exercising the large powers which the constitution vested in the imperial monarch, but which his grandfather had left in the chancellor's hands. His physical handicap, a withered right arm, the consequence of a difficult birth, had imbued him with a craving for self-assertion. It is possible that he suffered some brain damage at birth, which would account for his short attention span and lack of steady application. The manic element in his make-up caused even his entourage to doubt his sanity. He had, however, a quick grasp which, in the context of the deference due to him as a crowned head, deceived many into thinking him brilliant and gave him an aura of freedom from all earthbound restraints. He left no one in any doubt about what he thought was due to him as the ruler anointed by God. Two Latin tags which he used sum it up neatly: '*hoc volo, sic jubeo*', freely translated as 'my wish is my command', and '*suprema lex regis voluntas*' (the king's will is the supreme law), which he inscribed in the Golden Book of the City of Munich during a visit in 1891. His hasty, fitful, inconsistent input into most of the major affairs of his time had cumulatively a highly unfortunate impact. His many public gaffes and the scandals surrounding his court began, after a few years, to diminish the ample reservoir of monarchist loyalty existing among his subjects. In 1887, when it was known that, because of his fathers's fatal illness, his accession could not be long delayed, he allowed himself unwisely to be associated with Stoecker and Waldersee, who were intriguing against Bismarck and his cartel policy. Stoecker stood for the populist conservatism, anti-liberal and anti-Semitic and vaguely social-reformist, that was seen by some as an antidote to socialism's growing hold over the masses. Waldersee had political ambitions and was opposed to Bismarck's policy of 'keeping the wire open to St Petersburg'. After William's accession Bismarck was able to steer the emperor away from drastic foreign policy changes, but confrontation came over domestic affairs.

In May 1889, just when the old-age and invalidity scheme had passed into law, pit strikes on an unprecedented scale broke out. Nearly 90,000 miners were on strike in the Ruhr, around 140,000 in the whole of Germany. Troops were held in readiness, but Bismarck wanted to let the unrest burn itself out and thought it useful to give the middle classes something of a fright. The emperor wanted to show himself socially concerned at the beginning of his reign and received representatives of the strikers. Bismarck, with cynical realism, saw that the 'young master' would find it difficult to stick to the course of accommodation with the workers and that if it came to conflict again, he would still prove indispensable. In October he introduced a new anti-socialist law without a time limit. It would tie the emperor to the chancellor, but if the Reichstag refused to pass it, the ensuing constitutional crisis would equally make it impossible to get rid of him. The cartel parties wanted minor relaxations, with regard to the power to expel socialist agitators, but Bismarck, in spite of the emperor's plea at a crown council on 24 January 1890, refused to make any concessions. When the law in its existing form was then turned down, the Reichstag was dissolved.

The result of the elections made Bismarck's confrontational course look very threadbare. The cartel parties lost votes and seats heavily (see Appendix: Table 9). Their combined portion of the poll dropped from 47.3 to 35.4 per cent, their seats from 220 to 135. The Socialists now became the largest party with nearly 20 per cent of the vote, though only 35 seats. It still meant they had more than trebled their representation. The Progressives more than doubled their seats. The Centre lost share of vote, but with 106 seats reached their highest number. Bismarck's manipulation, which had succeeded on a foreign issue in 1887, now failed on a domestic one. More than ever it appeared that his policies had no future, but he still believed that he was indispensable to a government that could not now rely on any steady parliamentary support. For a few days it looked as if the emperor, under the shock of the election result, would go along with this. But Bismarck had underestimated the sheer pressure of opinion among public and parties to be rid, once and for all, of the chancellor's unscrupulous and inherently hopeless machinations. He had also underestimated William's desire to free himself of his overmighty servant, which, given his unrestrained egomania, took no heed of the future. Ominously the Kaiser boasted in public 'those who oppose me . . . I will smash'.

Ironically, Windthorst was in the end the only major figure prepared to continue playing ball with Bismarck. In a last desperate move the chancellor had an interview with him to explore the possibility of forming a centre-right coalition pivoting on Windthorst's party. The Catholic leader who had made a new school law the condition of his support, said after the meeting 'I come from the political deathbed of a great man.' This was on 12 March 1890. The final break came over this interview, with William complaining that he had not been informed about it; over a cabinet order of 1852, which Bismarck tried to use to prevent the emperor from consulting ministers separately; finally over relations with Russia, with William accusing Bismarck of keeping him in the dark over threatening troop movements. In fact Bismarck had just had a meeting with the Russian ambassador in Berlin about the renewal of the Reinsurance Treaty and saw no immediate threat. After repeated demands from the emperor that Bismarck submit his request to be relieved of his offices the chancellor did so on 18 March. The long drawn out process of Bismarck's dismissal showed German politics in a lurid light and the myths surrounding the event would do further great damage in the future. Bismarck's skill as his own propagandist was undiminished and he pursued his successors, from William down, with a relentless vendetta. Soon the many who had greeted his departure with a sigh of relief saw him as the wise old man in the Sachsenwald, the monumental founder figure, whose life work was being undermined by his incompetent heirs. In this way Bismarck continued to influence German affairs profoundly. Immediately, his departure made almost more of an impression abroad than at home. There was the famous Punch cartoon 'Dropping the pilot' and the Kaiser's remark, typical of his subaltern mentality, 'the course remains the same – full steam ahead' was widely quoted.

5   The Wilhelmine age

The growth of economic power

Bismarck's departure marked the end of an era, but the country which he had done so much to create was already very different from what it had been twenty years before. This contributed to the impression that in Bismarck's final decade political stagnation had cast a pall over a fast-moving society. Even in much of the standard historiography the extent to which Germany had already been transformed into an industrial society in 1890 is often not sufficiently emphasized. The Reich, which in 1871 had had a population of 41 million, had nearly 50 million in 1890. Urbanization was proceeding apace: fifty towns in the west of Germany, which in 1871 had a combined population of 2.63 million and therefore an average of 52,600, had by 1890 4.11 million and an average of 82,200. The proportion of the population living in cities of over 100,000 had risen from 4.8 to 12.1 per cent (see Appendix: Table 4). This was not only the result of a large absolute increase in the population, but of a huge east–west migration, from the agrarian to the industrial regions. Between 1880 and 1910 220,000 left East Prussia, 150,000 left the Posen province and 100,000 left West Prussia. In 1907 24 per cent of those born in these provinces had moved to other parts of the Reich, mostly the Ruhr and Greater Berlin. In the period 1870 to 1874, 33.8 per cent of the net domestic product came from industry, mining and transport, 37.9 per cent from agriculture and 8.15 from the tertiary sector (see Appendix: Table 2). The equivalent figures for 1890/4 are 40.6, 32.3 and 8.7 per cent, with most of the tertiary sector being related to industry. In spite of the slumps of the 1870s and 1880s the index of industrial production rose from 18.8 in 1870 to 39.9 in 1890 (1913 = 100), while total production rose from 29.2 to 48.7 (see Appendix: Table 8). Yet politically and ideologically there was a refusal to acknowledge the extent of the transformation.

Even in 1890 some of the economic and social features characteristic of the Wilhelmine age as a whole were already established. Railway building was the great promoter of growth in the middle of the century and when this was coming near to saturation point by the 1870s it was one of the reasons for the economic fluctuations between 1873 and 1896. Now three different sectors, machine building and the even more innovative production of chemical and electrical goods, were to take the lead in stimulating growth. In these sectors Germany occupied a favourable position and her relatively late industrialization was to prove an advantage, facilitating innovation in comparison with longer-established competitors. Machine and machine tool production not only accounted for a growing number of units, but was carried on in larger units employing larger numbers of workers. By 1913 secondary metal industries employed the largest number of workers of all branches, 1.9 million. The index of the metal industries rose from 7.5 to 23.8 (1913 = 100) between 1870 and 1890. As the names of Benz and Daimler indicate, Germany was in the van of developing the internal combustion engine and by 1897 Benz led in Europe with an annual production of 500 cars.

Germany became a world leader in chemicals and her success was largely due to the fruitful connection between fundamental research carried out in her well-developed system of higher education and its industrial exploitation. Although there was in the German universities a tendency to cultivate the non-utilitarian branches of knowledge there was, perhaps because of the prestige of Justus Liebig and the benefits he conferred on agriculture, an early close cooperation between university chemists and industry. Later industry developed its own research facilities and employed a large number of research chemists. This was particularly the case in the well-known leading firms that emerged in the German chemical industry, the *Badische Anilin und Sodafabrik* (BASF), Hoechst and Bayer. By 1913 the German chemical industry had a turnover that was 50 per cent greater than that of the USA, the second most important chemical producer. The electrical industries showed an even greater growth and here, too, cooperation with university physicists, in the much admired German *Technische Hochschulen*, played an important role. In 1887 the *Physikalische-Technische Reichsanstalt* (PTR, Imperial Institute of Physics and Technology) was founded, with official support and as a result of a long campaign by Werner Siemens. The famous physicist Hermann von Helmholtz became its head. The two leading electrical firms, Siemens and *Allgemeine Elektrizitäts-Gesellschaft* (AEG), the firm of the Rathenau family, were far ahead of their American and British competitors in world markets before 1914. The three sectors machine building, chemicals and electrical goods, were heavily involved in the export trade. Altogether Germany became a leading exporting and importing nation, lying even in the 1880s second only to Britain, along with the USA (see Appendix: Table 10).

The economy within which these technologically advanced industries flourished was basically a market economy. Many contemporary and subsequent commentators regarded state interventions and limitations of the market to be on a sufficient scale to warrant the use of terms such as 'organized capitalism' or corporatism. To protectionism there was now added a growing tendency towards the establishment of cartels. These had first made their appearance in the depression of the 1870s in the then dominant iron, coal and steel industries. Like protection they seemed an appropriate way of enabling these industries, then still establishing themselves, to ride out economic fluctuations. By 1887 only 70 cartels had been established, but by 1895 there were 143 and by 1910 there were 673. They were still mainly in the older industries, for in the newer chemical and electrical branches the field was in any case dominated by a small number of firms. In 1907 74 per cent of production in mining and 49 per cent in iron and steel was controlled by cartels. Agreements creating cartels were legally enforceable by a judicial decision of 1897. In the opinion of most German academic economists cartels were perfectly justified. It is more difficult to be certain to what extent they affected the market or provided protection against foreign competition. In spite of the high cartelization of coal mining British coal still supplied 60 per cent of the requirements of Hamburg in 1914 and 40 per cent of those of Berlin. There is, however, some evidence that in the areas where cartels were most effective, for example the Ruhr, wages were higher than in other German coal mining areas. Cartels were one indication that laissez-faire, or what Germans often called 'Manchesterism', was losing ground in the Wilhelmine period, compared to the position in the heyday of liberalism.

The preoccupation with the health of the agrarian sector and the fear of industrialism and urbanization, which, in a highly ideologized form, played so important a role in German affairs, was therefore already somewhat unrealistic at the beginning of the Wilhelmine age. Parallels can be found in other industrial countries, but the speed of German industrialization made fears of modernity particularly salient. There were losers, or those who felt themselves to be losers. They were to be found particularly among the lower middle classes, the petit bourgeoisie. In Germany this social stratum, difficult to define statistically, was usually divided into the old and the new *Mittelstand*. Among the old were various groups of artisans, butchers, bakers, candlestick makers, as well as small shop-keepers and traders. Such people had enjoyed a considerable degree of protection in the 'old-style' German city, with its control over settlement and guild regulation. With the foundation of the Reich they saw themselves fully exposed to the market economy, which appeared to favour other groups above as well as below them. They felt ground down between the upper millstone of successful entrepreneurs and the proletariat organized in increasingly threatening fashion by the socialists. Then there was the new Mittelstand, dominated by the fast increasing numbers of white-collar employees, among whom there was a growing number of women. In 1882 there were just over half a million of such employees, by 1895 the number had reached nearly a million. It was around 1890 that they were first recognized as a distinct social group statistically and legally. There is uncertainty about which social stratum these white-collar employees came from, whether they were upwardly mobile from proletarian backgrounds or whether they came predomi-nantly from formerly independent sections of the lower middle classes. In all probability the great majority came from the latter type of background. What is certain is that most of them acquired a status-conscious perception of themselves, seeing themselves as part of the Mittelstand and above the proletariat, whom they resembled in their economic circumstances. These developments were not specific to Germany, as the novels of H. G. Wells show. But in Germany the desire of the growing army of white-collar employees to separate themselves from even the upper echelons of the working class was particularly strong, going beyond objective factors of segregation, like educational qualifications or conditions of work.

The non-manual employees were a fertile recruiting ground for right-wing, nationalist, anti-liberal and anti-Semitic ideologies and organizations. Such an

organization was the *Deutsche Handlungsgehilfenverband* (Association of Commercial Assistants), founded in 1893, which by 1900 had 40,000 members, by 1914
144,000, or 40 per cent of organized white-collar employees. It was strongly
nationalist and excluded Jews from membership. Members of such an organization
did not always necessarily vote for right-wing parties, for these parties, with their
strong agrarian base, were agitating for much of the Wilhelmine period for higher
agricultural tariffs, which ran counter to the interests of those subsisting on
relatively modest wages. On the other hand there was little chance of either the
old or the new Mittelstand feeling other than threatened by the SPD (Social
Democratic Party of Germany), the title officially adopted in 1890. During the
twelve years of the anti-Socialist law Marxism had become the doctrine of the
party, even if the majority of members had only a hazy notion of it. Marxism, with
its prediction of the disappearance of intermediate classes like the petit bourgeoisie
into an increasingly impoverished proletariat, left the SPD seriously handicapped
in appealing to these classes. By 1911 the army of white-collars was successful in
having their separate and by implication superior status from the blue-collars
recognized by the establishment of a separate social insurance institute, the
Reichsversicherungsanstalt für Angestellte.

Modernity and cultural pessimism

Even the *Bildungsbürgertum*, that specifically German social grouping which has no
exact parallel in other major West European countries, felt itself among the losers
from the rapid transformation of their country. In the 1850s its great influence in
politics and in the bureaucracy of most German states was already coming under
challenge from the entrepreneurial class. The survival of a three-tier electoral law
not only in Prussia, but in most German larger cities, constantly reminded the
Bildungsbürgertum how they were losing ground to the really wealthy. Since 1870
the number of Bildungsbürger, as measured by those studying in universities and
Technische Hochschulen, had greatly increased, rising from under 20,000 to
32,000 and more than doubling again by 1914. However, it remained a very small
stratum in relation to the rest of the population. In 1855 the higher schools which
fed the institutions of tertiary education taught 3.5 per cent of the total school
population; by 1911 this proportion had only risen to 5 per cent. This expansion
was accompanied by a certain dilution of the high ideals of neo-humanism that had
traditionally inspired German higher education. Even in the schools the traditional
Gymnasium with its curriculum based on the classics catered for a smaller
proportion of pupils, while the percentage of those in *Realgymnasien*, with a more
modern curriculum, and in *Oberrealschulen*, with more orientation towards the
natural sciences, increased. In the universities there was more specialization and
vocationalism, which ran counter to the former emphasis on pure learning. The
acquisition of knowledge became subordinate to the acquisition of qualifications
useful for the furtherance of careers.

Much of this also happened in other advanced societies, but the close
association of the educated élite with the state and the importance of formal

qualifications made such developments particularly significant in Germany. There was more of a feeling of cultural crisis and cultural pessimism than elsewhere. The sheer speed of social transformation was as much an intellectual and spiritual challenge as a material one. Germany produced formidable social critics like Friedrich Nietzsche, but the cult made of them by many disorientated intellectuals was not paralleled to the same extent elsewhere. Nietzschean ideas, such the will to power, the superman and the death of God were vulgarized to underpin a crude nationalist drive for power and pathological hatred of parliamentarism, democracy and egalitarianism. There were lesser figures, self-styled social prophets painting with broad brush and high colour, who brewed up an often poisonous concoction of social Darwinism, chauvinism, racialism and anti-Semitism. Such were Paul Lagarde, Julius Langbehn and the English son-in-law of Richard Wagner, Houston Stewart Chamberlain. Their writings enjoyed wide popularity. They made it easy for educated Germans, Bildungsbürger, to be socially aware and anti-establishment from a radically right-wing point of view. There were also cooler, sharper analysts like Max Weber, who came to grips with the malaise of modernity felt with particular intensity in Germany. Weber was himself a product of the National Liberal establishment of the Bismarck years, but also very critical of it.

The Janus-faced nature of Wilhelmine society between modernity and reaction is also reflected in the arts. The euphoria engendered by successful nation-building produced a triumphalist, celebratory style particularly in the visual arts. It can be seen in the frequently reproduced painting by Anton von Werner of the proclamation of William I as German emperor in the Hall of Mirrors at Versailles or in the Reichstag building designed by Paul Wallot. Critics like Jakob Burckhardt or Nietzsche saw early that there was a discrepancy between the triumph of German nationalism and the quality of German culture. 'If only we do not have to pay too dearly for these enormous national triumphs in another area', said Nietzsche in November 1870, '. . . I consider the Prussia of today highly dangerous for culture'.

By the time William II came to the throne a reaction had begun against the triumphalism of the *Gründerzeit* and against officially sanctioned and patronized art. Then the emperor himself went to war against modernism and the avant-garde and decreed that art must continue to celebrate the glories of the Reich. In 1892 the authorities prohibited the play *The Weavers* by the prominent playwright Gerhart Hauptmann. Its theme was an uprising by Silesian weavers in 1844 and it gave a naturalistic account of the early proletarian milieu. The prohibition caused a prolonged battle in the courts, but when a judicial decision rescinded it the Kaiser publicly expressed his disapproval. The word 'pavement literature' (*Rinnstein-literatur*) came into use and William ostentatiously gave up the imperial box in the *Deutsche Theater* in Berlin. A group of leading German painters, most of them painting in a non-representational style akin to the French impressionists, among them Max Liebermann, Max Slevogt, Lovis Corinth and Käthe Kollwitz, formed the Berlin Secession when the official annual exhibition of Berlin Artists refused to hang a picture by one of them. In 1901, on the occasion of the inauguration of the Victory Avenue (*Siegesallee*) the Kaiser remarked: '. . . art which goes beyond the laws and boundaries set by Me, is no longer art, but factory work, commerce . . ..'

Similar clashes between traditional and modern art occurred elsewhere, notably Paris, but in Germany the establishment was exceptionally sensitive to such challenges and the conflict was highly politicized. Yet the Kaiser himself was in many respects eager to embrace modernity, especially where it could be demonstrated that modern science was enhancing German power. He took a leading part in the foundation of the *Kaiser Wilhelm-Gesellschaft*, a very highly profiled and well-endowed research institute, now called *Max Planck-Gesellschaft*, which represented the ability of imperial Germany to make pure research in all fields and its practical application work in tandem at its best. A lot of the money came from wealthy Jewish bankers and business men. Among the many prejudices that motivated the impulsive Kaiser anti-Semitism ranked high, but the men who were the leaders of Germany's pre-1914 economic miracle fascinated him and even if they were Jewish he would still admit them to his circle. William 'the Sudden', as he was called by his critics, was representative of his society in combining admiration of modernity with the most reactionary prejudices.

The changing structure of politics

In 1890 the German political framework was still as it had been established after 1866. Much of it was tailored to the personal requirements of Bismarck, but even he was finding it increasingly difficult to operate. In the remaining 28 years of the Reich the fundamentals of German constitutionalism, of the system of 'skirted decisions', did not change. The disjunction became ever greater between a fast moving social and economic scene and a political structure, which even at its inception was designed to preserve earlier conditions. This was an underlying cause of the eventual collapse of the Reich in 1918, but how important a cause is a matter of debate. There was also a great deal of change in the years up to 1914 and it can be argued that, if the war had not occurred when it did, the German political system might have undergone a successful, non-revolutionary adaptation.

After 1890 the importance of the Reichstag was almost continuously on the increase, in spite of the continuing and pervasive hostility to parliamentarism from the Kaiser downwards. The main reason was that in Germany, as elsewhere, the functions of the state were always growing and there was a commensurate growth in the need for legislation. The Kaiser might talk of the Reichstag as a pigsty, but the coup d'état with which Bismarck had so often flirted was ever more unrealistic. In order to get the laws passed without which it could not govern, the Reich executive had to arrange itself with the parties in the Reichstag. The same was true with regard to the financial needs of the Reich. These were growing not least because of increasing expenditure on armaments, particularly on the ambitious naval building programme. Ironically, the pet project of the Kaiser and of nationalist opinion, a large navy, therefore increased the government's dependence on the Reichstag. Bismarck had failed to find a satisfactory basis for the finances of the Reich and this failure continued up to 1914. It caused some of the big political clashes of the period. It was Reich legislation and revenues that were required, an indication of the ever greater coherence of the Reich. The individual person was increasingly conscious of being a citizen of the Reich. This affected the balance between Reich and Länder, which had been so carefully contrived by Bismarck to save the self-respect of the federal states while imposing the supremacy of Prussia. This change of balance impinged, however, most importantly on the balance between the Reich and Prussia, one of the key relationships of the Bismarckian constitution. Up to 1890 the growth of Reich offices had been slow and their heads had also been members of the Prussian cabinet. Now Reich state secretaries, in effect ministers, became increasingly independent and were making decisions on the basis of conditions in the Reich as a whole. Prussian conservatives complained that Prussia was being 'state secretarized' (*staatssekretarisiert*). The bulk of the expanded Reich bureaucracy, some 500 at the end of the 1870s, 2000 by 1914, was, however, still drawn from Prussia and the Prussian nobility was still much overrepresented in it, but the Reich interest had become stronger, the Prussian interest weaker.

The power of bureaucracy had long antecedents, particularly in Prussia, but to a lesser extent also in other German states. In the Wilhelmine period it continued to be the element that made a political system lacking coherence workable. All the chancellors following Bismarck were themselves drawn from the highest ranks of the bureaucracy. Until 1917, when the system was nearing disintegration, they were all Prussians, except Hohenlohe-Schillingsfürst, from 1894 to 1900, who was a Bavarian liberal Catholic *grand seigneur*, who had performed signal service for German unification when he was Bavarian prime minister in the 1860s. When the Conservatives became alienated from Caprivi, Bismarck's immediate successor, because of his policy of lowering tariffs on grain imports, much was made of the fact that he was not a real Junker, but a man 'without fields and crops'. In the eastern provinces of Prussia there was still a distinctly feudal flavour to the administration, particularly evident in the institution of the Landrat, who was the senior administrator of a district (*Kreis*). This office had since 1872 been more closely assimilated into the normal bureaucratic hierarchy and a Landrat could be moved from one district to another. Yet even in 1910 58 per cent of them were still drawn from the nobility and they were *par excellence* the officials who were expected to show loyalty in their politics. A high proportion of the Conservative deputies in the Prussian Chamber of Deputies were Landräte and they could lose their offices if they voted against the government. At the other end of the scale a huge number of railway and postal employees acquired the status of civil servants. For them even a simple vote for the SPD was a disciplinary offence and the expansion of civil service status to these groups was considered the most effective way of preventing a further rise of the SPD vote. In 1913 the postal service employed more than 260,000 persons with civil service status, the railways more than 200,000. Many of them had done service as non-commissioned officers in the army, a further assurance of their disciplined, conservative and anti-socialist outlook. In relations between the bureaucracy and the citizen a command style prevailed, even if actual abuses of power were contained by the rule of law, the *Rechtsstaat*. The military style of treating the public reached right down to the large army of lower grade civil servants, even to those in the postal service and on the railways, most of whom enjoyed the privilege of wearing uniforms. Authority was more liberally exercised in the western than in the eastern provinces of Prussia and in the southern states the administration was altogether more defeudalized. Nevertheless the exaltation of authority struck critical observers, native and foreign, as a prevailing characteristic of German conditions. When the high prestige of all things military is added, one could talk of 'General Dr von Staat' as the personification of the power conglomerate in the Reich.

One Prussian factor that was obstinately maintained was the Prussian three-tier electoral law. Those interested in the maintenance of the status quo clung to it with greater determination as the weight of the Reichstag based on universal manhood suffrage increased, while the pressure for change, from the SPD in particular, focused on the abolition of the three-tier system. There had to be some adaptation of it when at the beginning of the 1890s a mildly progressive income tax law kept the lowest category of earners free from tax. They had to be credited with a fictitious three-mark tax payment in the calculation of the classes and the three classes were no longer calculated for the whole of a town, but for various quarters within it. This meant that in poorer districts of a larger town even relatively modest taxpayers could move up into the second or first class. Even then the result was frequently absurd. In an expensive part of Berlin the chancellor might have to vote in the third class, while a rich sausage manufacturer was the sole voter in the first class. As the vote of the SPD rose inexorably, highly industrialized Saxony introduced a modified three-tier system. On the other hand some South German states, like Bavaria and Baden, extended the franchise. All this contributes to the impression that there was a great deal of unfinished business in the German political system on the eve of the First World War.

The departure of Bismarck inevitably raised the question of the relative powers of monarch and chancellor. William wanted to replace what had often been called a chancellor dictatorship with a personal regime of the emperor. Soon after Bismarck's departure he toyed with the possibility of breaking up the chancellorship into several offices, but soon dropped the idea. A personal regime in the full sense, with the emperor as the ultimate coordinator of policy, was never established. For this the Kaiser lacked the capacity for sustained effort, but in the 1890s, when weak chancellors like Caprivi and Hohenlohe held office, his influence was often decisive. Even under more methodical chancellors like Bülow and Bethmann Hollweg, he could still interfere decisively on specific occasions. It was difficult for anyone to transgress the limits set by the Kaiser's prejudices, for his ability to appoint and dismiss was still very great and ultimately included the chancellor himself. Bülow, who kept a tighter rein on his subordinates than his two predecessors, made it to the top by currying favour with the emperor and was as much a courtier as a politician. None of the chancellors after Bismarck had anything like his authority. They were bureaucrats, mostly from the Prussian bureaucracy, and like the rest of the bureaucracy considered themselves above politics. Under William II the independent influence of the military, and later of the navy in the person of Tirpitz, increased. Already under Bismarck the Prussian war minister, who represented the army in the Reichstag, was stripped of his personnel functions and these were vested in the emperor's military cabinet. Under William the chief of the general staff and the heads of the military and naval cabinets had easier and more frequent access to him than the chancellor. In addition he surrounded himself with military adjutants during the many months of the year when he travelled. Military attaches attached to the German diplomatic missions in many capitals could have direct access, through the general staff and the military cabinet, to the emperor and thus by-pass the civilian diplomats. The Kaiser was thus not the supreme coordinator of the decision-making process, but helped to fragment it. The decision to build an ocean-going fleet and the Schlieffen plan are the two most notorious example of decisions affecting fundamentally the course of German policy, the implications of which were never fully considered at the highest level.

German policy therefore became more militaristic in the direct sense under William II than it had been under Bismarck, who fought hard to maintain the supremacy of civilian control. The Kaiser's love of military pomp and circumstance and his predilection for the habits of the officers' mess also gave a further boost to what might be called societal militarism. After the victories in the three wars of unification the prestige of the army had rocketed sky-high, but it took time to overcome the distrust of the army that was evident in the Prussian constitutional conflict and in the aversion to Prussian militarism in southern Germany. Little of these negative attitudes was left by 1890. Throughout German society military dash and the brusque tone of command was much in favour. Nothing was more highly valued than the rank of reserve officer. It was open to those who completed the nine-year course in a Gymnasium, and later in the equivalent schools, to acquire a reserve rank after serving only one year (the *Einjährig-Freiwilligen Privileg*). It was proudly displayed on visiting cards and was one of the things that the wealthy, upper echelons of the bourgeoisie had in common with the nobility. Otherwise caste-consciousness kept these two groups still further apart than, for example, in Britain. The imperial court, and to an extent the higher positions in the army and even in the civil service, remained preserves of the nobility. Many of them were, however, inferior in wealth to the higher strata of the middle classes. It was yet another reason why attitudes to capitalism and the market society were so ambivalent in Germany. The prevalence of military values and attitudes did provoke much criticism and was the butt of jokes in journals like *Simplicissimus*, the German *Punch*. There was the incident of Captain Köpenick, when an ordinary artisan donned a captain's uniform and marched a troop of soldiers on the local town hall. Even the Kaiser laughed, but his laugh was, it was reported, one of satisfaction.

The political parties

By introducing universal manhood suffrage for Reichstag elections Bismarck had put the German political system ahead of most others in one vital respect. To his own increasing inconvenience he had allowed the political mass market to develop and nothing could stop its further advance in the Wilhelmine age. A good indicator of this advance is electoral participation. In 1871 it was 51 per cent, by

1887 it was 77.5 per cent (see Appendix: Table 9). There was some decline in the 1890s, with a low point of 68.1 per cent in 1898. At this point the normal period between elections had been lengthened from three to five years. Electoral participation then rose again, reaching 84.75 in 1907 and 84.9 per cent in 1912. Clearly the average voter believed that he was taking part in a process of significance to himself. This was despite increasing distortions in the electoral system. These arose mainly from the fact that the boundaries of electoral districts were never adjusted after 1871, in spite of enormous demographic changes. In 1871 50 per cent of electoral districts were within 10 per cent of the average size of about 20,000. In 1912 only 10 per cent were within the same divergence from the average size of over 36,000. Teltow near Berlin had nearly 340,000 men entitled to vote, Schaumburg-Lippe had 10,700. Even within a city like Berlin there were big differences: 5600 votes were required to win Berlin 1, 88,700 to win Berlin 6. On the whole, electoral districts with a large number of voters were urban, those with small numbers were rural. The system therefore put the SPD at a disadvantage and favoured the Conservatives, with their main base in the rural regions east of the Elbe, and to a lesser extent the Centre. The dual ballot system had always favoured parties that could make official alliances with other parties for the second ballot, such as the cartel parties. The SPD, and to a lesser extent the left liberals, were out in the cold. The SPD put up a candidate in virtually every constituency, to maximize their total vote. Most of their seats were won on the first ballot, but they got virtually no seats on the second ballot and the proportion of seats to votes was in the end low. With the National Liberals it was the other way round. Their voting base was scattered over urban and rural areas. Most of their seats were won on the second ballot.

The SPD and the free trade unions

The rise of the SPD and of the trade unions runs like a red thread through the history of Wilhelmine Germany. The fear and panic this inspired among their opponents explains a great deal. Repression and failure to integrate this huge labour movement positively into the political and social structures tied the party to a revolutionary rhetoric which disguised the non-revolutionary reality, but the rhetoric helped to freeze the defenders of the system into a rigid policy of exclusion. During the years of illegality Marxism had become the prevailing doctrine of the party. It made sense to leaders and activists who faced a totally hostile repressive state. To Bebel, the most influential leader, Marxism was, however, more a beacon of future hope than detailed prescription. The most widely read socialist tract was his *Die Frau und der Sozialismus* (*Woman and Socialism*), which was first published in 1879 and went into innumerable editions. As the title reveals it was a sketch of a socialist society free from exploitation and alienation. Its appeal lay in the contrast it painted between future paradise and present hell and the certainty it conveyed that paradise would be attained. It made light of concrete problems of social organization and economic production. At some stage the great transformation would occur, *der grosse Kladderadatsch*, a word which has the sound of the last trump on the day of judgment. It conveyed the expectation that sooner or later a great crisis would put an end to the capitalist system. This statement of faith helped Bebel to preside until his death in 1913 over a party in which different pragmatic and theoretical positions were constant sources of disunity.

The tension between reformism and revolution was evident when the party emerged from the period of illegality and never disappeared. Karl Kautsky and Eduard Bernstein were the two most influential theoreticians in the party. They jointly produced the Erfurt programme in 1891, which became the official doctrine of the party and was not revised till 1921. It combined a Marxist prognosis of the future, written by Kautsky, with a more practical section on the aims of radical social reform, from the pen of Bernstein, which served as a guideline at elections and for parliamentary activity. Major points in this section of short- and medium-term aims were the achievement of a genuinely equal electoral system and freedom of expression, equality for women, religion to be a private matter, schools to be secular, a progressive income tax, abolition of tariffs, factory legislation and an eight-hour day. The social insurance schemes against which the party had voted in the 1880s (see p. 85) were accepted. They were now mostly under the direct control of the Reich and functionaries of the SPD and the unions took a leading part in administering them. Therefore, by implication, the state was no longer regarded as a totally hostile institution. Kautsky's theoretical analysis can be summed up in the phrase that the SPD expects a revolution, but cannot make one, while its opponents cannot prevent one. It was a more theoretical and hard-edged version of Bebel's visionary statement of faith. On the whole the Erfurt programme served the party well in maintaining the loyalty and faith of its mass following, while not precluding the growing but always limited contribution to reform that the political realities allowed the party to make. It can also been seen as masking the increasing strength of reformism in the party. Ironically it was the unresolved nature of the German political system as a whole that allowed the SPD to live with its own contradictions.

As the voting strength, the membership numbers and the organizational structures of the party expanded, reformism became all but inevitable. In 1914 the party had nearly 1.1 million members, polled 4.25 million votes, nearly 35 per cent, and published newspapers with editions of nearly 1.5 million. Concurrently the membership of the trade unions associated with the party, known as the free trade unions, rose from about quarter of a million in 1895 to 2.6 million in 1913. While the party maintained its pre-eminence over the unions, the latter also exercised a pull in the direction of reformism. The party itself was the umbrella organization for a vast array of associations and institutions, ranging from sports clubs through women's organizations to the socialist press. This was the famous socialist sub-culture, a substitute for exclusion from similar associations in the rest of society. It is still a matter of debate among historians whether this subculture was a real counter-culture, or merely another way in which the hegemonic culture imposed itself upon the proletariat, another form of so-called negative integration. This is the term which a classical study used for the progressive absorption of the German working class into the rest of society and for the blunting of the revolutionary dynamic. Workers borrowing books from socialist lending libraries were, no doubt, taking out popular fiction more frequently than Marx's *Kapital*, while the members of socialist glee clubs were more interested in singing than socialism. It is not in dispute that a large army of paid functionaries came into existence. The growth of reformism was not so much due to the embourgeoisement of these functionaries, as to the unwillingness of leaders and functionaries to give the authorities an excuse for outright suppression. In this way the organizational expansion, impressive as it was, was yet another form of negative integration. Another factor working against a revolutionary concept of the party was the less repressive policy of the South German states. As soon as the anti-socialist law lapsed the Bavarian Georg von Vollmar advocated pragmatic reform and collaboration with governments and other parties, where something concrete was to be gained for the workers. As early as 1894 Socialdemocrats in the Bavarian Landtag voted for the budget, because they would not reject specific improvements for their voters. Towards the end of the 1890s Eduard Bernstein began to put forward a theoretical basis for reformism. By then there had been since 1896 years of renewed rapid economic growth, bringing with it a rise in real wages. The imminent collapse of capitalism could no longer be realistically expected. Bernstein presented an evolutionary version of Marxism, which rejected strict dialectical materialism and discarded concepts that looked outdated, such as the growing impoverishment of the proletariat and the disappearance of the classes between an ever vaster pauperized proletariat and a small stratum of exploiting capitalists. The party officially rejected Bernstein's theoretical revisionism, which to many seemed a dangerous dilution of the faith as well as threatening a split between the right and left of the party. The Bebel–Kautsky line of waiting in a political ghetto was in theory maintained, but in practice there many departures from it, especially in South Germany.

On the other hand, there was also a left wing, which sought to keep revolutionary activism, and not merely rhetoric, alive. The intellectual leader was Rosa Luxemburg, who with Karl Liebknecht and others advocated mass strikes against the obstinately defended Prussian three-tier electoral law. The mass strike presented a way out of sterile *attentism* and a means of stimulating and exploiting the spontaneity of the masses. To most trade unionists a general strike for political purposes meant 'general nonsense'. No more than the functionaries of the party did they wish to risk their organizations, which were achieving real gains for their members, by unnecessarily provoking the authorities. The rise of a left wing well fortified by theory meant that the Bebel–Kautsky line became a form of centrism. This helped to maintain the unity of the party between conflicting pressures and meant that it remained highly effective in mobilizing and keeping the loyalty of the constantly growing numbers of industrial workers. It had little success in appealing to the lower middle classes or to small farmers and agricultural workers. For them the Marxist prediction of doom for their class held no appeal. To theorists like Kautsky it did not seem worthwhile to dilute the Marxist perspective for the sake of such groups. As a result the party seemed to have reached the limits of its electoral potential on the eve of the First World War, but the mesmeric fear it inspired in the rest of the political spectrum was as great as ever.

The liberal parties

The SPD was the greatest beneficiary of the rise of a political mass market. The liberals found it most difficult to adapt to it. They had no coherent milieu to give them a secure base, as the SPD had the industrial workers, the Centre the Catholics and the Conservatives the East Elbian agrarian economy. Their claim to be the 'general estate' representing the best interests of the whole community had long been ringing hollow. The decline of liberalism beginning with the depression of the 1870s and the change of course on 1879 eroded their ideology. The National Liberals became almost indistinguishable from the Free Conservatives and to some extent even from the Conservatives proper. They supported the new German nationalism, a strong army and navy, colonial expansion and *Weltpolitik*. They were a Protestant party and therefore competed for the same voters as the conservative groups. They were in favour of secular education and opposed to the Centre on school policy, unlike the Conservatives, and clung to some remnants of the Kulturkampf. They were strongly anti-socialist, but opposed the more extreme proposals for the suppression of socialism. They represented rural constituencies in some parts of the country, for example Hesse, and had to heed the demands of the agricultural lobby for protection. Since an increasing number of their seats were won on the second ballot, the diversity of their voters made it particularly difficult to hold a consistent line. Given all the contradictory pressures to which they were subjected and the organizational difficulties they experienced they maintained themselves reasonably well. In 1890 they had 16.3 per cent of the vote and 42 seats. In the last elections before the war they had 13.6 per cent of the vote and 45 seats.

The position of the left liberals was even more difficult. The merger of the Secessionists of 1880 with the Progressives in 1884 into the *Freisinn* did not last. The veteran Progressive leader Eugen Richter stuck to his strongly oppositional line, still demanding real constitutional change, even when it had moved off the agenda, rejecting high defence expenditure and sticking to free trade. Some of the former Secessionists wished to move closer to the government, when this seemed possible after the departure of Bismarck. In 1894 the party split again, with the Richter group taking the name *Freisinnige Volkspartei* and maintaining a reasonable Reichstag foothold, the others under the name *Freisinnige Vereinigung* becoming a group of chiefs and few Indians. By the turn of the century there were efforts to reinvigorate the liberal movement. So-called Young Liberals tried to broaden the organizational structure of the National Liberals, by founding more local associations with an enlarged membership, instead of relying on small committees of notables operating mainly at election times. This development was made easier by changes in the law of association in 1899 and 1908. Prior to 1899 the national federation of political associations was prohibited and only when this prohibition was rescinded did it become easier to build up a representative structure on a national basis.

The Young Liberals also tried to move the party away from its conservative orientation and towards more cooperation with the left liberals. In the 1890s there were also some efforts at ideological renewal, a social liberalism, which gave a higher priority to solving the social question and meeting some of the concerns of the working classes, greater legal and social equality, more co-determination in the work place, better housing and development of the social insurance policy. This was to be combined with full acceptance of *Weltpolitik* and imperialism, whereas old-style liberals like Richter had been opposed to it. Indeed the material gains that were expected from successful imperialism would help to satisfy some of the material aspirations of the workers. Among those advocating this kind of liberal imperialism were Theodor Barth, who came from a another left liberal group, the *Deutsche Volkspartei*, based mainly in Württemberg, and Friedrich Naumann, a former follower of Stoecker. Naumann's book *Demokratie und Kaisertum* (*Democracy and the Imperial Monarchy*) was widely read and preached a form of conflict resolution very seductive for the many educated Germans who were longing for unity in their deeply riven society. Naumann's National-Social Party achieved little in the way of voter mobilization and in 1903 they merged with the Freisinnige Vereinigung. The death of Richter in 1906 and general political developments made it possible for the then existing three left liberal factions to reunite as *Fortschrittliche Volkspartei* (Progressive People's Party) in 1910. This enabled them to make a respectable showing in the elections of 1912, almost equalling the National Liberals in terms of seats. This was partly due to collaboration with the SPD on the second ballot, but the failure of many of their voters to follow this collaboration in the polling booth showed the dilemma of the party. Overall, liberals of all persuasions could not recapture the position their movement had held in the early years of the Reich, let alone the dominance they had once aspired to. They remained strong, however, in German towns, helped by the restrictive electoral laws that continued to prevail there, especially in Prussia. In Berlin in 1914 liberals had 98 seats in the municipal council, to the SPD's 44; in Munich they had 30 out of 60 seats in 1911; in Frankfurt they had 44 out of 71 seats in 1912. Given the spread and vigour of municipal activity, it was an important presence.

The conservative parties

The two conservative groups, the German-Conservatives and the Free Conservatives, also faced problems in getting to terms with the political mass market. The Free Conservatives did not really attempt it and remained mainly a parliamentary grouping, close to government and industry, in elections relying mainly on the prestige of individuals. By 1912 they had only 3 per cent of the vote and 14 seats in the Reichstag. The German-Conservatives survived rather better as a result of their close association with the *Bund der Landwirte* (Association of Farmers), founded in 1893 in protest against Caprivi's policy of reduced protection. The BdL was one of the first mass organizations, which mobilized large numbers of members through efficient countrywide organization and propaganda based on a distinct, populist ideology. It stridently asserted that farmers were the backbone of the nation and that without them Germany was doomed to decadence and decline. The BdL was a powerful reinforcement for the anti-modern, anti-urban, anti-liberal, anti-socialist and anti-Semitic chauvinist mentality rampant among significant social groups. In attacking the capitalism of the stock exhange and high finance it purveyed a mixture of anti-capitalism with strong attachment to property that was characteristically German. The distinction made between productive and parasitic capital usually had anti-Semitic overtones. The membership quickly reached 200,000 and was 330,000 by 1913. The BdL extracted pledges from candidates at elections and presented them with a 'list of transgressions' if they had voted against agrarian interests. National Liberals and even Centre party candidates had to submit to such coercion in rural areas, but the main links were between the BdL and the Conservatives. There was a considerable overlap between the leadership of both bodies and although the mass membership of the BdL came mainly from outside East Elbian Prussia, its leadership remained mainly in the hands of large aristocratic East Elbian landowners. It was, however, not merely a question of manipulation by the small agrarian élite, for there was much genuine community of interest between all types of farmers; for instance they all wanted to reduce imports of agricultural goods as far as possible.

The importance of the BdL to its survival was one reason why the Conservatives became less of a governmental party than they had been in the Bismarck period. The BdL, like the other nationalist associations that developed in the Wilhelmine period, was often anti-establishment, even though it received encouragement from the establishment and helped it to remain dominant. The other factor pushing the Conservatives into a populist direction was the rise of anti-Semitic parties. The 1880s had seen the rise of anti-Semitic agitation and propaganda, now definitely racial-biological and social-Darwinist. In Germany its ideological resonance owed much to the insecure nature of German national identity. Even the language used, *der Jude* (the Jew), *das Judentum* (something like 'the Jewish mentality'), reveals that anti-Semitism became, in the minds of anti-Semites, largely detached from the concrete presence of Jews. But Jews were also identified with specific modern developments that were perceived as damaging by particular groups, for instance department stores by small traders. Anti-Semitism also had an agrarian, anti-urban dimension. Margarine, a competitor for butter, was called *Judentalg* ('Jew fat'). Among farming communities in Hesse, where resentment of Jewish traders and money-lenders was endemic, an anti-Semitic agitator, Otto Böckel, won a Reichstag seat in 1887. Stoecker had already pioneered the use of anti-Semitism as a recruiting agent and now several small parties that made anti-Semitism their main plank made an appearance. They posed a particular threat to Conservatives in rural areas and in the Reichstag elections of 1893 won 3.5 per cent of the vote and 16 seats.

The Conservatives were thus exposed to populist pressures from anti-Semites, as well as from Christian-Social followers of Stoecker advocating further development of social policies to wean the workers from socialism. They were also caught between their traditional governmental orientation and opposition to Caprivi's pro-industrial trade policies (see p. 121). In 1892 the Conservatives adopted the Tivoli programme, which was monarchist, anti-parliamentary, anti-socialist and anti-Semitic, in favour of a strong national state with a strong army, but even more strongly agrarian and against the hated tariff reductions of Caprivi. The veteran party leader Helldorf, who had kept the party from its beginnings in 1876 on a pro-Bismarck course, was replaced by Hammerstein, the editor of the *Kreuzzeitung*, who had opposed Bismarck's cartel policy in 1887. In the ensuing years the Conservatives veered between supporting and opposing the government and above all clung to their agrarian base in East Elbian Prussia. They vehemently opposed any change to the three-tier electoral law. The threat from the anti-Semitic parties declined, because they were divided by sectarian and personal differences. This did not mean that anti-Semitism declined, for among those whose outlook was governed by nationalism it became widely accepted, even if its populist excesses were sometimes deplored. Nevertheless, the Conservatives felt by the eve of the world war that they had their backs to the wall. Heydebrand, their high-profile leader, said that he knew democracy would eventually come, but he would postpone it as long as possible.

The Centre party

Among the major players the Centre party had the most well-established milieu to rely upon, but it was also deeply affected by the changing nature of politics. During the Bismarck era its leadership consisted to a large extent of notabilities, drawn in many cases from the Catholic aristocracy of Silesia and Westphalia. These were the leaders most prone to make their peace with the government and grasp the concessions on offer to end the Kulturkampf, but Windthorst's presence contained these tendencies. He died in 1891 and by that time the leading Catholic aristocrats were also losing influence. The next generation of leaders, of whom Ernst Lieber was the most prominent, were much more in the mould of professional, middle-class politicians, and were anxious to exploit the pivotal role the Centre occupied most of the time. The assertion of constitutional rights became less of an issue for them, as it did for the other parties. They cooperated with the government even on defence matters, for instance they accepted the first naval programme of 1898. They wanted to escape from the 'cinderella' mentality that had for so long characterized Catholics. The mood among ordinary Catholic voters was often still anti-establishment and many shared to the full the attitudes of those who considered themselves losers in the modernization process. Most Catholics were socially conservative and as farmers and artisans wanted protection against the rigours of the market. They resented the underprivileged situation in which they still found themselves compared with Protestants, in wealth, education and many other significant indicators. But the politicians in the Reichstag did not need to be governed in their day-to-day tactics by such attitudes among their constituents, for they mostly sat for safe seats. They could rely on the fact that loyalty to their Church and religion was still strong among ordinary Catholic voters.

In fact Catholicism as a determinant of voter behaviour was in decline in the existing male electorate. It fell from about 83 to 55 per cent between 1874 and 1912. For working-class Catholics the SPD was an increasingly attractive alternative. In the last decade before 1914 some Centre leaders advocated broadening the base of the party beyond the Catholic milieu, under the slogan of breaking out of 'the Catholic tower'. Like the other parties the Centre acquired a network of associations to operate in the political mass market. The most important of these was the *Volksverein für das katholische Deutschland* (Popular Association for German Catholics), founded in 1890. It started with more than 100,000 members and had about 800,000 by 1914, with its main strength in the Catholic regions of West Germany. One of the most important tasks of these popular organizations was to counteract the influence of socialism among working-class Catholics. Even so, radical farming associations independent of the Centre sprang up particularly in South Germany. In Bavarian politics, for example, the *Bauernbund* run by the so-called 'farmers' doctor', Dr Georg Heim, exercised much influence and contributed to the revolution of 1918.

There were thus very conflicting pressures on the Centre Party, most of them arising from the social diversity of its followers. Even more than the other parties, it had little to gain from further parliamentarization and was therefore a powerful factor reinforcing the constitutional status quo. At the grass roots its existence provided alternative channels for radicalism and in particular set limits to the further rise of the SPD. Nationally it shored up conservatism and increasingly went along with nationalism, imperialism and *Weltpolitik*. In this way it had a kind of buffer function, absorbing and reducing what would otherwise have become more dynamic trends. Many of its leaders over-compensated for remaining badges of second-class citizenship by being loud in their hurrah patriotism. What others considered its opportunism, its tendency to pick up sweeteners from the government where it could, was much resented. None of the parties were, however, pushing for full parliamentary government with any determination. The constitutional halfway house enabled them to maintain their ideological purity and relieved them of having to make the compromises that would have been needed if they had been in coalitions sustaining an executive government. The majority believed that German constitutionalism was superior to Western democracy. As fear of the SPD rose there were those on the right who called for a coup d'état to end even the degree of constitutionalism that existed. The Reichstag's influence increased, but it remained in the antechamber of power.

Organized interests and lobbies

It had been Bismarck's intention to 'dry out' the Reichstag by creating institutions, such as an economic council, that would provide a forum for pressure groups and an alternative focus of influence to the parliamentary arena. This did not work out in an institutional sense, but the influence of non-party organizations grew mightily in the Wilhelmine period and limited the importance of the Reichstag and other parliaments. There were two kinds of influence these organizations were designed to exert: economic and ideological. The Bund der Landwirte, already mentioned, was founded to push the economic interests of the agrarian loby, but it also used propaganda heavily imbued with ideology to further its objectives. Other organizations, notably the pivotal Pan-German League, were mainly ideological, pushing what can be called a radical nationalism, supremacy of the German race in the world, elimination of internal enemies like social democracy at home. The older, more purely economic lobbies, such as the *Centralverband deutscher Industrieller* (Central Association of German Industrialists) and the Longname Association (*Verein zur Wahrung der gemeinsamen wirtschaftlichen Interessen im Rheinland und Westphalen* (Association for the maintenance of common economic interests in Rhineland and Westphalia) for short *Langnam-Verein*) became important, as we have seen, as a result of the conflict between free trade and protection in the 1870s. These bodies were mainly representative of heavy industry and were broadly protectionist. As German exports grew, the export-orientated industries founded their own Association of Industrialists (*Bund der Industriellen*), of which the young Stresemann became secretary. He was already a leading figure in the National Liberal party before 1914, showing the links between interest lobbies and political parties. The BdI was never as influential as the older CdI, for the important chemical and electrical industries had separate organizations. In 1909 a more ideological body, the *Hansabund*, was founded, as a kind of counter to the agrarian BdL. It tried to organize the consumer goods industry, trade and finance against the narrow concerns and illiberal ideology of the agrarians. It was a reinforcement to the liberal parties, but a broad industrial front against the agrarians proved impossible to organize, nor was it easy to convert the white-collar constituency to a more liberal orientation. Again attitudes towards the SPD, as it moved to its pre-war electoral high point in 1912, were a divisive issue. Heavy industry in the end had more in common with Conservative agrarians than with liberals willing to enter into electoral pacts with the SPD. In 1913 the CdI and the BdL came together in what they called the Cartel of the Productive Classes (*Kartell der schaffenden Stände*), which Stresemann renamed the cartel of greedy hands (*der raffenden Hände*). As a whole the mainly economic interest organizations were a powerful alternative to the political parties, sometimes reinforcing them, as the BdL did for the Conservatives, sometimes exposing them to internal stresses, as the BdL did to the National Liberals. The lobbies could deal directly with the government, though this never reached the point where they displaced the parties, the position Bismarck was aiming at with his economic council. They were, however, on at least an equal footing with the parties, since the latter were never part of the executive, as would have been the case in a fully parliamentary system.

The organizations which together constituted organized nationalism, often called the leagues, such as the Pan-German or the Navy Leagues, also had a complex relationship with the government and therefore with the course of German policy. To some extent, as recent research has shown, they were genuinely a movement from below and could become very inconvenient for the government. For this reason they have been seen as major cause for the bellicose and incoherent character of German foreign policy and diplomacy before 1914. It was, however, also the case that they received encouragement from the government and that various figures inside the ruling establishment used them to achieve their objectives. The best known example is Admiral Tirpitz and the Navy League. Tirpitz used the Navy League to give his policy of building a large ocean-going fleet popular backing. But the Navy League was not controlled by the government and the nationalist leagues collectively frequently put the government under pressure to achieve foreign policy successes by assertive and superficially virile international conduct. The Pan-German League arose out of the protest against the Anglo-German agreement of 1890, under which Zanzibar and some German colonial claims were exchanged for the island of Heligoland. Existing pro-colonial associations were already trying to enlarge Bismarck's limited colonial policy and were agitating for a German 'world position'. The title Pan-German League (*Alldeutscher Verband*) was adopted in 1894 and although never exceeding a membership of about 25,000 it became the central organ for radical nationalism. Germany was not only to be a world power, it had to mobilize all those of German race in Europe in a great continental empire. Racial and social-Darwinist ideas, spread by writers like Langbehn, Lagarde and H. S. Chamberlain, provided the secular religion which inspired the pan-Germans. Germanism was not only to be extended, but to be intensified and cleansed of internal detritus, such as Socialdemocrats, Jews and even Catholics. From its earliest days Alfred Hugenberg, soon to become a senior manager of the armament firm Krupp, was one of its leaders. At a later stage of his career he was, as leader of the German Nationalist party, to ease Hitler's path to power. The chairman of the Pan-German League from 1908 was Heinrich Class, who in the tense atmosphere following the SPD's election victories of 1912 published, under a pen name, a book *If I was Emperor*. It advocated a dictatorship, a hierarchical social order, conquest of *Lebensraum*; it opposed metropolitan cities, international finance capitalism and proposed to revoke the citizenship of Jews. It fitted in well with the 'backs-to-the wall' mood which gripped the Conservatives at this time. Not surprisingly the Pan-German League dissolved itself in 1939, when Class was still chairman, on the grounds that all its aims had been achieved. Although the Pan-German League had many establishment figures among its members, it also expressed a deep dissatisfaction with what was regarded as the defeatism of official policy. Much of its thrust was populist and oppositional, anti-monarchist at times, but men in the highest reaches of government were not above using it for the manipulation of opinion. In the second Morocco crisis of 1911, for example, Kiderlen-Wächter, the state secretary for foreign affairs, secretly encouraged it to fan the flames of outraged national sentiment. Ideologically the Pan-German League was close to the Eastern Marches Association, which had a larger membership and pushed the policy of Germanizing the areas of Prussia inhabited by Poles. Both leagues were in the business of creating a public atmosphere to support and radicalize official policy.

The Navy League was the largest of the nationalist organizations and more closely linked with official policy than the Pan-German or Eastern Marches Leagues. It was founded in 1898, when the proposals to build an ocean-going fleet was before the Reichstag. The chancellor and other high officials were early members and so were leading industrialists and it enjoyed the favour of the Kaiser, whose pet project the fleet was. It had close links to the news department which Tirpitz, an early public relations expert, established in the Reich Naval Office to forward his plans. Even when it started it had nearly 80,000 members and by 1913 it had 1.125 million. Even the Navy League was not always a docile handmaiden of official policy and from time to time there were attempts within the organization to radicalize it. The leagues were not the only expression of organized nationalism. Those who had served in the army were induced to become members of a *Kriegerverein* (warrior association), a veteran organization to be found throughout Germany. A new national federation of these associations, the *Kyffhäuser-Bund*, had 2.9 million members. All this by no means exhausts the list of organizations that gave expression to German nationalism. Its pervasive power showed itself in the building of countless national monuments, Bismarck towers, monuments to William I, like the one on the confluence of Rhine and Moselle at Coblence. German nationalism had become a huge secular religion, sometimes defensive, anxious to preserve what had been achieved, at other times radical and war-like. It could easily give rise to apocalyptic visions and its paranoid extremists saw the future in stark alternatives – *Weltmacht oder Niedergang* (world power or decline). It was a mood in which a great cleansing war might beckon as a welcome resolution of internal conflicts regarded as intractable and debilitating.

Historians with benefit of hindsight know that the Wilhelmine period ended in a disastrous war. Collapse and revolution realized the worst nightmares of the Wilhelmine doom-mongers. Gebsattel, a retired general and prominent pan-German, in a memorandum of 1913, which met with the approval of the Crown Prince, advocated a policy of the mailed fist abroad, at home a state of siege and suppression of the 'Jew press', and wrote to his friend Class that he longed for a 'redeeming war'. When there was so much of this kind of thinking around, not necessarily controlling policy but nevertheless close to the centres of power, it is impossible to ignore the dark side of pre-1914 German civilization, the chauvinism, militarism, authoritarianism, features which make it easier to understand why but twenty years later the Third Reich came into existence. Nevertheless, there was much about Imperial Germany at the beginning of the twentieth century that was widely admired even abroad, its educational system, its advanced technology, its high culture and much more. Most Germans living at the time thought they were progressing rapidly and the critics were a minority. It was just this feeling that the new century should be a 'German century' that induced hubris and also dark foreboding that it might all go wrong. The Achilles' heel was the political system, which lacked the power to integrate or provide legitimacy and failed to enable coherent decision-making to be undertaken. Chauvinism in one form or another was pervasive in pre-1914 Europe. In the end all the great powers preferred to risk war rather than accept any dilution of what they considered their vital interests. What distinguished Germany was that so many people of influence saw the alternatives so starkly posed between supremacy and total ruin.

6 Towards *Weltpolitik* and social imperialism 1890–1909

Domestic policy under Caprivi

Caprivi's appointment as chancellor, as of all the other six chancellors until the collapse of the empire, except Bülow, was almost casual and unpremeditated. Bismarck may have mentioned him at one point as a possible successor, but this was before he realized that his own tenure of office was coming to an end. General Leo von Caprivi had been head of the Reich Naval Office since 1883, succeeding Admiral Stosch, whom Bismarck had regarded with furious hostility as a friend of the Crown Prince. Bismarck clearly did not anticipate the relatively liberal disposition of his successor. Caprivi, as a man of sober common sense, but insufficient feel for the realities of political power, sought a way out of the intractable domestic and difficult foreign situation which he inherited. At home he turned his back on the dictatorial style of the later Bismarck years and sought to end the atmosphere of servility and Byzantine intrigue that had poisoned the top echelons of government. On the broader public stage he wanted reconciliation, particularly towards the working class. In this he was carrying out the intentions of the Kaiser, whose break with Bismarck was in large part due to William's refusal, after some prevarication, to follow the path of confrontation. A major consequence of the events surrounding Bismarck's fall was the lapse of the anti-socialist law. This made new initiatives in social policy almost a necessity. If repression was to be at least relaxed, there had to be more positive steps to satisfy the industrial workers.

Unfortunately for Caprivi, he was soon to find that the Kaiser had neither steadiness of purpose nor patience to follow a conciliatory policy for long. Caprivi's plan for relaxing domestic tensions had two major elements, further development of social policy, and a reduction of high tariffs particularly on grain imports, which would reduce prices for the consumer. The policy was based on a clear recognition that Germany's future was as an industrial nation, but this realistic appraisal came up against the powerful vested interests and ideological dogmas mentioned earlier. A third major plank of Caprivi's policy was to seek an accommodation with the Centre party, which seemed a necessity following the collapse of the cartel majority in the Reichstag in the 1890 elections. By meeting some of the Catholic concerns regarding denominational primary schools in Prussia, which required legislation in the Prussian Landtag, he hoped to induce the Centre to support his liberalizing trade treaties and a new enlarged army budget in the Reichstag. In the round

Caprivi wanted to promote a socially concerned conservatism from above, leaving intact the fundamentals of the Bismarckian settlement, strong monarchical–bureaucratic government with an infusion of legitimacy provided by limited parliamentarism. Even without the anti-socialist law there was still a great deal of repression and the SPD continued to be regarded as an enemy of the state.

The social policy initiatives of the early 1890s were mainly the work of Berlepsch, who had been appointed Prussian minister of trade following the departure of Bismarck. An international conference on factory legislation had met in March 1890 and, without reaching any concrete decisions, had put regulation of working conditions on the agenda. It was an area in which, partly owing to Bismarck's reluctance, Germany had hitherto lagged. When new proposals for the protection of labour were introduced in 1890, the SPD voted against them, suspicious of anything a hostile state was prepared to offer. When the law was passed in 1891 it contained restrictions on child labour and on hours of work, 10 for juveniles and 11 for women. There was a prohibition of night work for women and juveniles. In especially health-endangering processes maximum daily hours of work could be fixed and there were further regulations for safety at work. With some exceptions Sunday working was prohibited. In the following year a further law was passed for the protection of labour in the mining industry, which was not covered in the earlier legislation. These factory laws amounted to substantial and permanent progress in an area always of great concern to workers and were the most important part of Caprivi's social policy. They were further developed after the turn of the century. Earlier, in July 1890, a law had been passed to establish industrial courts, obligatory in larger, permissive in smaller communities. They consisted of an independent chairman and representatives of both employers and workers and could arbitrate in legal conflicts between the parties. It took some time for these courts to gain acceptance, particularly from the employers, but after the turn of the century and further improvements in the law, making it obligatory in all communities over 20,000, they became more popular. It was the beginning of a tradition of dealing with labour disputes by arbitration which was to become of great importance in German industry, though before 1914 decisions by industrial courts were not legally binding. This and the severe clashes between the increasingly powerful trade unions and the employers prevented the arbitration system from developing very far before the war.

The laws passed in the early 1890s did nothing to mitigate labour conflicts and, as in Britain, this was the most crucial area in the relations between labour and the state. Trade unions had been legal in Germany since 1869, but there were still many ways in which the authorities could try and break strikes. Attempts to strengthen the hand of the authorities in dealing with strikes became one of the most politically contentious issues in the later 1890s. In the circumstances Caprivi's gestures of conciliation would take a long time to show results. There was one further aspect of his legislation that became important in the long run, but made little immediate impact, the steps the legislation contained on the principle of co-determination. Under one of the laws promoted by Berlepsch it was obligatory to promulgate factory regulations in enterprises with more than twenty employees. In establishing these rules governing factory procedures the views of employees had to be taken into account. For theses purposes works councils could be set up on a permissive basis. The law concerning the mining industry also contained similar provisions. For the moment works councils, in the cases where they were set up, played no major role, though after another big miners' strike in the Ruhr in 1905 they were made obligatory in mining. It was, however, the beginning of a system under which labour relations were closely regulated by law and could be seen as another example of organized capitalism.

After 1892 there was little further activity in the field of social policy and soon repression was again in the forefront of the struggle against socialism. In the meantime tariff reductions, to be implemented by trade treaties with various countries, moved to the top of the political agenda. It could be seen as part of the effort to achieve greater social harmony, for it was meant to favour the consumer. Apart from the recognition that Germany was increasingly an industrial state, the trade treaties had the motive of improving relations with a number of neighbouring states and was a precursor of what by the turn of the century became endeavours to form a central European economic area under German aegis. The trade treaty with Russia, concluded in 1894, which caused the antagonism between the Caprivi government and the agricultural lobby to reach boiling point, had the purpose of preventing the further deterioration of relations with Russia. The first four trade treaties, with the two triple alliance partners Austria–Hungary and Italy and the two neutrals Belgium and Switzerland, received widespread support and even 18 Conservatives voted for them in the Reichstag. They reduced the tariff on wheat and rye from five to three marks fifty per 100 kilo. In 1892/3 there was a world-wide recession in agricultural prices which highlighted the uncompetitiveness of German grain and even meat producers. They attributed their difficulties to the reduction of tariffs and the hue and cry against Caprivi began in earnest. The BdL was founded in February 1893 (see p. 112). 'We must scream so that all the people can hear us, we must scream until it is heard in the parliaments and ministries – we must scream until it reaches the steps of the throne,' said a Silesian agriculturalist, and scream they certainly did. When trade treaties were concluded with Rumania in December 1893 and Russia in March 1893, countries that were real agricultural competitors, it was war to the knife. The *Kreuzzeitung*, still the flagship of conservatism in the press, proclaimed 'a war of annihilation against capitalist Liberalism, and all that goes with it'.

In the meantime Caprivi's 'New Course' of conciliation had proceeded along other lines. There were further reforms of the patrimonial jurisdiction in Prussia's eastern provinces, which, owing to resistance by the Conservatives, ended up rather half-hearted. There was some alleviation of the anti-Polish policies in the provinces of West Prussia and Posen, with the Polish language allowed some comeback in the schools. A Pole was appointed to the archbishopric of Posen. Some support was given to a Polish land bank, which created a more level playing field between German and Polish settlement aspirations. In his vendetta against Caprivi Bismarck strongly attacked this policy of accommodation with the Poles and this was, in 1894, the occasion for the founding of the Eastern Marches

Association. They were also known as *Hakatisten*, after the initials of the three founders Hansemann, the grandson of the founder of the Disconto-Gesellschaft (see p. 7), Kennemann and Tiedemann. Then there was the important Prussian tax reform, which also entailed the adjustments of the three-tier electoral law mentioned earlier. It was introduced in 1891 by the up and coming Prussian finance minister Miquel. Incomes under 900 marks were left untaxed and there was then a tax rate rising from 0.6 per cent at 900 marks to 4 per cent at 100,000 marks. The rates were modest enough, but the principle of a progressive income tax was thus recognized and there were allowances given for children. Joint-stock companies were drawn into the tax net and a capital tax, again at a modest level, was brought in two years later.

A rather different side of Caprivi's policy was revealed in proposals to reform the Prussian elementary school system by a return to more denominational teaching. Originally, in drafts prepared before Bismarck's fall, it was proposed to sanction a more balanced settlement between denominational and secular principles in the curriculum, supervision and regulation of schools. It had become a very sensitive matter during the Kulturkampf. There were two, essentially political, reasons why it was decided to strengthen the denominational principles once more, in proposals associated with the name of Zedlitz-Trützschler, who took over the Prussian ministry of culture in 1891 to carry them through. One reason was the fight against the socialists, which it was thought had to be waged even in the elementary schools by encouraging religious education. The other reason was that Caprivi depended on the Centre party in the Reichstag for the passage of his trade treaties and also for an expansion of the army, which he would in due course propose. In the Prussian Landtag he could dispense with the support of the Centre, but by giving them a sweetener there he hoped to make them more amenable in the Reich. The complicated interaction between Prussia and the Reich which Bismarck had created was becoming more difficult to control.

The Zedlitz school proposals encountered a storm of criticism from the liberal parties and from the Protestant Bildungsbürgertum in general. Prominent opinion formers like Treitschke and, further to the left Theodor Mommsen and Schmoller, signed a petition against them. Caprivi did not help matters by styling the proposals a decision against atheism and subversion, while opponents talked of capitulation to clericalism and obscurantism. What finally damned the Zedlitz proposals was the Kaiser's refusal, reversing his earlier support, to see them enacted against the votes of Free Conservatives and National Liberals. He was encouraged in this by Miquel, who thus took a position opposed to Caprivi. The Kaiser's bosom friend Philipp Eulenburg, at this time Prussian envoy in Munich, painted a frightening picture for his royal friend of a conspiracy against the Reich by the Centre party, by ultramontane and anti-Prussian Vienna, aided by the possible fall of the existing liberal Bavarian government and its replacement by another anti-Prussian Catholic one. Caprivi offered his resignation, which was not accepted, but he surrendered the Prussian premiership to Botho Eulenburg, thereby making coherent government even more difficult. The crisis of the Caprivi government showed the great power of the capricious Kaiser and of the camarilla surrounding him. The Kaiser's fiat was too inconsistently applied to amount to a 'personal regime' in the strict sense, but it was hardly the best way of governing a very divided and rapidly modernizing society.

It was not quite the end of Caprivi. Among his difficulties, quite apart from his own lack of tactical skill, was Bismarck's vendetta against him, although it made those who feared a return of the Iron Chancellor, among them Holstein, the *éminence grise* of the foreign office, reluctant to part prematurely with Caprivi. Holstein, who had originally been an acolyte of Bismarck, had in the late 1880s become part of the Waldersee–Stoecker fronde (see p. 88) against the old chancellor. Reluctant to come face to face with the Kaiser, Holstein influenced him through Philipp Eulenburg, though later these two intriguers parted company. The hostilities between Bismarck and the existing establishment reached an undignified climax, when Herbert Bismarck, seen as the heir of the Bismarck dynasty, married the Hungarian Countess Hoyos in Vienna in June 1892. In ill-judged moves the German ambassador in Vienna and his staff were instructed not to attend the wedding and in a personal letter the Kaiser asked the Emperor Francis Joseph not to receive his 'rebellious subject'. On occasion the Kaiser talked to his entourage about having Bismarck locked up. In January 1894 there was a formal reconciliation, when Bismarck paid the Kaiser a public visit in Berlin, but everybody knew that antagonism continued to smoulder.

There was no realistic chance of Bismarck returning, for when he stood in 1891 as a National Liberal candidate for the Reichstag in a constituency previously held by that party, he only narrowly squeezed in on the second ballot. He never appeared in the chamber, but the mere possibility that he might do so created panic in many quarters. Bismarck had nothing forward looking to offer. He now stressed the importance of the Reichstag as a countervailing force to the Kaiser's neo-absolutism, but he still advised the suppression of socialists as revolutionaries and the treatment of the left liberals as enemies of the Reich. He supported the agrarians to the hilt and allowed his name to be associated with the pan-Germans. He never ceased to castigate his successors as incompetents in foreign policy who were endangering the Reich. But however backward looking and driven by resentment his utterances might be, the Bismarck cult rose mightily and made life difficult for those ruling after him. His memoirs *Gedanken und Erinnerungen* (*Thoughts and Reminiscences*) were highly selective accounts of past history, when they were not outright distortions, but they continued to project his influence after his death. The extent to which he could still rouse hostile passions may be gauged from the fact that when the Reichstag wished to present him with a congratulatory address on his eightieth birthday on 1 April 1895, the motion was voted down by the Centre, the left liberals and the SPD.

Caprivi inherited a situation in which a further expansion of the peacetime strength of the army seemed advisable, not least because of the threat of a Franco-Russian alliance, but had been stalled by the parliamentary situation. It was desirable to spread the burden of military service more widely and justly, instead of allowing many exemptions, thereby also strengthening the reserves. Proposals put forward in November 1892 provided for an expansion of 72,000 men to nearly half a million, but they also contained the olive branch to the expected Reichstag opposition, of a reduction of the normal period of service from three to two years. This had been at the core of the great constitutional conflict thirty years earlier, but Caprivi had now secured the Kaiser's agreement to the reduction. A further olive branch was a reduction of the duration of the military budget from seven to five years. Since the normal life of a Reichstag had been extended from three to five years, this would mean that every Reichstag would have the chance to vote on a military budget. In the Reichstag the proposals were, as expected, opposed by the SPD and the Progressives, but the Centre, in a mood to take revenge for the failure of the Zedlitz reforms, also opposed them. A compromise proposal to reduce the increase of strength by 13,000, moved by a conservative Centrist and acceptable to the government, was voted down and the Reichstag was thereupon dissolved.

The elections, in June 1893, did not bring a clear-cut result (see Appendix: Table 9). The demagogic agitation of agrarians and anti-semites had some effect. The latter obtained 3.5 per cent of the vote and 16 seats, a result they were never able to better decisively. The Progressives had split into the dogmatic Richter party and the more pragmatic Freisinnige Vereinigung and lost heavily. Their vote in 1890 had been 16 per cent, obtaining them 66 seats; now the combined vote of the two factions was 12.6 per cent and their total of seats only 37. The further rise of the SPD caused alarm: their vote had risen from 19.8 to 23.3 per cent, their seats from 35 to 44. In terms of votes they were well ahead of all other parties. In spite of these inconclusive results Caprivi was now able to pass his military proposals for five years, providing for a normal period of service of two years and an increase of strength of just under 60,000.

In March 1894 Caprivi was able to pass the controversial Russian trade treaty, but his position with the Kaiser was becoming weaker. Botho Eulenburg as Prussian prime minister became an alternative centre of power and saw himself as Caprivi's rival and successor. Tensions were exacerbated by the court camarilla around the other Eulenburg, working at this stage with Holstein. Their machinations were exposed in the satirical journal *Kladderadatsch*, but it did not put an end to them. In due course the intrigue and scandal surrounding the imperial court would begin to drain the almost inexhaustible reserves of monarchist sentiment. The direct cause of Caprivi's downfall was, however, another attempt to deal with the rise of SPD and trade unions by repression, the issue that was also central to Bismarck's downfall. But whereas in 1890 it had been the chancellor who was in favour of confrontation and the Kaiser who wanted conciliation, now it was the other way round. For those who were in favour of exacerbating conflicts and bringing them to the point of explosion, Germans were beginning to use the word *Scharfmacher*, which can be loosely translated as 'confrontationalists'.

The Kaiser was disappointed that the social policy advances of the early 1890s were not reflected in an immediate decline of the SPD, and in his impulsive, hysterical way he veered to the opposite extreme. In 1891 he had already publicly declared that soldiers would have to obey his orders to fire on their own brothers, if socialist subversion made it necessary. He now came under the influence of the leaders of heavy industry who were alarmed by the extent of strikes and unrest in industry. C. F. von Stumm, the recently enobled West German magnate, was representative for their attitudes, so that this phase is sometimes called the Era Stumm. Stumm wanted to control the whole material and moral existence of his workforce in a patriarchal way, and was determined to keep out all hostile influences, such as trade unions and socialists. It was 'the master-in-the-house' (*Herr im Haus*) syndrome, the industrial counterpart of the regimental system. The Kaiser and others brought the possibility of new repressive measures on to the agenda by 1893, but Caprivi was unwilling, correctly pointing out that it would be impossible to get them through the Reichstag. There was again talk of a coup d'état, to curtail the Reichstag and universal suffrage, or abolish them altogether. The murder of the French President Carnot by anarchists in June 1894, one of a series of anarchist assassinations in the 1890s, stoked up the hysteria. The Kaiser and that section of opinion that thought like him saw no difference between anarchism and the German 'parties of revolution' (*Umsturz*), namely the SPD. In a speech in Königsberg in September 1894 the Kaiser called for a 'fight for religion, decency and order against the parties of revolution'. What precisely could be done without demolishing the rule of law was not easy to see and in the Reichstag there was no majority for abandoning the *Rechtsstaat*. Even the anti-Semite parties feared that a rigorous anti-subversion law might be turned against them. The question became tied up with the interaction between Reich and Länder law and with the rivalry between Botho Eulenburg and Caprivi. The Kaiser was in a quandary and at the end of October 1894 he dismissed both of them.

The chancellorship of Hohenlohe

Caprivi lacked political skill, but the course he wanted to steer, a moderately progressive conservatism imposed from above, made sense. If it had been given more of a chance, it might have spared Germany the frenetic political atmosphere that spilled over on to the conduct of foreign affairs, with fatal results. His failure highlighted the weaknesses of German constitutionalism and the choice of his successor confirmed them. The Kaiser wanted his 'own Bismarck', someone completely prepared to fall in with his wishes and competent to make them prevail in the political labyrinth. Philipp Eulenburg, prospecting for likely candidates, already had his eye on Bülow, but the time was not yet ripe. So the choice fell on Hohenlohe, aged 75, a stopgap who in fact lasted six years. He no longer had the mental or physical capacity to take initiatives and see them through, and personal financial difficulties made him dependent on secret subventions from the imperial purse. He did, experienced as he was and of the highest aristocratic provenance, have a certain capacity to resist the worst impulses of the Kaiser. It looked reassuring that a Bavarian and a Catholic could now be chancellor and Prussian prime minister, even though Hohenlohe came from an originally independent princely family and was a 'state Catholic'. The first three years of Hohenlohe's chancellorship saw the 'personal regime' at its height. Most of the Kaiser's assertions of royal self-will had to do with personalities, the 'fight against revolution', and most importantly with the complex of foreign and defence policy, including the building of an ocean-going fleet. In fact the Kaiser interfered often decisively in most major decisions and the only limit to the personal regime was his own ignorance, inconsistency and lack of a coherent plan. This still left the chancellor and the bureaucracy room to manoeuvre.

Hohenlohe inherited the anti-revolution proposals that had caused the downfall of Caprivi and Botho Eulenburg. It was known that he did not fully approve of them and therefore his own position was not involved in their eventual failure. Hohenlohe, like everybody else apart from some left liberals and intellectuals, shared the view that socialists were beyond the pale and presented a mortal danger to the existing order, but the divisions came on the tactics to be adopted in dealing with them. On the one hand there were the *Scharfmacher*, the Kaiser, Stumm, the Conservatives, the Bismarck fronde and many others. Others wanted legislation so drafted that it did not single out the SPD, but amounted to a general strengthening of the law on public order offences, breaches of the peace, incitement to violence and military indiscipline. The Centre and the Conservatives then extended the provisions to attacks on religion, on the churches and their teachings. This aroused a storm of public indignation among those who had reason to fear an extension of censorship and stirred up the old Kulturkampf passions. In May 1895 the proposals were voted down in the Reichstag.

This was by no means the end of the matter. The end of the recession in the mid-1890s produced not only a great rise in the membership of the free trade unions linked with the SPD, but a steep rise in strike activity. Improved statistics recorded 204 strikes in 1895, 483 with 129,000 participants in 1896, 578 with 63,000 participants in 1897. There was again much talk of a coup d'état, dissolution of the federation and its reconstitution without a universally elected Reichstag. Even Hohenlohe thought universal suffrage would eventually have to go, but preferred to wait until the Reichstag had cut the ground from under its own feet 'and could then be swept out like garbage'. Waldersee, who had lost the Kaiser's favour and been succeeded by Schlieffen as Chief of Staff in 1891, was back in circulation as the man to administer a policy of unalloyed repression. It was an illusion that such a policy was practicable, for there was not enough unity even between the federal states to promote it in the Bundesrat. It did put the frighteners on parties and politicians and set limits to their activities. In the case of the SPD it induced caution and a strategy of not provoking the authorities. Those who realized that the way forward might be to encourage the reformist tendencies in the SPD were a minority. In 1897 and 1898 the Kaiser returned to the attack, in a number of typically unrestrained speeches, calling for 'the protection of the right to work'. On his insistence the government worked out proposals, which the more liberal organs of the press quickly dubbed 'penal servitude proposals' (*Zuchthausvorlage*). Penalties were proposed for forcing workers to take part in collective action and for breaches of the peace in strikes, and restrictions were to be put on the right to picket. The proposals had no chance in the Reichstag in 1899, only the Conservatives wholeheartedly supporting them. The Kaiser's anti-socialist hysteria, shared by many of his subjects, was thwarted.

A number of issues arose during the Hohenlohe years which unleashed a fierce battle between liberalizers and their opponents. Again it was the Kaiser, egged on by the military element that played so large a part in his entourage, who insisted obstinately on a tightening of the laws on military discipline. The bone of contention was to what extent the administration of military justice should be open to the public and military judges should be independent, something which the Kaiser saw as an infringement of his powers of command. A great deal of political time and credit was expended before a compromise could be found. The Prussian minister of the interior Köller had to leave over the issue in 1895, although he was against the liberalization of military discipline. His colleagues in the Prussian ministry, including Hohenlohe, would not support him and pleaded with the Kaiser for his dismissal, whereupon he resigned. The Kaiser regarded this collective stand of his ministers against his own wishes as 'virtually republican behaviour' and made it clear that he would not tolerate such an attack, as he saw it, on the powers of the crown in future. It was a situation very similar to that which had contributed to the fall of Bismarck. Ironically the following year the minister of war, who by virtue of his office stood in a special relationship to the Kaiser, was forced out because he was too liberal on military discipline. The extent to which the personal regime was a reality should therefore not be underestimated. Personnel changes, in which the Kaiser's whims played a major part, reached a climax in 1897. Two men of great significance for the future came into positions of influence: Bernhard von Bülow became head of the foreign office, on his way to the chancellorship; Alfred von Tirpitz took over the Reich Naval Office and became the key figure in building a big navy. Hohenlohe, in his late seventies, was increasingly powerless, but Miquel, now Vice-President of the Prussian state ministry as well as finance minister, remained politically significant. Central areas of policy had been taken over by men whom the Kaiser regarded as the executants of his wishes.

Divisive social issues – lex Heinze and lex Arons

Two other controversies of these years highlight the clash between modernity and tradition and the profound discomfort caused by the uncertainty hanging over traditional values. They cut across normal allegiances and produced strange cross-party alliances. The first arose out of a murder case brought in 1891 against a Berlin couple named Heinze, from which it acquired the label lex Heinze. The case shed a lurid light on the big-city underworld of prostitution and crime and led to demands for legislation against such moral degeneracy. In 1892 proposals were drafted for more stringent penalties on prostitution, pimping and other moral offences, but they also contained provisions against corrupting publications. Unsurprisingly these proposals languished across two elections and parliaments, but were revived in 1899. The Centre party, with the support of Conservatives, proposed a strengthening of the penalties on offensive publications, pictures and performances. It was as if these parties were still seeking to revenge their defeat on the Zedlitz school law and on other attempts to impose Christian morality. Once more the old Kulturkampf mood was aroused in the opposite liberal camp and there was a fierce press campaign and many public meetings of protest. A Goethe Association, drawing into its membership academics, journalists and artists, was founded to spearhead the campaign against the lex Heinze. It would have exposed literature, painting and the theatre to more drastic censorship. The governments represented through the Bundesrat made it clear that they could not support the more extreme proposals. In the Reichstag, Centre and Conservatives, supported by a motley array of Poles, anti-Semites and other minority groups, fought a fierce battle for public morality, as they saw it. Even right-wing National Liberals finally manned the barricades against this onslaught. Ironically it was obstructive parliamentary tactics, hitherto unheard of, by SPD deputies that finally caused the more stringent proposals to be dropped. Thus it was the ostracised socialists, who professed to believe in the inevitable victory of proletarian man, who saved the day for the bourgeois values of free expression.

The second controversy ended less happily for the forces of liberalism. It concerned a Dr Leo Arons, a relative of the Bleichröder family, and hence acquired the name lex Arons. Arons was a physicist and a lecturer at the University of Berlin. His position was that of a *Privatdozent*, a grade peculiar to German universities, which did not carry the status of a *Beamter* (civil servant) held by full professors. Arons, besides being Jewish, was an active member of the SPD. When the University proposed to make him, in 1894, a professor extraordinary, which still did not carry civil service status, the Prussian ministry of culture refused to approve the appointment. It further decreed that Arons's right to teach, the *venia legendi*, should be questioned, in view of his political activities. The University refused to withdraw the *venia legendi* on the ground that this would infringe the freedom to teach. Leading figures in the academic world, including Mommsen and Helmholtz, supported this position. This assertion of liberality could not survive the intervention of the Kaiser: 'I will not tolerate a Socialist among my officials, therefore not among the teachers of our young at a royal institution,' he telegraphed, after Arons had spoken at a SPD congress in 1897. A law was prepared to subject Privatdozenten to the same disciplinary constraints as full professors. It was passed through the Reichstag in 1898 by the votes of Conservatives, Free Conservatives and right-wing members of the Centre. In 1899 the University, in a show of independence, refused to withdraw the teaching rights of Dr Arons under this law, asserting that his support of the SPD did not imply the intention to subvert the state. On appeal the Prussian ministry of culture decided the opposite and Dr Arons had to go. It set signals and shows the tight limits under which the rule of law operated. It was, however, not the end of the matter and in the new century there were a number of further cases which raised the question of freedom of expression in the academic world. In culture as in politics Wilhelmine Germany existed in a no-man's land between repression and liberality, the result of an uneasy juxtaposition of existential fear, Angst, and overweening confidence, hubris. The volatile Kaiser was an appropriate mouthpiece for this schizophrenic mood.

Fear of socialism, of the proletariat and of revolution made the Kaiser and the leading politicians in the mid-1890s look for new ways of rallying the counterforces, the classes that had a common interest in maintaining the existing order. They were the *staatserhaltenden Stände*, the classes upholding the state. Nationalism and increasingly *Weltpolitik* were the most effective social cement, reaching even the proletariat, Marxist rhetoric notwithstanding. But it required more immediate ways of making the Reichstag parties work together and find a common front against the SPD, when ideology and economic interest kept dividing them along different lines, as the clashes of the Caprivi and Hohenlohe years had shown. Miquel, whose influence had grown with the personnel changes of 1897 and who had the ear of the Kaiser, proposed a new form of *Sammlungspolitik*, essentially the same configuration that Bismarck had relied on in 1879 and again with the cartel of 1887. The Kaiser became the mouthpiece, proclaiming in June 1897 a programme of 'protection for the national labour of all productive classes, strengthening of a healthy middle class, ruthless repression of all revolutionary subversion and the heaviest penalty for anyone who dares to hinder his neighbour, who wants to work, in his freedom to work'. It foreshadowed the *Zuchthausvorlage*, but was also a slogan for the Reichstag elections due in 1898. In the new Reichstag the budget for naval expansion would be high on the agenda. As it was, Miquel's Sammlungspolitik was not very effective, because it could not do away with the deep divisions even among those who were now seen as staatserhaltend, including the formerly oppositional Centre. In the elections of 1898 the SPD rose by nearly another 4 per cent to 27.2 per cent and their seats from 44 to 56 (see Appendix: Table 9). There was no decisive shift among the other parties, the main losers being the two left liberal groups, but the number of their seats actually rose, because SPD voters often supported them on the second ballot. The Centre party remained essential for the passage of legislation: their vote dropped slightly, but their seats increased from 96 to 102. They gave support to governmental policies, but constantly required sweeteners for their diverse mass following.

Towards *Weltpolitik*

Conflicts over foreign policy had been an element in Bismarck's fall. An immediate reason for his departure was his refusal to 'cut the wire to St Petersburg', let alone contemplate a preventive war. A deeper reason was the dissatisfaction with his refusal to pursue a more active policy outside Europe, appropriate to a power with world-wide interests. Bismarck's complicated system of alliances and counter-weights, of keeping five balls in the air simultaneously, was admittedly reaching the point of no return. His principle of taking the pressure off the Reich in the centre of Europe by encouraging others to engage themselves on the periphery was also becoming more difficult. The Reich itself was bound to get more involved on the periphery and conflicts arising therefrom would have repercussions in the centre. These difficulties faced his successor and they were not made easier for him cope with by the myth, assiduously propagated out of Friedrichsruhe, that the master would have dealt with them more successfully.

Caprivi and his advisers, the new state secretary Marschall von Bieberstein and Friedrich von Holstein, the powerful continuity man in the foreign office, wanted to simplify the Bismarckian system by dropping the Reinsurance Treaty. It seemed to them incompatible with the triple alliance and that it might expose them to

Russian blackmail, should the tsarist government make it public. Although the Russians made a considerable effort to induce Berlin to renew it, the Caprivi government declined to do so. In retrospect this has come to look like a major error, made as soon as Bismarck's master touch had gone. In strengthening this impression Bismarck went so far as to make the treaty public in 1896. In fact there were many subsequent occasions when a restoration of the Russian–German relationship was on the cards and was seriously attempted. Nevertheless the non-renewal of the reinsurance turned out to be a first step towards alignments and alliances that led to war in 1914, in circumstances highly disadvantageous to Germany. A rapprochement developed between Russia and France, ideologically unlikely bedfellows, that by 1894 had become a definite alliance with military and economic underpinnings. Europe became divided into blocks, triple versus dual alliance, with an in-built hostility. Germany's principal partner was now Austria-Hungary, something that seemed to make sense in terms of Germanic kinship. Public opinion increasingly affected foreign policy, and cabinet diplomacy, as in essentials practised by Bismarck, was becoming a thing of the past. Public opinion supported the Austrians, Germanic brothers still seen as dominant in the Habsburg empire. It turned out to be dangerous, however, for Germany to be tied to a weaker partner such as the declining Habsburg empire, desperately struggling for survival. One reason why Bismarck had wanted to maintain the Reinsurance Treaty was that it provided a counterweight to Austria-Hungary and was a restraining influence on Vienna.

Another reason why Caprivi and his team allowed the Reinsurance Treaty to lapse was that they attached greater importance to an understanding with Britain. In this they were continuing Bismarck's policy, and the first major step, the treaty of July 1890 exchanging Heligoland for German claims in East Africa, had been prepared before he left office. Even this modest agreement came under attack from the colonial zealots in Germany and eventually led to the foundation of the Pan-German League. It exposed what turned out to be a major German miscalculation with regard to Anglo-German relations. The pressure for colonial and imperial development in Germany offered in subsequent years endless opportunities for friction with Britain, more so than with any other country. In spite of this the makers of German foreign policy, for instance Holstein, who was basically in favour of an Anglo-German alliance, thought that Britain's need of a German alliance was greater than Germany's need for a British alliance. The world-wide Anglo-Russian antagonism was considered to be so fundamental that it would compel Britain to 'come' to Germany. There was always fear that Germany would be left pulling British chestnuts out of the fire.

Thus misjudgments were made in Berlin about the British position, while the conditions for an Anglo-German alliance became less favourable. In the Near East the Anglo-Russian conflict declined, because for the British the Ottoman empire was replaced by Egypt as the major safeguard for the route to India. Thus it was Germany and her ally Austria who were left to confront Russia in the Balkans and in Asia Minor. German commercial and military involvement in the Ottoman empire meant that it was Germany rather than Britain that drew the Russian fire in that part of the world. In the Far East Japan emerged as a countervailing force to Russia and an eventual British ally, while the acquisition of European spheres of influence caused friction between all the powers concerned. Even more important than these diplomatic developments was the increasing Anglo-German antagonism over colonies, empire, markets and finally and most significantly, naval rivalry. These were matters that had a large resonance with public opinion in both countries and fostered pervasive and burgeoning mutual fears, which were beyond the control of diplomats. For all these reasons an Anglo-German alliance never happened and Britain and Germany became potential opponents. Even by the mid-1890s Germany's international position had therefore deteriorated, though not conclusively. For the German public this development was masked by the growing consciousness of power, but it was just this that made the conduct of foreign policy so difficult. Max Weber, the great sociologist, gave his inaugural address at Heidelberg in 1895 and declared in a frequently cited passage: 'We have to grasp that German unification was a youthful exploit, upon which our nation embarked in its old age, but which might have been, because of its high cost, better left undone, if it is to be the end rather than the starting point of a German world power policy (*Weltmachtpolitik*).' Weber was a liberal and immensely perspicacious. Others were more arrogant and less discriminating.

In 1891 the Triple Alliance was prematurely renewed and made more formal, largely to bolster Italy and prevent her from defecting to France. It was still hoped to attach Britain more closely to this block, and support for the British position in Egypt against France was an inducement. In the meantime, in July 1891, the visit of a French fleet to Kronstadt had signalled a closer alignment between Russia and France. A military convention between the French and Russian general staffs was signed in 1892 and later ratified, although the terms of the actual alliance remained confined to mutual consultation. This dual alliance turned out to be more important and enduring than was realized at the time. It was bolstered by the increasing commitment of French capital to the industrial development of Russia, which was proceeding rapidly at this time. The chances of Britain adhering to the other block had meanwhile diminished, partly because the fourth Gladstone government, which entered office in August 1892, was even less inclined than the preceding Salisbury ministry to enter into binding commitments, partly because colonial frictions got in the way. These arose from the German, British and American condominium in Samoa and even more over Central Africa. The British desire to consolidate a Cape to Cairo corridor conflicted with the German desire to link their footholds in East and Southwest Africa.

Caprivi's trade treaties were designed to strengthen the German hand in European diplomacy and this was particularly true of the Russian treaty of 1894, which was so strongly opposed by the German agrarians. But even in trade and economic affairs the Russian links with France proved more telling than those with Germany. The extent of the deterioration in Anglo-German relations was revealed at the turn of the year 1895–6 by the German reaction to the Jameson raid, even though by this time Salisbury, more sympathetic to an alignment with the Triple Alliance, was back in power. The Kaiser believed that Britain might be successfully threatened out of what he saw as her obstructive policy in many parts of the world by a block of the continental powers led by Germany. He seriously contemplated declaring a protectorate over the Boer republics and sending German marines to their assistance. He was with difficulty dissuaded from this course by the diplomats and by the logistical realities. Instead he sent the famous Kruger telegram in January 1896, congratulating Ohm Kruger, the Transvaal president, on having successfully repelled, 'without appealing to friendly powers', the bandits that had invaded his country. Great damage was done to Anglo-German understanding, long after the immediate circumstances had passed into history. The Anglo-German antagonism acquired sustaining currents in the public opinion of both countries which rose and receded, but never completely ebbed away.

An even more fundamental obstacle to Anglo-German understanding was created by the decision to build a German big-battleship fleet. After unification the German navy remained a coastal defence force. The expansion of German overseas trade and the acquisition of colonies inevitably widened the naval remit to trade protection and even coastal and Baltic defence came to be seen as more than a purely defensive task. By the 1890s a fleet of cruisers was seen to be a necessity and the Kaiser became a supporter of this idea. The complex arrangements of naval command gave him an almost greater say over the navy than he had over the army. In 1897 the state secretary of the navy, Admiral Hollmann, failed to persuade the Reichstag to vote funds for the expansion of the cruiser fleet. The naval budget had to be voted annually and the expansion of the army in 1893 had exhausted the Reichstag's willingness to increase defence expenditure. In June 1897 the Kaiser dismissed Hollmann and appointed Admiral Alfred Tirpitz in his place. Tirpitz came from a middle-class background and in the army would have had difficulty in rising as high as quickly as he did in the navy. He had come to the attention of the then Prince William when he escorted him to the naval celebrations for Queen Victoria's golden jubilee in 1887. Tirpitz had imbibed all the social-Darwinist views about the competition for power then fashionable; he proved himself a master of public relations and parliamentary management, even though he despised the Reichstag, but he knew and cared little about the finer points of international diplomacy.

Tirpitz had become an advocate of building large battleships, which were seen as the ultimate weapon of the time. The American naval strategist A. T. Mahan had developed the commonly accepted doctrine that large battleships, as fully armed as technology permitted, were the essential prerequisite for the exercise of world power. Tirpitz's position was therefore not exceptional, but he developed a German form of deterrence theory. There would be a period of risk, during which tensions with Britain would have to be contained, to avoid the danger of a 'Copenhagen', the preventive destruction of a Danish fleet by the British in 1807. Even at this stage the German navy would be able to break a close blockade of the German North Sea coast, something that had long been part of its remit, but which by the 1890s required larger ships, not the previously sufficient fast torpedo boats. After the risk period the German navy would be sufficiently powerful to inflict such losses on the British that the Royal Navy would be left fatally weakened against its world-wide rivals, the Russian and the French fleets. Thus Germany would no longer be dependent on British goodwill, but could assert its claims against the British imperial position where necessary. Britain would have to seek a German alliance on German terms. An anti-British element was therefore built into the naval expansion from the beginning, but the real naval armaments race between Britain and Germany did not begin till 1904–5 and attempts at an Anglo-German rapprochement continued for some years after 1897. The Tirpitz strategy left out of account the possibility that Britain might seek an accommodation with old rivals like Russia and France and new ones like Japan and the United States, which would enable her to concentrate a larger fleet in home waters. It did not foresee that Britain would stay ahead in the armaments race. Nor was it envisaged that a distant not a close blockade would become a most effective weapon against Germany. The big German navy proved the most expensive of white elephants as well as a huge albatross round the neck of German foreign policy.

For the moment the arrival of Tirpitz and Bülow in key positions was thoroughly in tune with the mood of German public opinion. In the debate on the first navy law, Bülow said, in December 1897: 'The times when the German left the earth to one of his neighbours, the sea to another, and reserved heaven, where doctrine reigns in purity, for himself, are over.' He concluded with the famous remark: 'We do not want to put anyone in the shade, but we want our place in the sun.' A few days before, in the race for influence and trade in China following the Japanese victory there in 1895, the Germans had seized the port of Kiaochow. It was to be a coaling station for the fleet that did not yet exist, but which would then be needed to protect the coaling station. Tirpitz calculated that the public enthusiasm for the navy, soon marshalled by the Navy League, would force the initially reluctant Reichstag parties to come to heel. Naval building would require long-term planning and once tied by a naval law, laying down the number of ships to be built over several years, the approval of the annual naval budget would become a formality. The naval policy was thus a means of controlling the Reichstag, putting the monarchy at the centre of German aspirations to world power and achieving something like a Sammlung of all nationally minded men, which might even have some attractive power for SPD voters. All this should not be exaggerated, for plenty of divisions remained. Conservative agrarians were never as keen on spending money on the navy as those sections of industry supplying the steel for the ships. Bülow might from time to time stress the importance of success abroad as an internal rallying mechanism, 'only a successful foreign policy can help, conciliate, appease, rally unify', but the policy was pursued for its own sake. There was no primacy of domestic policy, as has been argued against the previously prevalent doctrine of the primacy of foreign policy. A domestic national rally was a useful by-product, not the prime cause. Even without Tirpitz, Bülow and the Kaiser there would have been *Weltpolitik* and this would have entailed some naval expansion, as would the advance of technology. But that the navy became so much a cause for its own sake, which hijacked the conduct of foreign policy, was not inevitable. It was the result of personalities and above all of the lack of coherence in the German political system.

The Bülow years

The capacity of naval enthusiasm to rally the parties in the Reichstag was demon-strated when on a crucial division the first navy law was approved by 212 against 139 votes, with the Conservatives, the National Liberals, the small Freisinnige Vereinigung and a majority of the Centre voting for it, with SPD, Richter's Progressives and 30 Centre deputies against, in the the house elected in 1893. The second navy law of 1900 was passed by 201 to 103 in the House elected in 1898 and on that occasion there was virtually no opposition from the Centre. The first law provided for the building over six years of two squadrons, each of eight ships of the line, and this was doubled two years later, with an additional fleet of eight large and twenty-four small cruisers. There were further laws in 1906, 1908 and 1912, to keep pace with the British dreadnought programme. The Reichstag was thus tied to a long and expensive programme of naval building. The financial problems of the Reich, which Bismarck had never been able to solve, were further aggravated. This meant that in the longer run the Reichstag was more indispensable than ever, unless its powers were curtailed by a coup d'état. For the time being there was less talk of this and Bülow did not see a *Staatsstreich* as a realistic option.

The wide support for naval expansion did not exist on other issues and Miquel's Sammlung was no more effective than previous versions. The divisions between agrarians and industry and within each of the major parties became very apparent over another pet project of the Kaiser, the *Mittellandkanal*. The idea of Germany's big rivers from Rhine to Elbe flowing from south to north being linked horizontally from west to east had long been in the air. It took on fresh urgency with rapid industrialization. Great advantage was clearly to be gained from giving the great industrial centres of the Ruhr direct access by water to ports like Hamburg and Bremen and to other big inland industrial regions like central Saxony and Berlin. In its fullest form the Mittellandkanal was to run over a distance of 273 km from Duisburg on the Rhine to Magdeburg on the Elbe. The Kaiser threw the full weight of his authority behind the project. Openness to new and modern ideas was a positive aspect of his ebullient and impulsive character. On the other hand the project ran into bitter opposition from the agrarians, Conservatives and BdL. They feared that it would expose them to further competition from cheap foreign grain imports in some of the principal domestic markets. Beyond that they saw in it a symbol of the transformation of Germany into 'an exporting and trading nation dominated by big international capital'. The canal project was a matter dealt with in the Lower House of the Prussian Landtag. In this chamber, in the elections of 1898, the Conservatives won a third of the seats, while the SPD had none. On a vote in August 1899 the Mittellandkanal proposal was lost by over a hundred votes, the majority consisting of nearly all Conservatives and most of the Centre and Free Conservatives.

The Kaiser was as furious with the 'canal rebels' as he habitually was with the socialists. Since many of the Conservatives rebels held official positions as Landräte or in even higher offices they were disciplined by premature retirement, though most were later reinstated. It was one of the curiosities of the German constitutional position that officials could sit in parliaments, but those who were in effect the political leaders could not, by virtue of their membership of the Bundesrat, be elected to the Reichstag, though they could appear before it. Until the constitution was changed in October 1918, just ten days before the collapse of the empire, it remained a barrier to full parliamentary government. The Mittellandkanal project failed again in 1901. Thereafter, it got tied up with the question of the renewal of the Caprivi trade treaties and the level of agricultural protection. A reduced project, taking the canal as far as Hanover, was approved in 1905, but the full project was not taken up again until after the war and completed in 1938. The struggle over the Mittellandkanal showed how difficult it was to produce agreement even among the *staatserhaltenden Stände*. It also highlighted how great a divergence had grown up between the political situation in Prussia and in the Reich. The old sparse Prussian ethos, even if sometimes excessively idealized, was giving way to the expansive nationalism of the Reich. Constitutionally the expansion of Reich departments and activities was reducing the originally overwhelming administrative predominance of Prussia. What was left was the Prussian three-tier electoral law, the entrenched power it gave to Prussian conservatism and the way it blocked the representation of the SPD. The Prussian three-tier law became a principal target of attack for the SPD and others.

The canal controversy was connected with an even bigger issue, the question of tariffs. The Caprivi trade treaties were due to run out at the end of 1903 and a committee had been established at the end of 1897 to enquire into and take evidence on the policy to be adopted on their expiry. It was a kind of reincarnation of the Economic Council which Bismarck had established in the hope of emasculating the Reichstag. It was also part of Miquel's Sammlungspolitik, for it was realized that without an accommodation between agrarian and industrial interests political gridlock would ensue and there would be no hope of stemming the tide of socialism. The support of the Conservatives and the BdL for the first navy law of 1898 rested on the understanding that agrarian interests would be duly respected when it came to the revision of tariffs. The Conservatives could not oppose a national objective such as the navy, but *Weltpolitik* did not initially arouse their enthusiasm. The alliterative slogan '*ohne Kanitz keine Kähne*' ('no boats without a state grain monopoly', a proposal made by Count Kanitz, an agrarian leader) was coined. The passage of a new tariff law became a major preoccupation during the first two years of Bülow's chancellorship. On the basis of the committee of enquiry's report the Bundesrat proposed a minimum tariff which was a compromise between the levels negotiated in the Caprivi treaties and the level demanded by the BdL. There was a bitter battle in which the deputies of the Conservatives, Free Conservatives and Centre in particular, the supporters of the agrarian interest, were subjected to great pressure from the BdL. Bülow managed to get his compromise through in December 1902, after a long night session brought on by obstruction from the SPD. It looked as if the government could now count on a fairly stable majority, made up of the cartel parties, Conservatives, Free Conservatives and National Liberals, with the addition of the Centre. Even without the extreme demands made by the BdL the tariff amounted to a considerable impost on consumers, castigated by the SPD as 'bread usury' (*Brotwucher*). It has been calculated that if a British worker at this time had gone to Germany and maintained his spending habits, his cost of living would have risen by 18 per cent.

Social policy under Posadowsky-Wehner

To compensate the consumer and to reduce the appeal of the SPD, the Bülow government reactivated the social policies which had stagnated since the Era Stumm, the later years of the Caprivi period. The new initiatives were mainly the responsibility of Count Posadowsky-Wehner, who had been state secretary of the treasury under Hohenlohe and from 1897 secretary of the interior and vice-chancellor. They were not of a very major character, but included further restrictions on child labour, which reduced the employment of children of fourteen, the compulsory school age, from more than half a million in 1898 to 14,000 by 1913. There were improvements in the accident and invalidity insurance and the extension of the labour courts already mentioned (see p. 120). Similar courts were established for white-collar employees, who were also given the benefit of the laws which restricted hours of labour for factory employees. There was thus an effort to reach out to the fast increasing category of white-collar employees, whose political orientation tended in any case to the right and whom the SPD and the free trade unions were clearly failing to attract. The rapid expansion of the unions and their organizations was itself being facilitated by changes in the law of association in the late 1890s, which previously had prohibited the federation of 'political associations' and their recruitment of women and apprentices. These prohibitions always posed the potential danger of prosecutions for the unions. The free trade unions were since the 1890s federated in a General Commission of the Free Trade Unions of Germany. The chairman of the commission, Carl Legien, became a powerful figure in the labour movement, whose influence strengthened the reformist tendency. There was also in these years a considerable development of Christian trade unions linked to the Centre party. The big expansion of the free unions and great strikes like the 1889 Ruhr miners' strike had made Catholics aware of the threat that the socialist unions posed for their following among the industrial working class. In 1894 a union of Catholic miners was founded and similar foundations followed in other trades. These unions were federated in 1900 in a central association of Christian unions, whose general secretary Adam Stegerwald became an important figure in Centre party politics, just as Legien did in the SPD. The effect on the Centre party of its working class wing was to strengthen the demand for social progress and to make cooperation with the government more conditional on the fulfilment of such demands. The expansion of unionism largely passed the old liberal Hirsch–Duncker unions by and their numbers stagnated, reaching 122,000 by 1910. Their ideology of social harmony between capital and labour did not fit into the militant labour relations climate of the decade before the war.

Small-scale, slow-acting improvements in social policy, such as those promoted by Posadowsky-Wehner, could not wean the voters from the SPD. The gulf between the labour movement and the state was sustained by a great show of mutual hostility of the symbolic kind. The Kaiser spoke in public of 'unpatriotic fellows'and 'bandits not deserving the name of Germans', while the SPD deputies remained seated when there were three cheers for the Kaiser. Above all the tariff law of 1902 showed how much the state was still in the pockets of the Junkers. This was reflected in the Reichstag elections of 1903 (see Appendix: Table 9). The SPD vote rose from 27.2 to 31.7 per cent, their seats from 56 to 81. It was largely at the expense of the left liberals, so it made little difference to the overall balance in the Reichstag, where the Centre was still necessary for a government majority. Friedrich Naumann made an ambitious effort to bridge the social gulf with his new party, the National Social party. He tried to combine the social concerns of the better elements in the Stoecker group with liberal imperialism. His electoral showing was negligible.

Bülow's social imperialism

Bülow could not stop the electoral rise of the SPD, but up to a point his practice of social imperialism had a calming effect on the domestic political conflicts. Like Tirpitz, Bülow played effectively upon public opinion and its growing receptivity for *Weltpolitik*, but more than Tirpitz Bülow was driven by the pervasive sentiment of imperialism rather than being its manipulator. The result was a certain aimlessness and simply a determination to assert a German presence wherever it was remotely possible. This did not help in the fundamentally difficult German security situation as the newcomer in the centre of Europe. The makers of German foreign policy, Bülow, the Kaiser, Holstein and others were still inclined to over-play their hand, thinking that other powers, like Britain or Russia, had greater need of the Germans than the Germans had of them. The influence of economic interests can easily be overestimated. The idea that economic interests had to be pursued and markets opened was more important than the reality. Germany had entered the competition for the Chinese market and had acquired Kiaochow in 1897 (see p. 133). The exploitation of the market and of railway concessions had mostly to be carried on in cooperation with British businesses and banks and did not fulfil expectations. There was more of a realistic German economic interest in the penetration of the Ottoman empire. German capital had become engaged in the building of the Anatolian railway in 1888, but Bismarck and his immediate successors had been very cautious in involving German diplomacy in support of this penetration. The German involvement received a big fillip from the Kaiser's visit to the region in 1898, when in a speech in Damascus he styled himself the protector of Moslems all over the world. The Baghdad railway, the extension of the Anatolian railway which never in fact reached Baghdad, became a very important element in German perceptions of their imperial destiny and German influence in Turkey, economic and military, became sufficient to make her a German ally in the First World War.

German colonial and imperial involvements stretched right round the globe by the turn of the century, but hardly justified themselves on a strict cost/benefit analysis. They greatly complicated the German position on the crucial security problem. Bismarck's principle of keeping Germany secure by encouraging the great powers into expansion and potential conflict on the periphery was, as it were, stood on its head when Germany participated in so many peripheral conflicts. There was never any realistic possibility of undoing the Franco-German antagonism. At the time of the Fashoda crisis in 1898, when Britain and France clashed at the source of the Nile, France would have welcomed some German support, but Germany would not risk British hostility over a matter so marginal to her interests. There were times when the German–Russian relationship improved, but there were too many reasons why the former close relationship could not be permanently restored. The German economic penetration of the Ottoman empire was one, the virtual exclusion of Russian grain from the German market after the new tariff law of 1902 was another. The project of an alliance with Britain, or her adhesion to the Triple Alliance had been on the agenda since the late Bismarck years and came back into view between 1898 and 1901. It would have been the last opportunity when such an alignment might have been possible, for thereafter it was made impossible by the German naval programme. Joseph Chamberlain, the British colonial secretary, anxious to clear the decks for conflict with the Boer republics, began to raise the possibility of an Anglo-German alliance in 1898. It still had ideological mileage, the brotherhood of Germanic nations, but the tide of public opinion in both countries was running against it. There was a press war, which rose in intensity during the Boer war, but a visit by the Kaiser to Britain in 1899 was designed to show that official circles in Germany were not swayed by the anti-British emotions of the public. There were many causes of friction all over the world, though also several attempts, as over the Portuguese colonies and spheres of influence in China, to resolve them. The pro-Boer sentiment in Germany proved useful in helping the passage of the second navy law in 1900. But the real reason why the Anglo-German alliance did not come about was that the Germans still overestimated the British need for it, were still afraid they might be pulling British chestnuts out of the fire, while in the last resort it might make little sense for the British.

Bülow, still relying on the advice of Holstein, believed that the 'free hand' was still the best policy for Germany, but the loud, indiscriminate and aimless assertion of German claims here, there and everywhere was hardly a good way of pursuing it. When the Boxer rebellion occurred in Peking in 1900 the Germans insisted that the international contingent to suppress it should be led by the ageing Waldersee. He had not left Germany when contingents from the naval forces sent out to quell the rebellion had already succeeded in their task. Nothing but irritation was achieved for Germany in China. Similarly, when the international peace conference called by the Tsar met at the Hague in 1899, the Germans took it upon themselves to reject disarmament in principle, thus enabling other powers who had no serious intention to disarm to shelter behind that position. In the unlikely event of a general disarmament agreement, the German naval building programme would have had to be stopped, but the policy of the 'free hand' was meant to continue until the German navy was sufficiently powerful to threaten the British into an accommodation with the Triple Alliance on German terms. When in 1903 Bülow was warned that the British might in fact seek to remove their many differences with both France and Russia around the globe by seeking agreements, he made light of it. Smooth courtier that he was he wrote with disdain: 'we can treat such matters with a dose of hair cream' (*pomadig*). Bülow's complacency was no doubt fuelled by the fact each of the many movements within the great clock-work of world diplomacy did not have to be taken too seriously. Yet Britain, sobered by the expenditure of resources required to subdue the small Boer republics, had already taken steps out of 'splendid isolation' by an alliance with Japan in 1902, while the Triple Alliance was fraying at the edges. Italy was becoming an uncertain partner against France, and Austria-Hungary was weakened by internal problems. The renewal of the Triple Alliance in 1901 no longer meant much.

In 1904 there were two major developments, the formation of the Anglo-French Entente Cordiale and the outbreak of the Russo-Japanese war, with contrasting implications for Germany. The Entente Cordiale was a major blow to German diplomacy. It was a world-wide clearing-up operation, removing causes of conflict between the two major colonial powers. The most important aspect was that France finally gave up the spoiling position she still retained over Egyptian finances. In return Britain gave up what remained of her position in Morocco. Holstein's reaction was: 'England and France are hardly likely to attack us . . . but we will be unable to make any overseas acquisitions. I do not want such acquisitions, but masses of people are shouting for them and wonder, why there is nothing in it for Germany . . .' In so far as Bülow was pursuing social imperialism, the Anglo-French agreements were bound to disappoint the expectations of vocal German chauvinists and put his government under pressure to achieve countervailing successes somewhere. The Anglo-French accords were not directed against Germany, but stemmed from the British desire to avoid imperial conflicts, following the strains of the Boer war; for the French the Russo-Japanese war and the fear of being sucked into it or else lose the Russian alliance was one of the motives for seeking an accommodation with Britain.

The entente did, however, give the lie to the long-standing German calculation that Anglo-French and Anglo-Russian hostility were irreducible facts of the international system. There was beginning to be talk of encirclement, attributed to an inordinate degree to Edward VII personally, because his visit to Paris in 1903 seemed to have created the right atmosphere for the Anglo-French understanding. An early version of the Schlieffen plan was elaborated. Alfred von Schlieffen had succeeded Waldersee as chief of staff in 1891 and, in contrast to his predecessor, had no political ambition. He was a pure technician of war and had worked hard on the strategic problem posed for Germany by a possible two-front war. His solution was an attack first in the West, which would subdue France by a large enveloping operation through Belgium and Luxemburg, originally also Holland, to be a followed by an Eastern campaign to defeat Russia. The circumstances of 1904 and 1905, in particular the Russo-Japanese war, led to renewed consideration of a preventive war against France in the General Staff and the German foreign office. It did not come to that at this juncture, but the Schlieffen plan was certainly known to the civilian authorities, including successive chancellors. Its political implications were, however, never fully discussed. Thus, almost by default, another burden was put upon the conduct of German foreign policy, in addition to the pursuit of a great navy. The lack of coherence and clarity of concept among Germany's top decision-makers was glaring.

For the moment the war in the Far East masked any deleterious effects of the Entente Cordiale on the German position. When Russian warships on their way to fight the Japanese in the Far East fired on a British fishing fleet at the Dogger Bank tensions rose. There was talk in Berlin of a Russian–German continental alliance against Britain, to which France might be forced to adhere. The Nordic states would be forced to cooperate against a possible 'Copenhagen' type preventive strike against the German navy, still in process of construction. The notion of a struggle for survival between Germany and Britain, the new against the old world power, was taking a stronger hold in both countries. It did not come to that at this stage, but the Russian defeat and the revolution of 1905 in that country had a profound influence on the future course of events. Russian ambitions were turned back towards Europe, with implications for the long-standing rivalry with Austria in the Balkans. For Britain any threat from Russia now receded behind the threat from Germany and the maintenance of the Ottoman empire against Russia was past history. The way was opened for a removal of Anglo-Russian sources of conflict further afield. A preventive war against France, which Schlieffen and Holstein were toying with, was opposed by the Kaiser, but the opportunity to inflict a humiliation on France and show up the fragility of her ties to St Petersburg and London was too good to miss. This was done by asserting Germany's own claims in Morocco. On 31 March 1905 the Kaiser made a spectacular landfall at Tangier and declared Germany's interest in Moroccan independence. The French foreign minister Delcassé, architect of the Entente Cordiale, was forced to resign and the status of Morocco was submitted to an international conference.

In the meantime the Germans bent every effort to exploit Russia's moment of weakness to force her into a realignment of alliances. The Kaiser met his cousin, the Russian Tsar Nicholas II, at Björkö on 4 July 1905 and cajoled him into signing an alliance. The meeting had been carefully prepared by Bülow and his advisers, but the Tsar's ministers were against such a sacrifice of the Franco-Russian relationship. The Tsar was soon forced to put the Nicky–Willy agreement into cold storage. Russian ministers were not prepared to jeopardize the French alliance and French capital flows into Russia, or to participate in a continental league against Britain. Bülow and his advisers were annoyed that the Kaiser, on his own authority, had limited the agreement to Europe, when they had hoped that one of its advantages would be renewed Russian pressure on India. It was too late for a fundamental recasting of power blocks which might have reversed the deterioration of the German position. The international conference to settle the future of Morocco met at Algeciras in January 1906, but it did not bring the diplomatic gains the Germans had anticipated. They hoped that the pressure on France would become so strong that not only would she have to accept a retreat in Morocco, but it would be demonstrated that the Anglo-French entente was of little use to her. The French would be forced into a reconsideration of her alliances and become amenable to participation in a continental league alongside Germany, a calculation similar to the one that had led to the Björkö treaty. Again it proved to be a miscalculation. The Algeciras conference itself was not well handled by German diplomacy and Germany found herself in the end isolated, supported only by Austria-Hungary among the great powers. German threats against France were bluff, since neither the Kaiser nor in the end Bülow wanted to go to war over Morocco. If the intention was to weaken the ties between London and Paris the opposite was achieved. A Liberal Government had just come to power in Britain when the Algeciras conference met and Sir Edward Grey had become foreign secretary. Although balance of power politics went against the grain with the radicals in the large Liberal majority at Westminster, Grey was a liberal imperialist and did not want to show weakness at the beginning of his period of office. In public he maintained such pledges as the previous Conservative government had given to France over Morocco. Behind the scenes he sanctioned the Anglo-French staff conversations, which went on intermittently over the next few years. Grey made it clear that they did not commit Britain to come to France's assistance in case of a German attack, but the inevitable implication was that Britain could not afford to let France go to the wall. The Algeciras conference reaffirmed the sovereignty of Morocco, which in the circumstances was a formality, and reasserted the 'open door' principle, giving all the the powers economic access. It was not a German defeat, but the economic penetration France had already established was not reduced and the high German hopes of achieving a realignment of alliances were certainly disappointed. Significantly Holstein resigned as counsellor in the German foreign office in April 1906, just as the Algeciras protocols were being signed. His relatively lowly position had disguised the important role he had played in German foreign and even domestic affairs at least since the fall of Bismarck.

In the meantime the Anglo-German naval rivalry was intensifying. The Russo-Japanese war and its naval battles had shown the importance of very large battleships, heavily armoured and gunned and endowed with high speed. In Britain and the United States the design and building of Dreadnoughts as the ultimate deterrent was being initiated. Admiral Fisher, who became the First Sea Lord in October 1904, calculated that the German navy, increasingly seen as the main potential enemy, would be handicapped in introducing ships of such size by their inadequate docking and canal facilities. The first Dreadnought was launched by Edward VII in February 1906. Tirpitz, on the other hand, saw that the introduction of such ships would virtually negate the usefulness of existing warships and would therefore wipe out the advantage of numbers which the British navy had hitherto possessed. In Britain it was thought that the financial weakness of the Reich would make it impossible for the Germans to win a naval arms race. In Germany the British willingness to finance such a race was underestimated and too much importance was attached to the pacifism of the Liberal left in the House of Commons. Tirpitz, who had been so successful in building up naval enthusiasm, found that radical elements in the Navy League and elsewhere were pressing him to go even faster than he originally wanted to go. The navy law of 1906 provided for the building of Dreadnought type ships of 25,000 tons in place of previously planned ships of the line. Significantly the Freisinnige Volkspartei, the old left liberal party of Richter, who had died in March 1906, now also voted for it. Even this was not enough for the Navy League, which mounted a massive campaign for even faster building, invoking the name of the Kaiser. It was certainly the case that the Kaiser wanted to build up the navy, whatever the cost, financially or in terms of foreign policy problems. In another navy law of 1908 it was envisaged that four large battleships should be launched every year until 1912, though this timetable could not in the end be quite sustained. Not unnaturally the British response was to keep pace, and in 1908 the popular campaign 'we want eight and we won't wait' became part of the run-up to Lloyd George's people's budget of 1909.

Although this naval arms race placed a heavy burden on Anglo-German relations, it was not bound to set the two countries on a collision course. From time to time efforts were made to reach an understanding on limiting naval building, the last of them the Haldane mission of 1912. However, Britain retained her advantage as a naval power and the Tirpitz calculations about using the German navy as a means of pressure came to nothing. In fact the German naval building programme did not fit into any coherent policy and became an end in itself, and an irrational one at that. There was a good deal of unease in Germany, following Algeciras, that Bülow's *Weltpolitik* was not achieving anything but 'encirclement', *Einkreisung*, which in fact was a kind of self-exclusion, *Auskreisung*. The criticism of Bülow, and often of the Kaiser for his ill-judged interventions, was not coherent either, because it was counterbalanced by attacks from the radical chauvinists, who criticised official policy as lame and wanted even more machismo. By and large the German mood was still optimistic. From 1902 to 1907 the economy was on a rising curve, the forward march of the technologically advanced German industries continued unabated, and in spite of the higher tariffs real wages were rising. The contribution made to German prosperity by the formal imperialism of her African and Asian colonies and the informal imperialism of the Baghdad railway was negligible. The German colonies accounted for 0.25 per cent of German exports and 0.7 per cent of German imports. But colonies and navies were accoutrements of the well-dressed world power which no German government could give up.

Domestic politics in the later years of Bülow

The new peak of electoral support achieved by the SPD in the 1903 Reichstag elections strengthened rather than weakened Bülow's position. Fear of the socialists was the one thing all the other parties had in common and enabled the government to rely on a minimal consensus in the Reichstag. Bülow and Bebel needed each other. In the first party congress following the 1903 elections, held at Dresden in September 1903, Bebel made sure that electoral success and the many other tendencies strengthening reformism would not result in a dilution of revolutionary theory, expectation and rhetoric. The revisionist theory of Bernstein was rejected and so was any theoretical opening of the party to the lower middle class and to farmers. In the South German states such an opening had become a necessity of practical politics. In the Reich the rigidity of the national party line made it possible for the opposite camp, from Bülow down, to claim that any hope of making the SPD into a reformist party within the system was a chimera. Millerandism – Millerand was the French socialist who had assumed a cabinet post in 1899 – was not going to work in Germany. In 1904 a National Association against Social Democracy (*Reichsverband gegen die Sozialdemokratie*) was founded with the blessing of the government, to coordinate the struggle against the SPD. It had the support of the cartel parties, but the Centre, with its own trade union and working-class wing, and the left liberals remained outside it. In 1905 big strikes in Germany, notably in the Ruhr mines, and the Russian revolution of that year led to discussions in the SPD about the role of the mass strike in achieving political advance. At the Jena party congress of September 1905 the revisionists and the new left, led by Rosa Luxemburg, supported the concept of the mass strike as a way out of mere waiting (attentism), but from different motives. Rosa Luxemburg saw the mass strike as a means of keeping alive the spontaneous revolutionary drive of the masses (see p. 110). The revisionists around Bernstein saw it as a response to the refusal of the ruling élites to remove the two major blockages obstructing democratic progress, restricted access by the voter to the franchise and restricted access to power by the parties. There was a sense that the Bebel–Kautsky strategy of proletarian purity on the one hand, and the refusal of the imperial establishment and its supporters to move on matters like the three-tier electoral law on the other, was foreshadowing a kind of stalemate. Under cover of revolutionary theory and rhetoric, the energies of the labour movement, party and unions, were being diverted into electioneering and organization, but eventually these would reach their limit, particularly if they were not to reach out from the industrial proletariat to other groups in society. At the same time the SPD, by continuing to inscribe revolution in tablets of stone, made integration into the political system difficult and made it easier for the ruling élites to keep the political status quo. It took defeat in a world war to break this logjam.

Bülow was thus able to continue without any fundamental resolution of the domestic problems, just as he could not resolve the underlying security dilemma of the Reich. In both areas postponement of solutions allowed the problems to fester. *Weltpolitik* helped to maintain the feel-good factor, but it was expensive. The chronic shortfall in the income of the Reich, which even Bismarck had been unable to cure, was becoming very serious. The indebtedness of the Reich rose from less than 500 million marks in 1887 to 5 billion on the eve of war. The proportion of defence expenditure to total public expenditure at Reich level was in fact declining and if it had been possible to introduce effective federal taxes, in particular an income tax, as Bebel advocated, it should have been possible to put the finances of the Reich on a sounder basis. The fragility of the party support on which the Bülow government could rely in the Reichstag made it impossible. The Centre party agreed to the virtual abolition of the Franckenstein clause, under which the revenues from customs and other dues were remitted to the federal states. The price was a further step towards the liquidation of the Kulturkampf, a modification of the expulsion clauses of the anti-Jesuit law of 1872. The treasury secretary Stengel then proposed more far-reaching changes, the main element of which was to be an inheritance tax. In the end this was levied only on distant beneficiary relatives and a third of it went to the Länder. This and a few other tax rises did little to cure the financial malaise of the Reich. As a concession to secure these meagre advantages expense allowances were introduced for Reichstag deputies. Bismarck had fought hard against such allowances, to prevent the rise of professional politicians. By now all parties needed them and so did the government, for without them there was often no quorum in the chamber and legislation was delayed.

The Centre party was essential for most of what the Bülow government did, but its ability to run with the hare and hunt with the hounds caused resentment. Kulturkampf passions were still simmering. They were highlighted by the appointment of the historian Martin Spahn, son of the leading Centre party politician Peter Spahn, to a chair at the University of Strassburg in 1902. The establishment of a Catholic theological faculty at Strassburg had been an aim of the Reich government since the days of Bismarck, the intention being to strengthen the pro-German element among the Catholic clergy of Alsace-Lorraine. This involved lengthy negotiations with the Vatican, which had not reached a conclusion by the turn of the century. The appointment of Spahn was an attempt to improve the atmosphere by increasing the very small number of Catholic professors, but it was done over the objections of the Strassburg philosophical faculty, in which Spahn's chair was to be located. There was a furious outcry from the predominantly Protestant German academic profession. Theodor Mommsen, the persistent critic of the establishment, published a widely noticed article on the need to maintain teaching and research entirely free from any dogmatic preconceptions and ties. The Spahn case became the most bitterly fought cultural controversy of the time and is eloquent testimony for the continuing deep-seated suspicion and contempt for Catholicism among leaders of public opinion.

The basis on which the Bülow government worked with the Reichstag, a combination of the cartel parties with the Centre, was therefore insecure. It was held together by the glamour of *Weltpolitik* and depended on the appearance of success in national self-assertion. The threat from the SPD and the trade unions helped it to survive. In 1906 Bülow's grip weakened. Following the only half-disguised failure of Algeciras the chancellor himself was absent for six months after a heart attack. For years he had played a delicate game of treating the Kaiser with the courtier's sycophancy, while persuading him to tone down the tactless and arrogant speeches that attracted criticism in the Reichstag and among the general public. The so-called 'prophets of doom' speech the Kaiser made in November 1906 revived these criticisms. William said he 'would not tolerate prophets of doom. Those who were not suitable for work should emigrate and find a better land to live in.' Bülow was blamed for not keeping the Kaiser firmly within his constitutional limits, but the monarch was easily displeased when his chancellor did not seem to defend him sufficiently fiercely. William had reason to feel vulnerable, for once more the scandals surrounding his court, his friend Philipp Eulenburg, the circle at Eulenburg's seat Liebenberg, homosexuality and spiritualism, were resurfacing. Again Maximilian Harden, the editor of *Zukunft* (Future), was the source and information came to him from Holstein, who deeply resented his removal earlier in the year.

On his return from sick leave in November 1906 Bülow decided to strengthen his position by turning against the Centre, the focus of so much resentment. A factor in this decision was the criticism that came particularly from the rising Centre politician Matthias Erzberger about the German colonial administration in South-West Africa. Erzberger, a native of Württemberg, represented the populist, anti-establishment element in the party, that was sceptical and unimpressed by the cosy relationship that often existed between the Centre party leaders in the Reichstag and the government. He was well informed about conditions in South-West Africa through the Catholic missions there. A fierce colonial war had raged in the colony since the beginning of 1904, directed in the main against the rebellious Herero tribe. The Germans had to deploy some 20,000 troops in the colony and put the rising down with great brutality, exterminating about 60,000 Hereros, something like three-quarters of the tribe. Supplementary estimates of 60 million marks had to be passed to finance the war. Just as Algeciras had fuelled doubts about *Weltpolitik*, the Herero rising highlighted the doubtful utility of the German colonies. To meet these criticisms Bülow appointed Bernard Dernburg, a Jewish banker, director of the colonial department in the foreign office in the autumn of 1906. He became state secretary of a separate colonial office in 1907. He had good links with the business world and tried to persuade investors that there were advantages in channelling money into regions where Germany had direct control.

Bülow saw in the Centre party's opposition to German colonial policy, in which so much German self-esteem was involved, a chance for a new party alignment. The death of Richter and the abandonment by his party of his permanent opposition to defence expenditure also facilitated such a realignment. When the Centre, following Erzberger rather than its established parliamentary leaders, joined the SPD in opposing supplementary estimates for the South-West African campaign in December 1906, Bülow dissolved the Reichstag. The so-called Hottentot elections, a phrase coined by Bebel, became a contest between what was now called the Bülow block, the cartel parties joined by the left liberals, against Centre and SPD. It was a successful mobilization of nationalist–imperialist sentiment, shown by the record electoral participation, up from 76.15 in 1903 to 84.7 per cent (see Appendix: Table 9). The campaign of the block parties, particularly their cooperation on the second ballot, was coordinated by the National Association against Social Democracy. Neither SPD nor Centre lost votes, but they lost share of votes, most of the previous non-voters responding to the nationalist slogans. The Centre's loss of share was so slight that the number of their seats actually rose by five. The SPD suffered their first real setback, dropping from 31.7 to 28.9 per cent. Their loss of seats was drastic, from 81 to 43. The Bülow block had 220 out of 397 seats.

Bülow looked like the strong man, but his triumph proved an episode and not an enduring shift of forces. The difficulties Bülow encountered in keeping his block together for a definite purpose, such as solving the Reich's financial problem or curing the most glaring and divisive features of the Prussian electoral law, illustrate the continuing deficiencies of the German constitutional system, which the passage of time had done nothing to alleviate. In a parliamentary system, parties governing together in a coalition, as is usually the case in a multi-party system, are continually compelled into compromises if they wish to retain office and power. The German political parties did not have office or the power derived therefrom, hence they were not amenable to these compulsions. They could not topple the chancellor, only make life difficult for him. The chancellor could not discipline them by threatening resignation and loss of office. Moreover the proliferation of lobbies and interest groups negotiating directly with the government put the parties on their mettle to defend the interests of the groups linked to them regardless of the public interest. The whole system was seriously lacking in integrative power and this became particularly evident in the remaining years before the outbreak of war. The Hottentot elections showed that Bülow had succeeded, for the moment, in replacing this absence of integrative power by the appearance of successful *Weltpolitik* and world power. Among the well-informed there may have been doubts about this success, anxiety about encirclement, apocalyptic presentiments about the stark alternative of *Zusammenbruch* (collapse). A majority of the general public, particularly the Protestant bourgeoisie, still felt good about Germany's manifest destiny, if only the internal disintegrative forces could be kept at bay. A strong dose of social imperialism was essential to the task of governing Germany and Bülow, Tirpitz, even the Kaiser, in their different ways, had supplied it. In these circumstances an essentially superficial but smooth operator like Bülow cultivated complacency and refused to take seriously the signs of Germany's deteriorating position. After the elections a few personnel changes were designed to cement the Bülow block at home. The most important was that Posadowsky-Wehner, too closely identified with a progressive social policy to please the Conservatives, left and was succeed as interior secretary and vice-chancellor by Bethmann Hollweg.

Germany's international position deteriorates

With hindsight and in a longer perspective the Anglo-Russian entente of August 1907 was another sign of the deterioration of Germany's international position. Britain and Russia removed a number of long-standing irritants in their relations. The most important agreement was over Persia, where a British sphere of influence in the south and a Russian sphere in the north were recognized. The entente was in no way directed against Germany, and Izvolski, the Russian foreign minister, had secured Berlin's approval of the Persian part of the agreements. Nor was it the case that Anglo-Russian relations ran smoothly henceforth. The left wing of the the Liberal majority in the Commons had no love for the Russian autocracy. But the assumption of irreducible Anglo-Russian hostility, for long one of the bedrocks of German diplomacy, was no longer valid. Against that, the German political and economic penetration of Turkey, symbolized by the Baghdad railway, did not exactly find favour in St Petersburg. For the Germans this was their one imperial project where clear gains could be demonstrated and even greater ones antici-pated. When in 1908 the Sultan Abdul Hamid II was overthrown by the Young Turk revolt, the German stake in Turkey seemed for a moment in jeopardy. The Young Turks, initially disposed towards closer links with the western powers, found, like their predecessors, that the German interest was useful as a counterpoise to the interference of the older imperial powers and it continued. The German government rather than German banks and business were the driving force, for the latter often preferred sharing the risks with French and British competitors rather than going it alone.

The Young Turk revolt sparked the next major European crisis, over Bosnia. The Turkish reformers wanted to create a homogeneous modern state and thereby threatened to disturb the status quo in what remained of Turkish control in the Balkans. The Austrians wanted to use the opportunity to annex Bosnia and Hercegovina, which they had administered since 1878. They were afraid of the irredentist pull emanating from Serbia in these territories and elsewhere in the Habsburg dominions. Russia on the other hand exercised a kind of informal patronage over their Serb fellow-Slavs. The relative quiescence that had prevailed in the Balkans in the previous years owed a good deal to the fact that the conflict between Russia and Austria in this area was less acute, largely because the Russians were fully engaged in the Far East. An agreement between Russia and Austria over Bosnia-Hercegovina appeared to have been reached in September 1908, but the Russian quid pro quo, an opening of the straits to Russian warships, did not not materialize, because it had not been agreed by the other major powers. When the Austrians in October 1908 formally annexed Bosnia-Hercegovina, the Russians felt duped and called for an international conference. By this time two men had assumed office in Vienna, Aehrenthal as foreign minister and Conrad von Hötzendorf as Chief of Staff, who felt the survival of the multi-national Habsburg empire required a strong line to be taken against Serbia, as the focus of nationalist aspirations among Slav nationalities inside the empire. If such a strong line should lead to war with Russia, Aehrenthal, Conrad von Hötzendorf and others like them felt that Berlin was bound to support them. In fact this was precisely what happened in this crisis. Although German interests were not directly involved and by now required support for the Turks, Berlin felt bound to demonstrate *Nibelungentreue* (the loyalty of the Nibelungs) to their one remaining ally. This position was strongly supported in the Reichstag, outside the ranks of the SPD. This time Russia, still weak from her defeat by Japan and in no way ready for war, had to beat a retreat. It looked like a considerable triumph for the central powers, but the crisis had an ominous resemblance to the one that six years later started a world war. Even some of the personalities were already in place. It was, moreover, an empty triumph, because it confirmed rather than weakened the power relationships that were already adverse for the Reich. The Russians felt sore and did not forget. Mistrust grew in London and Paris.

The *Daily Telegraph* interview and the fall of Bülow

As the Bosnian crisis reached its climax events occurred that were eventually to bring about Bülow's downfall, the episode of the Kaiser's *Daily Telegraph* interview. During manoeuvres in Alsace William had conversations about Anglo-German relations with Colonel Stuart Wortley, who had been the Kaiser's host at his seat in

Hampshire. William was persuaded to allow his remarks to be consolidated into an 'interview', which appeared in the *Daily Telegraph* on 28 October 1908. The intention was to improve the atmosphere in Anglo-German relations, soured by the slanging match about naval building programmes on both sides of the Channel. The Kaiser sought to portray himself as a candid friend of England, who had supplied a military plan worked out by the German general staff to help the British to win the Boer War. He had also frustrated the plan of an anti-British continental league by revealing it to Queen Victoria. He was one of a small pro-British minority in Germany and the German navy was not a rival of the Royal Navy, but a potential future ally in the Far East. These ill-judged remarks caused uproar in both countries. In Germany it was felt that the Kaiser had demeaned himself and that it was the worst of a long line of indiscretions which Bülow had promised to restrain but had failed so to do. It came at a moment when the Eulenburg trial precipitated by Maximilian Harden's attack was already casting discredit on the Kaiser and his court. On this occasion the Kaiser had in fact caused the text of the interview to be submitted to the chancellor. Bülow was on holiday at the time, did not read it, but passed it on to the foreign office where it was approved by a minor official. The Kaiser was therefore highly resentful of the lukewarm way in which the chancellor protected him and felt that he had been betrayed. It was the end of his relationship with Bülow and although he could not get rid of him at that point, he did so as soon as the chancellor's position in the Reichstag was undermined. The Kaiser hardly helped himself by going hunting at the height of the crisis and by making the chief of his military cabinet perform a ballet dressed in a tutu, in the course of which the 56-year-old Count Hülsen-Haeseler dropped dead. The Kaiser never understood that his antics, so far removed from the normal world of his subjects, caused deep public unease. Even the Conservatives joined in the attack on the Kaiser, who thereby felt doubly betrayed, but there was no united front between the parties on what should emerge from the crisis. There were demands that the chancellor's responsibility to the Reichstag should take a more concrete form and should become more enforceable. The SPD, the left liberals and some on the extreme right wanted to bring Bülow down, so that he would have been held responsible for what happened in a more than formal sense. Such a move could have led to a full parliamentarization of the system, but the other parties were not ready for that. The last thing the Conservatives wanted was a further strengthening of the Reichstag, where they had 15 per cent of the seats, when they held a third of the seats in the Prussian Landtag. The affair of the *Daily Telegraph* interview showed that one of the pillars of the German political system, a strong and popular monarchy, was seriously weakened.

The cohesion of the Bülow block, including as it did the left liberals, required at least some genuflection towards liberalism. There was one major piece of legislation of a clearly liberalizing kind passed in 1908, a new Reich law on association. There had been a relaxation of the association laws, which originally prevented any national affiliation for political purposes, at the end of the Hohenlohe era in Prussia (see p. 111), but the law on association and assembly was still subject to much local and Länder variation. The new *Reichsvereinsgesetz* (Reich association law) by and large removed restrictions on association and assembly that were no longer compatible with modern notions of the rule of law. It was very significant that membership of political associations and participation in political meetings was now opened to women. On the other hand the law contained provisions clearly designed to help the German language in the on-going battle between Poles and Germans in the eastern provinces of Prussia and also with French speakers in Alsace-Lorraine. These provisions were slightly mitigated by being suspended for twenty years in areas where more than 60 per cent of the population was non-German speaking. The really big liberalizing measure would have been a reform of the Prussian electoral law. This question was fairly and squarely on the agenda. Both liberal groups wanted it, though there was no agreement on how far the reform was to go. A liberal ideologue like Friedrich Naumann, without much of a political following but influential among the articulate classes, saw it as a question of life or death. The SPD was beginning to move towards mass demonstrations in favour of a fairer law. Baden and Bavaria had already broadened their franchise; Saxony, which had slipped back to a three-tier system in 1896, reduced the degree of discrimination by a provision, introduced in 1909, which gave higher income groups additional votes. On the reform of the Prussian system Bülow could only prevaricate, for he would have lost the support of the Conservatives if he had made a real move. The issue would not go away and the speech from the throne at the end of 1908 at least recognized the need for change in principle.

Even more pressing than the reform of the Prussian electoral law was the reform of the Reich finances. The so-called 'little reform' of 1906 was inadequate to meet the constantly rising expenditure and an annual shortfall of 500 million marks was recognized as the gap that needed to be closed by increased taxation. The Bülow government proposed to meet four-fifths of this target by raising four major consumption taxes, on spirits, wine, beer and tobacco. This burden on the consumer was to be counterbalanced by extending the inheritance tax introduced in 1906 to the immediate heirs, spouse and children. Even then it was only to be levied on estates exceeding 20,000 marks. This inheritance tax sparked off a bitter battle. The Conservatives called it an attack on the sanctity of property, on the rural way of life, on the family, in short 'the first step towards communism'. They simply refused to put the power to tax property into the hands of a chamber elected by universal suffrage. The question also got tied up with the problem of the Kaiser and his conduct, raised by the *Daily Telegraph* affair. The Conservatives had infuriated William by associating themselves with the calls for restraint in his conduct. They were, however, by no means disposed to go along with the attempts by left liberals and the SPD to use the occasion for a major constitutional shift. It had also become clear that the Kaiser was only waiting to get rid of Bülow. The Centre party went along with the Conservatives, partly because they also wished to defend agrarian property, but even more because they wished to take revenge on Bülow. The government proposals were narrowly voted down in June 1909, with left liberals and the SPD supporting them. For the first time the SPD had supported a major financial proposal at national level. The Kaiser's first reaction to Bülow's defeat was to talk of a coup d'état again, an eloquent testimony of the extent to which lines had got crossed in this cauldron of recrimination and bitterness. It would have been a coup d'état to force through a law supported by liberals and social democrats and opposed by conservatives and catholics. The Kaiser's fighting mood was short-lived and a day later he accepted Bülow's resignation with scarcely disguised relief. The announcement of the resignation was delayed for a fortnight to allow the tax proposals to pass in a modified form. The inheritance tax fell, the consumption taxes remained and there were stamp duties on financial transactions, cheques and bills of exchange. The taxes were a flagrant example of class egotism, the agrarians led by the big landowners, at their core the Prussian Junkers, against the consumers, the workers, industry and commerce.

7 Stagnation at home, 'encirclement' abroad 1909–1914

The chancellorship of Bethmann Hollweg

The collapse of the Bülow block meant that for the next few years the government had to rely mainly on the Black–Blue block, the reactionary–clerical coalition. The result was the reconstitution of a united left liberal party, the *Fortschrittspartei*, and the foundation of the *Hansabund* (see p. 116). Even the National Liberals were forced to the left. Their gradual adaptation to the political mass market and reduced reliance on notabilities had made them more responsive to their predominantly big-city voters. But when it came to asking their supporters to cast their votes for a SPD candidate on the second ballot, National Liberal and even Progressive voters often preferred bourgeois solidarity. An alignment left of centre from the National Liberals to the SPD was therefore as fragile as the Bülow block had proved to be. Intellectuals like Naumann talked of a coalition from Bassermann to Bebel. Ernst Bassermann was the leader of the National Liberals in the Reichstag. But even in Baden such a coalition proved short-lived. There the Black–Blue block was even stronger than in Berlin and forced liberals and socialdemocrats together. Contrary to the line laid down by the Bebel leadership, the Baden SPD, following their Bavarian counterpart, collaborated in passing budgets, from which their followers stood to benefit. After a while the Baden National Liberal voters turned against a policy of collaborating with those whom they considered their natural enemies. To keep the SPD united Bebel had to pay regard to his left wing, and to keep the National Liberals together Bassermann had to keep in with his right wing. It was a long way from the SPD left to the National Liberal right. The events culminating in the fall of Bülow therefore showed the German political system in a state of comprehensive immobility. The Kaiser could not remove Bülow while he enjoyed parliamentary support, but he could have maintained him in office, had he wanted to, even after his finance reforms had been defeated. He was still free to choose his successor. Party combinations remained fragile and the parties preferred their freedom to choose allies to forcing the chancellor of their choice on the monarch. They paid for their unity and dogmatic purity with the price of immobility and they were in hock to the interests and lobbies to which they were linked. The Centre party provided a kind of buffer zone for the system. It limited the gains the SPD could make in working-class areas that were predominantly Catholic, but in the Reichstag it could ally itself with the Conservatives.

Bethmann Hollweg, treasury secretary and vice-chancellor, became Bülow's successor as chancellor. It was said that Bülow suggested him, hoping that his limitations would highlight his own qualities in retrospect. Bethmann was both by background and experience a bureaucrat. The roots of his family were in Frankfurt and in banking and his grandfather had headed the liberal-conservative Wochenblattpartei in the 1850s (see p. 12). He was therefore not a Junker, and the family estate of Hohenfinow was but recently acquired, but even as a young prince Wilhelm had stayed there. Bethmann was a brilliant administrator, but had no experience of foreign affairs, the field that was to dominate his chancellorship. This was held against him, but in fact he quickly acquired a grasp of the subject. The problem was not that he lacked the knowledge and the right ideas, but that the system did not give him the legitimacy and power to make these prevail. Much the same was true of domestic affairs. He tried to steer a right of centre, moderately reformist conservative course, but more often than not he could not carry his intentions into practice in the bitterly divided Reichstag. Bethmann personified the notion of 'goverment above politics', deeply rooted in Germany and Prussia, but it was a concept whose time had passed. He neither could nor would go against the Conservatives, because he wanted to preserve the existing power constellation, nor would the Kaiser have kept him in office if he had not done so. He wanted to uphold the privileged position which the mainly Prussian aristocracy still occupied in the state, through their hold on the court, the army and the bureaucracy. At the same time he recognized that the hold of the SPD on the masses could not be broken by repression and that therefore some accommodation with the social-democrats was necessary. Their cooperation would be required if it came to war, but this was an eventuality Bethmann hoped to avoid. The new chancellor's policy was one of living with rather than solving problems. He called it the policy of the diagonal, but it looked more like squaring the circle.

Bethmann's first major domestic project was the reform of the Prussian electoral law. Bülow had toyed with it but drawn back, but in principle king and government had accepted the need for change. The reform proposals put forward in February 1910 were modest enough. They amounted to a modification, but not an abolition of the three-tier system. The amount of taxes to be taken into account in calculating the classes was to be limited to 5000 marks. This would have done away with the situation in which in some electoral districts a handful of high tax payers could determine the outcome in the first and even in the second class. About 13,000 of the wealthiest electors would have seen their power reduced. Factors other than tax would in future count in the classification, such as education, public service and professional experience. It was called 'rewarding the carriers of culture' (*Privilegierung der Kulturträger*). Elections were still to be open, but now direct, without an intervening tier of electors. It was calculated that the numbers in the first class would be nearly doubled, in the second raised by nearly a quarter, and in the third reduced by about seven per cent. Even this modest reform was blocked in the Prussian Landtag by an unholy alliance of Conservatives and Centre, the Black–Blue Block. The Conservatives at bottom wanted no change, the Centre would have wanted the Reichstag electoral law, but knew it was unattainable. The two parties, which had already brought down Bülow, decided on a manipulation of the electoral law in their mutual interest, Bethmann could not risk a break with the Conservatives and unwisely withdrew the proposals.

The SPD between reformist pragmatism and revolutionary rhetoric

The failure of Bethmann's electoral reform proposals was a clear demonstration that even a limited change in a flagrantly undemocratic law extending over two-thirds of the nation was impossible. It was a lesson not lost on the socialdemocratic movement, where Bebel was pursuing his own version of the chancellor's diagonal. On the one hand the collapse of the Bülow block, the move of the liberal parties to the left and events in the South German states had opened up the possibility of collaborating with sections of the bourgeoisie; on the other the inability of the system to reform itself pointed to the use of pressure, violence, ultimately revolution as the only way forward. After a short economic recession in the years 1907 and 1908 the German economy was growing again and this increased the membership and the militancy of the unions. In spite of economic growth real wages were virtually stagnating as a result of the tax and tariff policies, putting burdens on consumers. The years 1909 and 1910 saw some big and bitter strikes. A strike in the Mansfeld coalfield in October 1909 led to the use of troops. From April 1910 there was a three months lock-out in the building industry, which affected 170,000 workers. From August to October 1910 the whole shipbuilding industry was paralysed. In 1910 as a whole nearly 370,000 workers were involved in strikes and lock-outs and more than nine million working days were lost. In September and October there was unrest in the working class districts of Moabit and Wedding in Berlin, with street fighting between workers and police, resulting in hundreds of injured and some dead. At the same time, with Bethmann's moderate Prussian electoral reform proposals coming before the Prussian Landtag, there were big demonstrations in favour of a reformed franchise. The biggest was the so-called Berlin streetwalk of 6 March 1910, which is said to have brought out quarter of a million demonstrators. In these demonstrations middle and working classes came together, whereas the strikes tended to push middle classes and liberal parties to the right again.

To complicate matters further, in July 1910 the Badenese SPD, in a deliberate gesture, passed a budget in collaboration with the liberal parties and attended a levee of the grand duke. A month later the Kaiser, still a slow learner when it came to keeping his mouth shut, made one of his threatening, grandiloquent and ridiculous speeches: 'Regarding Myself as an instrument of the Lord, I go My way without regard to the fashions and opinions of the day.' In the atmosphere of unrest, strikes, police and troop interventions it aroused the customary inclination in the SPD leadership to avoid provoking the authorities. The party leadership, with Bebel himself often absent at his villa on Lake Zürich owing to ill-health, used its time-honoured tactic of concealing day-to-day pragmatism behind revolutionary rhetoric. It thus maintained party unity between 'Baden and Luxemburg' and left the party in the Reichstag free to decide its tactics. The Baden SPD, led by Ludwig Frank, the most promising of the younger reformist leaders, and Rosa

Luxemburg, the most creative figure on the left, both wanted to escape from the immobility and lack of future strategy that was characteristic of the centre. The arguments for reformism seemed unanswerable and the only responsible way of improving the condition of the German working class. On the other hand there was also much plausibility in the strategy of generating revolutionary spontaneity advocated by Rosa Luxemburg. The discontent and alienation of the masses was palpable, the illegitimacy of the state flagrant. For the moment there was, however, no practical alternative to the 'diagonal' as pursued by Bebel and Kautsky, more or less in unison, any more than there was to Bethmann's 'diagonal'.

The minority problems of the Reich: Poles and Alsace-Lorrainers

Bethmann applied his policy of alleviating problems by emollience to the two major nationality problems that faced the Reich, Alsace-Lorraine and the Poles in the eastern provinces of Prussia. Caprivi's attempts to steer a more conciliatory course towards the Poles had long been abandoned and the clash of rival nationalisms had taken on a fiercer note. On the German side the flames were fanned by the Eastern Marches Association, also known as the Hakatisten (see p. 112), which by 1913 had 48,000 members and a considerable capacity to influence official policy. But the Poles had reacted strongly against the German settlement policy begun in the days of Bismarck and designed to shift the ownership of land from Poles to Germans. Even fiercer conflict was provoked by attempts to impose the German language in schools, particularly for religious education. School strikes, resulting in prison sentences for some parents withholding their children from attendance, made emotions run high. The Polish leadership was no longer aristocratic and clerical, but middle-class, national-democratic. In Upper Silesia there was no Polish aristocracy, hence for a long time no strong Polish nationalism, and the Centre party represented Catholic Germans and Poles. This had changed by the beginning of the new century and Adalbert Korfanty, the first Polish Nationaldemocrat to be elected from Upper Silesia, entered the Reichstag in 1903 and became a conspicuous representative of Polish nationalism. In spite of all official support, the progress made by Germanism against the Polish element was inconsiderable. The settlement policy did slightly increase German landholding and counteracted the westward emigration in the province of Posen, where the largest number of Poles in Germany lived, but the much higher Polish birthrate meant that the population balance continued to shift slightly in the Polish favour. The Jews, tending culturally towards Germany but politically towards the left liberals, had a low birthrate and high emigration rate and were in consequence a declining element. It was precisely such statistical facts that aroused the nationalist hysteria of the Hakatisten and their supporters. Superior German culture was seen to be under biological threat, social-Darwinist Angst ran high. In 1908 Bülow brought in a new settlement law which established the principle of expropriation as a means of strengthening German landownership in Posen. The chancellor wished to placate the Hakatisten and was at that point no longer dependent on the support of the Centre. Some Conservatives, though otherwise supporters of Germanism in the east, jibbed at establishing expropriation, even with compensation, as a principle and liked cheap Polish seasonal labour. Bethmann Hollweg thus inherited a situation in which the Scharfmacher had had their way and, as in other respects, he tried to reduce the temperature. In 1910 the new castle in Posen was inaugurated by the Kaiser and numerous prominent Poles were invited to the celebrations. They found themselves under attack as conciliators in the nationalist Polish press. Bethmann himself came under attack from the Hakatisten for not making enough use of the expropriation legislation and as a result he tightened the screw again in 1912. On the eve of war the tensions between the rival nationalisms ran as high as ever. The only factor restraining Polish nationalism in Prussia was the fact that the Prussian state was clearly a less despotic and arbitrary taskmaster than the Russian, though perhaps worse than the Austrian. What there was of the Prussian Rechtsstaat with regard to the Poles gave them some room for manoeuvre. The Polish question was a microcosm of the situation that faced Bethmann Hollweg on the larger stage of international policy.

Alsace-Lorraine was the other big internal nationality problem. To avoid complications in establishing the federal structure of the Reich, Bismarck had not given these two previously unconnected regions full federal status, but made them a Reichsland, directly ruled from Berlin through a Statthalter. There was much pro-French sentiment, at least among the articulate classes, and the pull of French culture remained strong. As a constitutional anomaly, without the full federal status of other parts of Germany, there was a sense of second-class citizenship. Administration by German officials was not popular and often repressive. The Kulturkampf stoked up antagonism among the mainly Catholic population. Gradually more local autonomy was given and this encouraged those who were prepared to accept that their region was part of the German Reich and would not return to France in the foreseeable future. To set the seal on this acceptance the status of Alsace-Lorraine within the Reich would have to be normalized, so that the inhabitants could feel on a par with the citizens of other parts of the Reich. To such a settlement Bethmann Hollweg now turned his hand, but it was bound to raise at least two thorny problems. One was how to fit Alsace-Lorraine into the federal structure without disturbing its delicate balance, the problem Bismarck had side-stepped. The second contentious issue was what electoral system should be introduced. It could not be the Prussian three-tier one, which was now not acceptable anywhere south of the Main. But the Conservatives would fight universal suffrage tooth and nail, as breaching the dam they had constructed against it. The Bethmann Hollweg proposals gave Alsace-Lorraine three votes in the Bundesrat, but they could not be cast if they were decisive in giving Prussia a majority. The franchise was to be equal and without this the SPD and the left liberals would not have supported the new constitution for the Reichsland. It was the first time that the SPD was consulted and supported a major legislative proposal that actually became law. It was a clear indication that revolutionary rhetoric and gestures had lost their full meaning in practice. The Conservatives were bitter in their opposition and for them, as for the chauvinist section of opinion, the chancellor was irremediably soft, a *Schlappmacher*.

Bethmann Hollweg's foreign policy

It was to become a major incubus on the chancellor's conduct of foreign affairs that there were so many who believed him to be a *Schlappmacher*. It made it that much more difficult for him to do what common sense clearly dictated he should do: reduce tensions and loosen the formation of blocks potentially hostile to Germany. The highest priority was a reduction of the Anglo-German antagonism and this could only be done if the naval arms race was scaled down. So far all attempts to defuse the Anglo-German naval race had foundered on the refusal of the Kaiser and Tirpitz, backed by much vocal opinion, to accept any limitation of the German rate of building. The only condition on which they would agree to such a limitation would have been a British declaration of neutrality in a war involving Germany. This would have seriously curtailed the British diplomatic freedom of manoeuvre, running counter to the traditional British aim of a balance of power in Europe, and was therefore unacceptable to the British. Even this fundamental difficulty in Anglo-German relations was, however, not beyond hope of resolution and in other respects, colonial and Balkan questions, Bethmann Hollweg did achieve a certain relaxation of tension with Britain. It required a good deal of courage in face of the loud-mouthed machismo displayed not only by the nationalist leagues, but across a wide party spectrum in the Reichstag. Had Germany been a fully parliamentary country the conduct of foreign policy would not necessarily have been easier. The chancellor himself did not want to turn his back on *Weltpolitik* and in the existing climate that would have been an impossibility. He did not, however, want to damage the security of the Reich in Europe for the sake of ill-defined or non-existent colonial advantages.

It was therefore unfortunate that the first big crisis of Bethmann's period of office, the second Morocco crisis, did just that and so inflamed public opinion that it further reduced the chancellor's freedom of action. In fact the signals had been set in favour of Franco-German economic cooperation in Morocco by an agreement of February 1909, but one German firm, the brothers Mannesmann, was not satisfied and started to stir up opinion. The pan-Germans and the Central Association of German Industrialists took up the cudgels on behalf of Mannesmann and the German stake in Morocco and in March 1910, long before the crisis came to the boil, the Bethmann Hollweg government was accused in the Reichstag of weakness in the representation of German interests. In these years the National Liberals were especially to the fore in beating the patriotic drum, to compensate for their turn to the left in domestic affairs. Stresemann, the up and coming young man behind the party leader Bassermann, complained on 15 March 1910 in the Reichstag, with reference to Morocco, that German interests abroad were not being asserted with sufficient vigour, when recent events in the Near East had shown that only a policy of strength brought dividends. It was in fact the case that the French were strengthening their military hold on Morocco at this time, in face of growing disorder and loss of control by the Sultan. This culminated in the occupation of the capital Fez in April 1911, a step which could undoubtedly be interpreted as a breach of the Algeciras agreements and of the Franco-German agreement of February 1909.

By this time Kiderlen-Wächter was state secretary for foreign affairs. Bethmann had wanted to appoint him when he took over the chancellorship, but having once been part of the Kaiser's inner entourage, he had incurred the monarch's displeasure by ill-judged remarks and had been exiled as ambassador to Bucharest. He was an experienced diplomat and wanted to use the situation in Morocco, favourable to Germany in international law, to improve both the foreign and domestic position of the Reich. The French would be made to see that they could not ignore German interests, that their alliances, particularly the entente with Britain, could not help them and that they were therefore well advised to seek conciliation with Germany, a policy which had considerable political support in France. If Franco-German understanding became a fact, then the whole block system with its unfavourable implications for Germany would fall to the ground. Domestically the government would be seen to have made firmness pay. Kiderlen did not want war with France, for he knew that the Kaiser was strongly opposed to war for a secondary issue like Morocco, but he calculated that going to the brink would work. As the crisis progressed, virtually all Kiderlen's anticipations were falsified by events and the opposite occurred. He deliberately stirred up the expectations of the German public by contacts with Heinrich Class, the chairman of the Pan-German League.

The big bang of the fist on the table came with the dispatch of the gunboat *Panther* to Agadir on 1 July 1911. The move was received with great acclaim by the German press and public opinion, the SPD's party paper *Vorwärts* being virtually the only major dissenting voice. The German public was led to expect that Germany would secure a chunk of Southern Morocco, whereas the government knew that the most that could be secured would be compensations in Central Africa, which would give Germany access to the Belgian Congo. Kiderlen-Wächter was forced to move towards an increasingly threatening posture *vis-à-vis* France and this evoked hostile reactions, particularly in Britain. On 21 July 1911 Lloyd George, generally regarded as the leader of the Radical and pacific element in the Liberal government, was authorized to fire a warning shot across the German bows, in a speech he was due to make at the Mansion House that evening. British and German public opinion was now roused to a high state of mutual hostility. There was a considerable risk of war and when there were rumours that the Kaiser was unwilling to go to war over Morocco, even he came under attack. Germany did not really want war, even Tirpitz thought the navy was not yet ready for it, and Kiderlen's bluff was not helped by a stock exchange panic in September. In the final settlement in November 1911 the German gains were disappointing: all claims to Morocco were abandoned and the compensation was the transfer of a large but valueless tract of territory from the French Congo to the German Cameroons.

When the Reichstag met in the autumn the screams of disappointed chauvinism were deafening. Even the leading Centre party spokesman Count von Hertling, soon to become Bavarian prime minister and six years later the last but one imperial chancellor, said that too high a price would be paid for peace if it was bought at the cost of Germany's world position. Bethmann had great difficulty in pleading for a more rational assessment. Attacking the Conservative leader

Heydebrand he said: 'To bring, for the sake of utopian plans of conquest and for party purposes . . . the national emotions to boiling point, means to compromise patriotism and to throw away a valuable asset.' Only Bebel castigated the armaments race and the flirtation with war and said prophetically: 'The time will come when the bugles of war will sound throughout Europe, 16 to 18 million men will answer, the flower of the manhood of the various nations, and armed with the best murder weapons they will fight each other on the battlefield . . . the bourgeois world is approaching its twilight of the gods [laughter]. Be assured it is approaching.' It was seven years to the day to the collapse of the empire.

The repercussions of Agadir

The Agadir crisis carried a real risk of war and it involved public opinion as never before. Bethmann and Kiderlen might have liked to return to secret diplomacy, as did Sir Edward Grey and most of the other principal players, but it was no longer possible. Bassermann, the National Liberal leader who vied with the Conservatives in the stridency of his nationalism, demanded that the Reichstag be kept more fully informed about the conduct of foreign policy. Far from loosening the ring of encirclement, as it was seen in Germany, Kiderlen's conduct of the second Morocco crisis had tightened it. The Anglo-German antagonism, reflected in the press and public opinion of both countries, became more intense. In Germany Britain was now seen as the chief obstacle everywhere to legitimate German aspirations to world power. Anglo-French defence cooperation became closer, on land and sea. In the minds of men like Helmuth von Moltke, the chief of staff and nephew of the victor of 1870, the notion of preventive war was being more actively entertained.

Germany was on the eve of Reichstag elections, due in January 1912. The hysterical attacks on the government's alleged weakness owed something to the fear that these elections would give even greater strength to the SPD and so it turned out. Electoral participation rose to its highest level, nearly 85 per cent (see Appendix: Table 9). Resentment at the selfish behaviour of the Black–Blue block over taxation led to a considerable drop in the Centre's vote, from 19.4 to 16.4 per cent. Many Catholic workers were no longer casting their vote according to their religion, but according to their economic interest. The Conservative loss of votes was slight on the first ballot, but their loss of seats considerable, from 60 to 43. The Free Conservatives got only 3 per cent and 14 seats, and were becoming marginal. The National Liberals lost slightly in terms of votes, more in terms of seats. The now united left liberals, the *Fortschrittspartei*, gained votes, but lost seats. The leaders had made an agreement with the SPD to cooperate on the second ballot, but this was not popular with voters in either camp and produced many left liberal abstentions on the second ballot. All the seats won by the left liberals were won on the second ballot, because the SPD gave them a clear run and because middle-class voters saw them as the lesser evil to the SPD. The big gainers were the SPD, with nearly 35 per cent of the vote, 28 per cent of the seats, 110 seats out of 397. It was a sensational result and it moved the SPD to the centre of all political calculations.

The ghettoization of the party, as well as its own refuge in revolutionary rhetoric, was becoming ever more unreal. Nothing could disguise the deep divide that ran through the German body politic. How much of the socialdemocratic surge was due to economic factors, how much to the loss of prestige suffered by the establishment in the Morocco crisis, is debatable, but the former was undoubtedly more important. What few outside the socialist camp noticed in their panic, was the fact that the SPD had nearly exhausted its voter potential. Between 1903 and 1912 it vote had risen by only another three percentage points.

The elections left Bethmann without any majority in the Reichstag on which he could rely, but this mattered less than it would have done under a parliamentary system. It accorded with what had always been his concept, to govern 'above parties'. He still could not, nor did he intend to, go against the in-built conservatism of the system, the mesh of influences that resulted from monarchy, Junkers, Prussia, bureaucracy and army. No further constitutional or systemic change came onto the agenda. Yet so many elements in this conservative power complex felt they had their backs to the wall and that Bethmann could not be trusted to defend the system to the hilt. This engendered more than ever an apocalyptic mood: that there would after all have to be a coup d'état at home and a war abroad to cut the gordian knot, to fight off 'the combined attack of the golden and of the red international, both of them manipulated by the Jews'. To shore up the conservative position organizations to stimulate populist chauvinism were more than ever necessary. A new organization the *Deutsche Wehrverein* with a large individual and corporative membership appeared, led by the retired General Keim, who in the Navy League had already proved himself a scourge of the establishment through his radical nationalism. Nationalist organizations and opinion pounced on any sign of backsliding and softness in the Bethmann Hollweg team. The two Conservative parties, the German-Conservatives and the Free Conservatives (also known as Reichspartei) had previously often been suspicious of mass organizations. In the earlier stages of the naval expansion the mainly Prussian and agrarian Conservatives had not always been in the forefront of *Weltpolitik*. Now Conservatives could see only too well that mass organization, beyond the economic mobilization achieved by the Bund der Landwirte, was a necessity. Altogether the new right became more radical, social Darwinist, racist, anti-Semitic, in favour of force and preventive war. Two widely read books were indicative of the mood, Heinrich Class's *If I were Emperor* (see p. 117) and Friedrich von Bernhardi's *Germany and the Next War*. Bernhardi extended the social-Darwinist view of the necessity of imperial expansion into the cultural sphere: 'We have fought for our national unity and thereby for our European power position in the last two great wars, but now we face the greater decision, whether to become and maintain ourselves as a world power and to obtain for German culture and outlook the respect which is its due across the globe and which so far it has not been given.' It was not necessarily the view of the majority of the public or of the inner circle of the establishment. A book published anonymously by the chancellor's private secretary, Kurt Riezler, articulated the widely held view that the growing economic interdependence of the major powers made war less likely and more irrational. Opinions about a future war were shaped on the one hand by the survival of the notion of war as an an instrument of policy. From this point of view it was possible to contemplate a preventive war. The opposite view was that war had become so technological and total that it could no longer be controlled. Such contradictory speculations were not confined to Germany, as Norman Angell's famous book *The Great Illusion* shows. In 1913 75 per cent of German exports went to Europe and 54 per cent of German imports came from Europe; for Britain the equivalent figures were were 35 and 44 per cent.

Their electoral victory also posed problems for the SPD. This was highlighted by the events surrounding the elections to the Reichstag presidency when the new chamber was opened in February 1912. According to tradition, Scheidemann, one of the leaders of the SPD as the largest party, was elected the first vice-president of the parliament, Spahn of the Centre as president and a National Liberal as second vice-president. Scheidemann's election caused a storm of protest among the middle-class public. It was remembered that a few years earlier Scheidemann had declared that breach of their word was among the noblest traditions of the House of Hohenzollern. The two other members of the Reichstag Presidium resigned and their places were taken by members of the Progressive Party. When it came to the customary audience with the Kaiser, Scheidemann, following the feelings of his party, refused to go. The Kaiser then refused to receive the Reichstag presidium and a new one, without Scheidemann, was elected. The gulf that divided the German body politic was deep enough in reality, but it was constantly reinforced by rhetoric, gesture and symbolism.

Much of the Bebel–Kautsky strategy had been designed to persuade the party's mass following that the development of organization and the piling up of electoral majorities would result in concrete improvements for the workers, might even be the prelude to the great 'Kladderadatsch'. No such results followed, because the party could not translate its strength into action and the bourgeois parties were frozen into even greater immobility by the strength of the socialist threat. For years the party leadership had avoided provoking the authorities too much, lest repression would again damage the movement so painfully built up. There was also a reluctance to take opposition to navalism, *Weltpolitik* and bellicosity too far, lest the party be successfully tarred with the brush of treason and lack of patriotism, as had been the case in the Hottentot elections. The revisionist–reformist wing was increasingly inclined to give some support to national defence, sensing that at the grass roots patriotic pride was a force to be reckoned with. There was even a small group, centred round the journal *Sozialistische Monatshefte*, which argued that the SPD should not turn its back on *Weltpolitik*. Bebel, who died in 1913, was genuinely convinced that German policy, as seen for example in the second Morocco crisis, was driving the world towards a catastrophic war. Just before his death he warned the British foreign office, through the German consul in Zürich, about the ultimate aim of the Tirpitz naval programme and urged them to stand firm, if peace was to be saved. Had this become public he would have been accused of high treason, a charge which the opponents of the SPD were in any case habitually flinging against the whole socialist movement. After Bebel's death the new generation of party leaders, among whom Friedrich Ebert was to become the most prominent, were even more inclined to make sure that the party should not look unpatriotic. Otherwise there was immobility. In theory the SPD wanted fully parliamentary government, but since they knew they could not get it, at least in the short run, their only role was opposition. There was less talk of a block 'from Bebel to Bassermann', for it was quite unrealistic and did not continue even in Baden.

Efforts to reduce Anglo-German tension

Between the intransigence and growing radicalism on the right of the political spectrum and the continued exclusion of the SPD, Bethmann Hollweg, with his policy of the diagonal, somehow survived. In the last resort he depended on the emperor, another factor among the many that circumscribed his freedom of movement. In foreign affairs an accommodation with Britain was still his highest priority. Soon after the Reichstag elections, in February 1912, Lord Haldane, the secretary of state for war, visited Berlin. His mission was prepared by Albert Ballin, the Jewish chairman of the Hamburg–America shipping line and friend of the Kaiser, and Sir Ernest Cassel, the financier of German-Jewish origin, friend of Edward VII and grandfather of Edwina Mountbatten. Ballin and Cassel were representative of that section of business, finance and industry that was well aware of the growing economic interdependence of Britain and Germany. The aim of the Haldane mission was to find a way out of the naval arms race. In Berlin Haldane's arrival had been preceded by an intense tussle between Bethmann Hollweg and Kiderlen-Wächter, on the one hand, and Tirpitz, backed by the Kaiser, on the other. The chancellor wanted meaningful negotiations with the British that would include a curtailment of the German naval building programme. This would also fit in with the financial aims of Bethmann and his treasury secretary Wermuth, to maintain the balance between revenue and expenditure achieved by the reforms of 1909. Bethmann was in fact faced with a rise in the size of the army and of expenditure on it, something that would help to contain the pressure for more spending on the navy. For Bethmann the security of the Reich in Europe always had priority over *Weltpolitik*, which was popular but had meagre results. It was one of the curiosities of the German situation that the army had not been expanded in proportion to the increase in the population. The extent to which the annually available manpower was recruited and trained in Germany lagged behind that of other continental European powers, for example France. This was largely due to the fact that the still predominantly Prussian aristocratic senior officers of the army feared an expansion that would dilute the homogeneity of their force. More Socialdemocrats would be found among the other ranks and more members of the middle class among the officers. This view was, however, being contested by Colonel Ludendorff, one of the few staff officers of bourgeois origin and a military technocrat of great ability. He argued in a memorandum of 1912, written on the basis of the Schlieffen plan, that it was urgent that the available manpower should be more fully recruited and trained. He became temporarily *persona non grata* and it was not till the following year that his recommendations were at least partially implemented in a major army reform. A minor increase, of 29,000 men, was agreed by the Reichstag in June 1912, supported not only by the right wing parties, but also by the Centre and the Progressives. The German lack of urgency in exploiting their manpower potential is sometimes cited as an argument in favour of their peaceful intentions immediately before 1914, but it is more likely to be further evidence for the absence of coherence in the German decision-making processes.

In the meantime the Haldane mission had ended in failure. The German position still was that they would agree to a major slowing of their naval building programme only in return for a British declaration of neutrality in a continental European war. In the German view the acceptance of naval limitations was tantamount to becoming a junior partner to the British Empire in the world outside Europe. In the British view a far-reaching declaration of neutrality would mean the acceptance of German hegemony on the continent. The negotiations were complicated and so were the positions held by different elements in the inner circles of government on both sides of the water. On the German side Tirpitz was still wedded to the view that he could build a navy sufficiently powerful to threaten Britain to such an extent that she would have to become Germany's ally on German terms. He still felt that he could reduce Britain's naval advantage, based on having 'two keels to one', to 'two keels to three'. Bethmann had some success in detaching the Kaiser, at least temporarily, from backing Tirpitz by a threat of resignation, but in the end the Germans were not satisfied with what the British offered in terms of neutrality, while the British could not accept the slightly reduced rate of naval building on offer from the Germans as sufficient. The German naval proposals of 1912 went ahead and the views of Tirpitz prevailed over those of the chancellor. It was another indication of the weakness of political control over vital military and naval decisions under the German system, and of the chaotic decision-making process at the very top. An important consequence of the failure of the naval negotiations was a further closing of ranks between Britain and France. The staff conversations between the two countries received more official recognition and a naval understanding enabled Britain to concentrate more of her fleet in home waters. This more than ever invalidated the calculations on which the great Tirpitz naval building programme was based. Yet the German public enthusiasm for the navy was undiminished and in the Reichstag the SPD was the only major party voting against the naval law of 1912. When the British talked of the German navy being a luxury, while the British was a necessity, German nationalist opinion felt this to be an 'impertinence'.

The Balkan wars

It was, however, not the end of the efforts of Bethmann Hollweg and Kiderlen-Wächter to bring about a détente in Anglo-German relations. The next major European crisis, the first Balkan war in the autumn of 1912 brought Britain and Germany together in a form of crisis management that enabled a major European war to be avoided on this occasion. The Young Turk regime in Constantinople had attempted a renewal of the Ottoman empire and a tightening of central control, but the Italian seizure of Libya in February 1912 showed that the Turkish empire was as close to collapse as ever. This emboldened the Balkan states, Serbia, Bulgaria and Greece, to aim for the final liquidation of Turkey in Europe. The impending conflict faced Germany with difficult decisions. On the one hand she had extensive interests in Turkey, which were considered by some to be the most important and potentially rewarding aspect of *Weltpolitik*. On the other hand a further rise of nationalism among the Balkan nationalities affected Austria-Hungary and also held the possibility of conflict between Russia and Austria. It remained fundamental for German policy that Austria-Hungary had to be sustained. The outbreak of war in October 1912 produced a Turkish defeat, but Bulgarian troops failed to take Constantinople. For some weeks there was a considerable risk of war between Austria and Russia, for the emergence of a Greater Serbia was seen in Vienna as a mortal threat. A general European war dragging in all the major powers, on the pattern that did in fact occur in July 1914, could not be excluded, since Russia would have to take the side of Serbia.

When war scares were at their height in December 1912, the Kaiser, in a panic and veering between fear of war under adverse conditions and determination not to abandon Austria in an extremity, called a meeting, on 8 December, of his closest military and naval advisers, but without the knowledge of Bethmann or Kiderlen. The mood of the Kaiser may be gauged from a note which he made on the same day for his foreign secretary: 'In an eventual struggle for existence, which the Teutonic race in Europe (Austria, Germany) will have to fight against the Slavs (Russia) supported by the Romance race (France), the Anglo-Saxons will be found on the side of the Slavs. The reason: Envy. Fear of our becoming too powerful.' The 'war council' of 8 December 1912 has often been seen as a preparation for the war that eventually came in 1914. Moltke, the chief of the General Staff, said he considered war inevitable and the sooner it came the better. Tirpitz pleaded for a delay of 18 months, to complete the widening of the canal linking the Baltic and North Seas, and to allow for the building of more submarines. There was talk of preparing public opinion for war through the press. The meeting had in fact hardly any concrete consequences and Bethmann and Kiderlen remained in control of diplomacy. But the meeting showed that the hysterical mood of sections of the German public was shared by some of the top decision-makers. The ideas of a fight to the finish for racial supremacy and of preventive war had become common currency.

For the moment these ideas did not prevail. It was largely due to the cooperation of Britain and Germany that a conference of the ambassadors of the great powers met in London on 17 December 1912 and for many weeks afterwards to produce an agreed settlement for the Balkans. It proved difficult for the great powers to impose their will on the smaller Balkan countries and to control what was going on in the region. Serbia wanted an outlet on to the Adriatic, while it was still the chief concern in Vienna to prevent Serbia from exercising an irredentist pull on the nationalities in the Habsburg empire that threatened its disintegration. German diplomacy had no direct interest in checking Serbia and had some promising commercial interests there, but could not afford to allow its Austrian partner to be weakened or humiliated. If it came to a racial clash between Teuton and Slav, the

Germans had to back the Teutonic element and its pre-eminence in the Habsburg dominions. There were also other considerations, the German stake in Turkey, the maintenance of the Triple Alliance, which required attention to the Italian interests in the Adriatic. Even more important was the cooperation with Britain in controlling the Balkan situation, which provided some antidote to the failure to end the naval arms race. The preliminary peace concluded in London on 13 May 1913 did not end the Balkan turmoil, for only six weeks later, on 29 June, Bulgaria, which had borne the brunt of the fighting against Turkey, attacked its former allies, Serbia and Greece, who were joined by Rumania in the second Balkan war. In this second phase Vienna tended to back Bulgaria as a means of containing Serbia, whereas Berlin favoured Greece and Rumania, with whom the Hohenzollerns had dynastic ties. Among the many reasons why a year later, in the July crisis of 1914, the Germans felt they had to back Austria to the hilt was that they could not afford to repeat the lukewarm attitude towards their principal ally that they had shown the year before. Berchtold, who had become Austrian foreign minister in 1912, sometimes wondered during the Balkan wars of 1912/13 if his country might not be better off if it switched alliances.

Europe had frequently teetered on the brink of war during the Balkan crisis. This strengthened the hands of those in the German General Staff who were asking for a further substantial increase in the size of the army. The minister of war, Heeringen, who had hitherto resisted a large increase on grounds of quality, logistics and political reliability, now gave way and in March 1913 proposals were put forward to increase the strength of the army by 117,000 men and 19,000 officers and non-commissioned officers. The size of the army was to rise from 750,000 officers and men to 816,000 by October 1915. The total rise was much less than the 300,000 figure that had been demanded by Ludendorff, to which Moltke, the chief of staff, had given his backing. Bethmann Hollweg managed to stave off further naval increases, which would have acted as a provocation for the British. The army expansion raised once more the question of Reich finances, for the settlement over which Bülow had fallen four years earlier was now definitely inadequate. Increased taxes on property became unavoidable and a once for all capital tax levied by the Reich was agreed. The SPD voted for this tax, though opposing the army increases as such. A majority of the party thought it was important to establish the principle that the propertied classes should bear the brunt of the burden and that the Reichstag could levy a direct property tax. A left-wing minority of the Reichstag SPD deputies would have preferred to oppose the whole package of army expansion and its finance and to dare the government to dissolve the Reichstag on this issue. The majority felt that such a tactic would enable the government to stage a rerun of the Hottentot election, with the SPD being branded as unpatriotic. It was another sign that the party was being driven towards reformism by circumstances, even though the official centrist line of Bebel and Kautsky remained in tact. The divisions and eventual split in the SPD which the war would cause were being foreshadowed.

The Conservatives, on the other hand, opposed the finance package, thereby emphasizing their isolation. Even for the sake of national security they were unwilling, so it looked, to abandon their privileged social and political position. In the debate on the army expansion a great deal of bitterness against this privileged position surfaced across the political spectrum outside the Conservative ranks. Three of six cavalry regiments demanded in the government proposals were deleted and other symbols of military feudalism, such as duelling, came under attack. The radical nationalism of the chauvinist leagues was mainly middle class and impatient of such relics of aristocratic privilege. The SPD was publicly anti-militaristic, whatever its ordinary voters felt, but even in the two liberal parties aristocratic exclusivity in the army was no longer acceptable. The leader of the beleaguered Conservatives, von Heydebrand und der Lasa, openly admitted that they were only delaying as long as possible the inevitable onset of parliamentariz-ation and democracy, but the Prussian aristocratic–agrarian stranglehold on key centres of power like court and army remained in tact. The foundation of yet another league, the *Preussenbund* (Prussian Association), indicated that they were unwilling to surrender. The Centre party now abandoned the Blue–Black block, their alliance of the previous years with the Conservatives. The Centre was much more conscious of having to maintain the loyalty of Catholic working-class voters and possibly expanding its base beyond Catholicism. The Christian trade unions played their part in some of the big labour conflicts of this period. Nevertheless the Centre party was still part of the broad national consensus on army expansion and on a policy of strength abroad.

For Bethmann Hollweg the problem remained that there was no secure majority for the government in the Reichstag when political and ideological polarization was greater than ever. This ideological clash meant that the political parties were more important again, as opposed to lobbies and interest groups, which had at one time almost by-passed them. But no new coalition between the parties was in sight. Bethmann could not shout *Weltpolitik* from the housetops, the way Bülow had done, to distract from domestic conflict, because it was now too dangerous. There was no major progress in social policy after 1911, which had always been conceived in official circles as a way of either weakening the hold of the SPD on the workers or strengthening the reformist tendency within the SPD. Such alleviating strategies were condemned as soft on the confrontationist right, which for this purpose included not only the rabid anti-socialists of the nationalist leagues, but also sections of heavy industry. On the other hand there was no majority in the Reichstag for right-to-work legislation, which would have curtailed the freedom to strike and to picket.

There was a new version of Sammlungspolitik, the Cartel of the Productive Classes (see p. 116), relying heavily on the *Mittelstandsideologie*, the idea that the middle classes, from wealthy industrialists down to artisan and white-collar workers, were the backbone of a healthy nation. In fact the Mittelstand had become a nebulous concept, because the middle classes were now very diverse and lacked almost any homogeneity. The cartel hardly became politically operational, but on the other hand the Hansabund, once the hope of left liberalism and the exporting industries, also lost impetus. There were differences on tariffs, due to be reviewed in 1917. Industry as a whole opposed the more extreme protectionist demands of the agrarians, because of their effect on the basic cost of living and the level of wages. The non-tariff protective devices on which the farming community insisted, for example the system of import vouchers and stringent veterinary controls, were not liked by industrialists. On such issues the differences between heavy industry and the exporting commercial and financial sectors remained considerable. Then there was the fundamental division between those who envisaged a reform of the system, parliamentarization, curtailment of the monarchical power, defeudalization of the military, and those who wished to stop all such developments and looked to a resolution by coup d'état, caesaristic leadership and war. The dividing line ran through the parties. Among the National Liberals, for example, there were those, sometimes known as Old National Liberals, who wanted to stress anti-socialism and were prepared to associate with the Conservatives in a new cartel. The Young National Liberals, of whom Stresemann was typical, were anti-socialist, but not prepared to accept the totally backward-looking policies of the Conservatives. They saw *Weltpolitik*, the aggressive development of markets for the dynamic export industries, as the key to growing prosperity that would take the edge off domestic social conflicts. Ernst Bassermann, the leader of the party, a Baden patrician, displayed much ingenuity in keeping the party united.

The Zabern affair

The stalemate in the German situation was strikingly illustrated in the Zabern incident, in November 1913. In the small Alsatian garrison town of Zabern (Saverne) it was reported in the local newspaper that a young lieutenant had told his recruits that if they got involved in a dispute with a local, for whom he used the expressly forbidden derogatory term *Wacke*, he should use his weapons to put him down and would be rewarded by him personally with ten marks, to which his corporal said he would add a further three. The military command in Alsace tried to hush up this incident and refused the advice of the civilian governor to remove the offending young officer. As a result there were peaceful demonstrations by the civilian population in Zabern, which were dealt with heavy-handedly, with numerous arrests, by the military authorities. This interference by the military in the maintenance of law and order caused a storm of indignation among the German public. In the Reichstag Bethmann Hollweg had to admit that there had been a breach of the law by the military authorities, but his condemnation of their conduct was somewhat restrained. The minister of war, von Falkenhayn, put most of the blame on the press and still defended the military on the basis of the imperial power of command, and the chancellor did not contradict him. All this caused great indignation in the Reichstag, which passed a vote of censure on the chancellor by 293 to 54 votes. Only the two conservative parties supported the chancellor, but only the SPD demanded his resignation. He somewhat ironically referred to the 'so-called vote of no-confidence', when a few days later, on his return from seeing the Kaiser, he made it clear that he would not draw any consequences from it. Once again an opportunity to enforce the will of the elected parliament was missed. The majority against the chancellor was a purely negative one. In the meantime the Kaiser's reaction to the Zabern incident had been determined by the *maison militaire* that surrounded him and he covered the conduct of the military authorities in Alsace with his power of command. The commanding general remained in his post, while the civilian governor resigned. Any benefit derived from the constitutional reforms of 1911 in Alsace-Lorraine was lost. Although Bethmann Hollweg managed in the end to obtain a regulation, which defined more narrowly in what circumstances the military authorities were entitled to intervene in cases of civil disorder, the extra-constitutional position of the military, covered by the imperial power of command, remained intact. The Zabern incident showed again that a move forward towards a fully parliamentary system was blocked and that the exceptional position of the military was an essential part of the blockage. On the other hand there was now a limit beyond which the public was not prepared to see the military exercise their extra-constitutional position.

There was a dysfunction between the retarded nature of the German constitutional and political system and the advanced state of many of Germany's economic and social arrangements. The political system was, however, defended not merely because those whose privileges were tied to it were stubbornly refusing to give them up. The radical nationalist ideology of the pan-Germans and others like them amounted to an assertion of the superiority of this system to decadent Western democracy and primitive Slav despotism. This made it doubly difficult to remove the blockages to change. On the other hand the enormous socio-economic changes that had taken place in the quarter century of the Wilhelmine era was bound to lead others, not only socialists brought up on Marx but the more liberal section of the middle-class world, to the conclusion that reform was urgent. Hence the deep, but also shifting polarization of the different camps. Nobody could ignore the socio-economic transformation. Germany by 1913 had a population of 65 million and was second only to the United States in its share of world industrial production. Britain, with a smaller population, had dropped to third place. The figures for share of world trade are equally striking: in 1880 Germany had just over a tenth of world trade, Britain well over a fifth. By 1913 Germany ran Britain a close second, with 12.3 against 14.2 per cent, with the USA in third place at 11 per cent. In 1890 the per capita social product in Britain was 1130 (1970 US$), against 729 in Germany, by 1910 the figures were 1302 to 958. Germany was the fifth richest state in Europe, but the three countries coming between Britain and Germany were small, Belgium, Denmark and Switzerland.

Cultural clashes

There were non-political symptoms of the tension between a high level of modernity and the tradition, authority, hierarchy and patriarchy reinforced by the constitutional and political straitjacket. There was a level of generational conflict probably more pronounced than in other European societies. In the closing years of the old century there developed, from small beginnings known as *Wandervogel* (wandering bird), a youth movement that formed a counter-culture to the rigid codes governing bourgeois behaviour. Its members were boys, and soon also girls, mostly from upper middle-class backgrounds attending the Gymnasien. They went on excursions into the countryside, gathered round camp fires, sang folksongs, cultivated comradeship and sought escape from the constraints of the parental home and the strict discipline of the German school system. It was a quest for nature, sincerity, truth, inwardness; it implied criticism of the regimentation and bureaucratization of life, of the complacent, self-satisfied existence of their elders. The so-called *bündische Jugend* had many variants and sub-groups and spawned a diverse ideological penumbra, which defies categorization into left or right. Many of those who were adolescents before 1914 and survived the Great War owed their intellectual formation to this movement, but they could end up Communist party members or Nazi storm troopers. The early groups were pronouncedly male, but after girls formed their own groups there were many mixed groups, aiming at a natural relationship of the sexes and a comradeship between them. This implied criticism of the hypocrisy and double moral standards of bourgeois society. In the youth movement the attitude to sexuality was ascetic rather than libertine. By 1913 the bündische Jugend had 25,000 members and another 75,000 had passed through these groups. In October 1913 there was a legendary meeting of two or three thousand members of the *Freideutsche Jugend* (Free German Youth) on the Hohen Meissner in the Harz mountains, which passed the following resolution: 'Free German Youth wants to form its own lifestyle, by its own determination and responsibility, and with inner truthfulness. It will insist on this inner freedom in all circumstances.' For all its desire to escape from societal constraints, the bündische Jugend also shared many characteristics of this society. It cultivated the apolitical as superior to political commitment and provided an escape from real engagment with reform and change. There was much celebration of the hero, the leader, the Volk, a romanticising of solidarity and the pre-industrial idyll, but only the exceptional tensions that had built up in German society could give rise to such a movement and make it so influential.

Youth sought escape from societal restraints in pre-war Germany and so did women. The German women's movement was similar to that in other European countries at this time and developed round similar issues, educational and professional opportunities, problems of special concern to women, such as prostitution, abortion and later on birth control. The early appearance of a socialist proletarian party caused a deeper divide in the women's movement than elsewhere, just as it did in the body politic as a whole. There was great diversity of aim and orientation among organized middle-class women, but they nevertheless managed to set up a federal body in 1894, the *Bund Deutscher Frauenvereine* (Federation of German Women's Associations), which through its affiliated organizations had some three to four hundred thousand members by 1913. It was a markedly moderate movement and there were few radical feminist voices within it. It was slow to take up the demand for political rights for women, particularly the right to vote, but it did affiliate, in 1907, a previously separate *Verband Fortschrittlicher Frauenvereine* (Federation of Progressive Women's Associations), dedicated to the push for women's right of political participation. The BDF kept its distance from the socialdemocratic women's movement, which had championed the right to vote from an early date. Bebel had a special commitment to women's rights, social and political, and had managed to include the demand for female suffrage in the Erfurt programme of 1891. Even within the socialdemocratic women's movement, part of the socialist sub-culture, there were many differences of view and emphasis. The radical/reformist divide in the party as a whole also affected the SPD's women's section and had additionally divisive issues to cope with. There was the question of priorities, whether the class or the gender emancipation was more urgent. The radical feminist position had a high profile because one or two charismatic women, Rosa Luxemburg and Clara Zetkin the best known, were its protagonists. There were obstacles to female emancipation even in the labour movement, for the trade unions were predominantly male organizations which often saw women as rivals in the workplace. In a country where the equal suffrage for all men was as yet so imperfectly realized and the subject of a great political and ideological battle, the right of women to vote became a subsidiary matter. There was no militant women's suffrage movement in Germany, as there was in Britain. The breaking of sexual taboos was as traumatic a process in Germany as anywhere. Freud wrote in German and his views, as those of other prophets of a new psychology, had an early airing in the German-speaking countries. New sexual mores, implicit in the emancipation of women, were a massive challenge in a society where there was so much patriarchy and hierarchy. German nationalism, with its cult of virility, was rooted in an intensely masculine consciousness that found it difficult to retreat from the subjection of women.

The German artistic avant-garde in the decade before 1914 provides yet a further illustration of an exceptional degree of dissonance, protest and counter-cultural intensity. In painting, German expressionism became internationally significant, when the previous German impressionist school, itself a shock for the officially approved art, had still been somewhat imitative. Expressionism moves completely away from the representational, seeks out the chaos and turmoil beneath reality, goes beyond categories of beauty and ugliness, reflects the destructive forces below the conscious. It holds up a mirror to a society which sees itself as ordered and whole, but is in fact decadent and disintegrating. In the nature of the case expressionism was not a 'school' and not coherent, but the various groups and individuals in Germany that can be roughly labelled expressionists have retained their resonance for later generations. There was the *Brücke*, with painters like Kirchner and Schmidt-Rottluff, individuals like Kokoschka, the *Blaue Reiter*, with Kandinsky, later a leading abstract painter, and Marc and Macke, both of them casualties of the First World War. In literature a dramatist like Frank Wedekind depicted Lulu, femme fatale, a challenge to all sexual repression and hypocrisy, but also destructive of those who succumb to her as well as of herself. Alban Berg turned Lulu into an opera and was himself a practitioner of the twelve-note system associated with Schönberg. In music, where Germany had for long been the leader, there was also the feeling that traditional forms had reached the end of the road and that there had to be a completely new way forward. Even the last giant of German music, Richard Strauss, experimented with atonalism in two of his operas before 1914, *Salome* and *Elektra*, though he turned away from it again. One of the literary expressionists, Kasimir Edschmid, summarized their aims: 'The world exists. It would be pointless simply to repeat it. But it is the great task of art to trace this world in its ultimate convulsions, in its true essence.' But, as Max Weber remarked, this artistic counterculture could only exist as a counterpoint to that which it condemned. Across the arts therefore the radical break with tradition that is often associated with the Weimar Republic was already under way before 1914. The general public turned its back on this experimentation and the Kaiser's rejection of all modernism reflected its tastes more accurately than did the avant-garde. When William visited the National Gallery in Berlin in 1913, Valentini, the chief of his civil cabinet, made sure that a newly purchased picture by the impressionist Slevogt was hung, but only after the monarch had left the room in question. The acceptance of modernism even among the Kaiser's entourage does provide a clue to the creative tensions beneath the superficial triumphalism of Wilhelmine society in its later years. It is tempting see in this juxtaposition of doubt and assertiveness, in this mixture of doom-laden Angst with claims to world domination, a prelude to the catastrophe of war, itself both feared and desired.

The coming of war

The second Morocco crisis and the Balkan wars had not led to a general European war, but the July crisis of 1914 did. The final crisis should, however, not simply be seen as a repetition of the previous constellation or a recurrence of the same tensions leading by sheer force of repetition to final explosion. For such a con-clusion the situation was too complex and too many factors were simultaneously at work. Even some of the fundamental alignments, such as the alliance between Berlin and Vienna, were not irreducible factors. Just as the decision-makers of Vienna from time to time asked themselves whether the German alliance was still worthwhile for them, so there were voices in Germany questioning whether the maintenance of the ramshackle and decaying Habsburg empire was still in the German interest. There can be no doubt that the Balkan wars had improved the climate of Anglo-German relations and in most respects this improvement lasted right up to the July crisis.

Nevertheless some of the basic factors at work in the previous few years proved in the end more powerful. As far as Germany was concerned, Bethmann Hollweg and his circle of advisers were operating within narrow confines in seeking to maintain and advance their country's position as a world power while avoiding an immediate war. The pressure of what one might call pan-German bellicosity, but which extended in varying degrees of intensity through the political spectrum, was relentless. Even the slightest sign of flexibility in German diplomacy was greeted by loud screams of indignation by the chauvinist section of opinion and their organs in the press. A middle-of-the-road politician like Bassermann said, in connection with the army expansion of 1913: 'We have remained, in the course of our splendid ascent, a peaceful people. But we are in a new epoch, with new tasks, and the number of people and the amount of goods we have to defend has become greater.

What the blood of our fathers has achieved we do not want to lose. The number of our enemies is greater, but we can cope with any danger.' This defensive/offensive spirit infected the decision-making machinery and among the military took the form of an increasing disposition to preventive war. Even those who like the chancellor, at times the Kaiser, and many others, who realized that a general war might turn into an uncontrollable catastrophe, believed in strength, in the necessity of world power, in the impossibility of accepting retreat or loss of prestige. It was an article of faith that other powers could be made to do by a show of force what they would not otherwise willingly do.

The improvement of Anglo-German relations in the year before the outbreak of war produced two important colonial agreements. One, in August 1913, concerned another division of the Portuguese colonies in Africa, the second since 1898. The Germans wanted to consolidate an area in central Africa that would stretch from the Atlantic to the Indian Ocean and which, it was hoped, would eventually include the Belgian Congo. Belgian public opinion was divided on the decision to take over, as state territory, this large and important area which their king, Leopold II, had acquired by dubious means. The Portuguese colonies were in a sorry state and it was likely that sooner or later Portugal would be open to an offer to sell them. The German government had actively pushed, through banks like Deutsche Bank and Warburg, for an expansion of German investment in Mozambique and Angola. The British, in an early form of appeasement, were now prepared to meet German aspirations to a considerable extent, provided other interested parties, like France, were not neglected. In China there was also cooperation between British and German firms and banks, with both governments prepared to assist such cooperation, where necessary against third parties. This was the kind of quiet diplomatic and economic penetration, mainly in cooperation with Britain, which the Bethmann Hollweg government favoured. Unfortunately such a slow patient policy, which, as with the Portuguese colonies, the Germans did not want prematurely disclosed, could not easily satisfy strident nationalism at home. Anglophobe chauvinists could easily jump to the conclusion that perfidious Albion was offering meaningless concessions at the expense of others. Reliance on the increasing economic strength of the Reich, the approach favoured by the chancellor, would pay off only in the long run.

The other important Anglo-German agreement concerned what was widely regarded as the most promising venture of German financial imperialism, the Baghdad railway. In the Ottoman empire German economic penetration was also linked with political and military penetration, so that this area was becoming a sphere of German influence. It could be seen as an extension of a Central European economic block under German aegis, a concept which leading German industrialists saw as more realistic and promising than colonial acquisition in Africa. The German influence in Turkey was, however, still in competition with other powers, Russia, Britain and France. Moreover, the German contribution to the heavy investment required by the railway project was limited by what the restricted German capital market could bear. Cooperation with the other major providers of capital was therefore inescapable. Russia was economically not much in the running, but was still sensitive on the Straits question. This led to a short sharp crisis when in December 1913 a German general, Liman von Sanders, was appointed Inspector-General of the Turkish army and, unusually, commander of the Turkish army corps stationed in the Constantinople area. The situation, which nearly led to war, was resolved by a face-saving formula, under which Liman von Sanders was made a Turkish marshal, which relieved him of the command of the Constantinople army corps. The German military influence in Turkey, on top of her economic engagement, held out prospects that Germany would acquire an important sphere of influence reaching down to the Persian gulf when the long-expected collapse of the Ottoman empire would eventually occur. It was also evident that the build-up of German power on Russia's southern flank was exposing her to the hostility from St Petersburg that had previously focused on Britain. On the building of the Baghdad railway and on the oil concessions, in the long run even more important, there were long Anglo-German negotiations leading to agreements in the spring and summer of 1914, one on the railway as far Basra on 15 June 1914. The Germans had to make many concessions to British interests, for especially the government in New Delhi was concerned about a possible German penetration to the Persian gulf. French interests, financially still very important, had also to be considered. The Germans had, however, reason to be satisfied with the settlement, which left them with a potentially important stake in the area. To Bethmann Hollweg and his advisers it looked as if their patient policy of pursuing *Weltpolitik* without war and in junior partnership with the British empire was paying off.

The next great European crisis was to show, however, that agreement and collaboration with Britain on the periphery, coming after many years of friction, was not sufficient to counteract the fears and tensions produced by naval rivalry and fundamental security concerns on both sides. The assassination of the Austrian heir to the throne, Archduke Franz Ferdinand, and his wife at Sarajevo on 28 June 1914 produced a situation which seemed to offer the Bethmann Hollweg government a chance to achieve an easement of the German 'encircled' situation through a policy of calculated risk. Resolute Austrian action against Serbia would evoke some sympathy throughout Europe, though this was a factor that may well have been overestimated. In the circumstances there was, however, a good chance that the Austrians by swift action would stabilize the fragile condition of their multi-national empire. Many in Vienna, including the chief of staff Conrad von Hötzendorf and the foreign minister Berchtold, had been looking for such an opportunity for some time. Russian aspirations in the Balkans would be decisively set back. From the German point of view a degree of Russian humiliation might bring leading circles in St Petersburg to the conclusion that they would need to revise their existing system of alliances. They might even be inclined, this was a distant German dream, to replace their alliance with France and semi-alliance with Britain by a German link. There were other considerations among the ruling élites in Berlin. The military leaders, Moltke prominent among them, were still toying with the idea of a preventive war, the strategy they had advanced at the 'war council' of 8 December 1912. By 1917 Russian military capabilities would have fully recovered from the defeat of 1905 and the construction of railways in the western regions would make a more rapid mobilization possible. The basic premiss of the Schlieffen plan would be invalidated. If war was sooner or later inevitable, the sooner it came the better, so the military argued. Even Bethmann and his circle were overtaken by a certain fatalism about the probability of war that made the calculated risk acceptable. The chancellor's policy of collaboration with Britain had just lost credibility within the inner circle of decision-makers by reports, reaching Berlin through secret channels in May 1914, of Anglo-Russian talks about naval cooperation in case of war with Germany. Sir Edward Grey's public denial of such contacts did not enhance his credibility in German eyes. Fear of Russia increased and reinforced the argument that Austria as the only reliable remaining ally must be fully backed. All these debates, and others among the decision-makers, were echoed in a less-informed and cruder fashion among the general public and in the press. The pressure of nationalist opinion was such that the last eventuality that the government could contemplate was concession and conciliation, let alone a diplomatic setback.

These were some of the factors behind the so-called blank cheque which Berlin gave Vienna, namely that decisive action against Belgrade would receive full and unconditional German backing. The blank cheque was issued on the assumption that Vienna would act swiftly, while the tide of sympathy was flowing in its direction. Meanwhile the German government would maintain a public attitude of unconcern, emphasized by the fact that many of the leading players, including the Kaiser himself, were on holiday. The Austrians, however, did not come up to scratch. There was divided counsel in Vienna, with the Hungarian prime minister Tisza in particular opposing strong action against Serbia. It was not until 14 July that the decision was taken to despatch an ultimatum to Belgrade designed to lead to war. Its despatch was then further delayed until 23 July, after the departure from St Petersburg of the French President Poincaré, who had been there on a state visit. In any case the Austrian mobilization process was so slow that action against Serbia could only be taken by 4 August. All this meant that the original German strategy was unravelling, which was to use a limited war between Austria and Serbia, unleashed when public opinion was behind the former, to loosen the ties between Russia and the West. But it was too late and would have been too humiliating to revise this strategy now. Berlin, having encouraged Vienna to act, could not and would not now restrain it. Nor was it willing to press on Vienna the various offers of mediation that were now forthcoming, particularly from London. The German chancellor still hoped for a diplomatic triumph, while avoiding a general European war. The Kaiser, on his return from his northern yachting trip on 28 July, thought that a diplomatic success was in the bag, with the almost complete acceptance by Belgrade of Vienna's humiliating demands, and that further action was unnecessary. If Germany was unwilling to urge on its Austrian ally anything that looked like a retreat, then Paris and even London were unwilling to risk their relations with Russia by pressing strongly for compromise. Thus the crisis ground inexorably on, with mobilization timetables increasingly dominating events in the final hectic days. Under the constitution Moltke and the general staff were not under the control of the chancellor and had immediate access to the Emperor. To the last the chancellor hoped that he could rescue his strategy of securing a diplomatic triumph without war, but the deadlines to activate mobilization procedures progressively reduced his room for manoeuvre.

As war became increasingly inevitable, it was Bethmann Hollweg's main concern to make Russia look like the aggressor, particularly for domestic consumption, and in this he was successful. He knew that without the collaboration of the German labour movement the war could not be fought and that the German worker would respond to the call of the fatherland if it appeared to be under attack from the dark, reactionary forces of Tsarism. He took steps to prevent any repressive measures against the SPD, such as the arrest of their leaders and of prominent trade unionists. Such moves might well have been made by some of the commanding generals who would assume special powers under the state of siege that would come into operation on the outbreak of war. The chancellor had no direct constitutional power over these commanding generals, but he made sure that the minister of war, Falkenhayn, recommended that no arrests or other provocative steps should be taken, even though the Kaiser was demanding them. Contacts were made between officials and SPD leaders to counteract the impression, widespread in the SPD press, that the crisis was being exacerbated by the warmongers in Vienna. As for the British position, Bethmann hoped to the last for neutrality, but he knew that once the military machine was rolling Belgian sovereignty would be infringed. This swung British public opinion in favour of intervention. The policy of Grey had in any case made such intervention difficult to avoid. In Germany the British declaration of war reinforced the impression that the fatherland was under attack from powerful and envious rivals and had to be defended at all costs.

8 Germany during the war years 1914–1918

All the belligerent nations of Europe entered the war in an orgy of patriotic fervour. It is legitimate to doubt the depth and nature of this phenomenon, for everywhere it eventually gave way to a disillusionment so profound that horror of war became the dominant emotion of the interwar years. There was fear and anxiety as well as euphoria and enthusiasm. It was the opinion-forming classes that showed most enthusiasm, and there was less of it outside the large cities. For the moment, however, the fever of war was real enough, for without it the relentless slaughter could hardly have been sustained for four years. Nowhere was the enthusiasm provoked by the outbreak of war a more defining experience than in Germany. Suddenly the hitherto deeply divided German society appeared to experience a feeling of total solidarity in defence of the fatherland. It was 'the spirit of August', a unique moment of national uplift, celebrated in innumerable poems, recalled ever after by all those who wished to mobilize the German national spirit. It was encapsulated in the Kaiser's remarks, made on the advice of Bethmann Hollweg to the Reichstag deputies assembling in his Berlin palace before the meeting of 4 August: 'I no longer see parties, I see only Germans.' The most important political aspect of this spirit of national unity was the decision of the SPD to support the war. The German declaration of war did not require ratification by the Reichstag, but the initial credits to fight the war had to be voted by that body. There was also to be an enabling act which conferred on the Bundesrat almost unlimited powers to control and mobilize the German economy. In the Reichstag the attitude of the hitherto ostracised party was crucial. After the party presidium had by a majority decided to support the vote of credit, the parliamentary party followed suit, by a majority of 78 against 14. A three-line whip was imposed, against 24 dissenting votes. It fell to Hugo Haase, the chairman of the party and an opponent of the vote of credit, to declare the support of the party for the war at the crucial Reichstag sitting on 4 August. Not long ago the SPD had remained seated in the Reichstag when a cheer for the Kaiser was demanded; now by coupling the future of people and fatherland with the name of the Kaiser, they were able to join in the general patriotic acclamation.

It was again a defining moment. Bethmann's clever diplomatic manoeuvres, making Russia appear the aggressor, had helped the SPD to reach this decision. So had events like the murder on 31 July of Jean Jaurès, the French socialist leader, who only days earlier had sought to use international socialist solidarity to prevent the war. The crucial factor, however, was the patriotism of the German working class and the fact that it had long moved beyond the apartheid state from which the party and the unions still suffered. In this it did not differ from the working classes in the other belligerent countries, but they were not represented by parties as powerful and at the same time as politically ostracized as the German SPD. Nationalism was the reality, international working-class solidarity was the shadow, nation came before class, and this fact was most strikingly and with the greatest consequences demonstrated in Germany. Even many of those SPD Reichstag deputies who had clung to the traditional anti-war position of their party became convinced, as they travelled to Berlin for the crucial meetings of 3 and 4 August and witnessed the mood of the country, that the party would be committing suicide if it did not support the war.

The labour movement's change of course fundamentally altered the nature of German politics. The existing discrimination, which had kept avowed adherents of the SPD out of even lowly state employment on the railways and in the post office, had to end. The leaders of the party had to be treated by the government as partners, while they for their part expected their cooperation to be honoured by far-reaching changes, for instance abolition of the Prussian three-tier electoral law, at least after the anticipated victorious end of the war. This was, however, not what the massed forces of the right hoped for from the war. They expected it to stabilize the existing order and for this reason, as well as for others, would settle for nothing less than total victory. Only such a *Siegfrieden*, as it was usually called, would, by enabling the German people to enjoy the fruits of victory, reconcile them to the traditional distribution of power. The SPD's decision to support the war therefore defined the new battleground in German domestic politics, but before the domestic battle was reopened there was the *Burgfrieden*, the peace within the castle, the declared intention to refrain from all party fights and divisiveness. The German Burgfrieden was not in essence different from the position in the western democracies, where the outbreak of war also brought about a truce between the parties. In Britain, for example, party activity in the constituencies officially ceased and by-elections were no longer fought. But in the western democracies it was easier to sustain the party truce, for it was soon institutionalized in coalition government. In Germany the Burgfrieden made the public airing of dissent, mainly over war aims, difficult and therefore in the end doubly divisive.

Everything now depended on the fortunes of war. The German generals, led by the younger Moltke, had, in pressing for war, taken a colossal gamble. They had staked everything on putting into practice the basic concept of the Schlieffen plan, a swift annihilating campaign against France. The German right wing would wheel through Belgium and surround Paris and the French armies from the west. For the sake of this strategic concept they had tied their political leaders to the violation of Belgian neutrality, which made British entry into the war all but inevitable. For the Schlieffen plan to work everything had to go right and in war it rarely does. Moreover the plan, based on the elementary military principle of concentrating attack in one sector, had been substantially modified. Moltke could not bring himself to leave the sector along the Franco-German frontier in Alsace and Lorraine as thinly held as the plan envisaged. It was in this sector that the French armies tried to mount their offensive, for it was still universally accepted that in war attack was everything. The Germans had considerable success in stopping this offensive, but in achieving it they violated the principle of concentrating their forces on their right wing. Somewhat later more troops were detached from what was meant to be the decisive enveloping movement to stop the Russian incursion into East Prussia and to take Antwerp. In the decisive phase in September 1914 the German right wing was only half as strong as it should have been. It could push the French and British back, but it could not envelop and crush them. There were serious shortcomings of command, communication and logistics which deprived the Germans of the decisive victory that was vital to them. Moltke was a weak commander, failed to coordinate his lower commanders and lacked the communications system to keep a tight grip on the situation. The initial German mobilization was a masterpiece of railway planning, with a train crossing the Hohenzollern Bridge over the Rhine at Cologne every ten minutes. But the move through Belgium was slower than expected, partly because of fierce Belgian resistance. German measures to crush the Belgian guerilla tactics, uncomfortably reminiscent of the French *franc-tireurs* in the war of 1870, attracted international condemnation, adeptly exploited by Allied war propaganda. During the decisive battle of the Marne Marshal Joffre kept his nerve, while Moltke lost his. The German commander now feared that his own flank was overexposed and the liaison officer he sent out, Colonel Hentsch, ordered a pull-back of the line. The German gamble had failed, Moltke suffered a nervous breakdown and was temporarily and then permanently replaced by his deputy General Falkenhayn.

Little of this drama penetrated to the German public. On the face of it the German armies had advanced victoriously deep into France and the battle of the Marne was made out to be no more than a minor rectification of the front. Public attention was diverted by the successful reversal of the Russian 'steam roller' incursion into East Prussia, the only substantial violation of German territory that was to occur in four years of war. The heroes of the German counterattack in the East were Hindenburg and Ludendorff, respectively Commander in Chief and Chief of Staff of the Eastern Command. Hindenburg, whose impressive looks disguised a less than impressive intellect and personality, had been recalled from retirement at the age of 67. His function was to provide a figurehead for Ludendorff, who as a military technician was first-rate, but also had ruthless ambition and a brutal will to power. Ludendorff had overcome the obstacles to promotion that had dogged him before 1914 as an officer of bourgeois origin by the role he played in the seizure of Liege in the opening weeks of the war. In the battles of Tannenberg and of the Masurian lakes two Russian armies were largely annihilated in late August and early September 1914 and a powerful myth was created for the German public. Even so sober a politician as Bethmann soon saw Hindenburg and Ludendorff as the winning combination and their mythical stature among the people as a political fact that could be exploited. It escaped attention that the Russian enemy remained militarily a scarcely diminished part of the problem of fighting a two-front war. In the West Falkenhayn did try to keep the battle moving by trying further attacks between the Aisne and the Channel, but the technology of war had reached a point where the defence was stronger than the attack. In the final stages of these battles, in November 1914, the heroism of young volunteers who freely gave their lives impressed itself deeply on the public in Britain and Germany. The name Langemarck, where German volunteers fresh from the universities were mown down in their hundreds, became a symbol of unquestioning self-sacrifice in defence of the fatherland, similar to the associations assumed in Britain by Ypres and the poppies of Flanders. After another year or two of butchery not much of this spirit survived in either country.

German war aims

The spirit that prevailed at the outbreak of war in Germany and that gave rise to the Burgfrieden did not last long. It was an instinctive mobilization of the national will to survival in face of a perceived mortal threat and for the moment made it irrelevant what the aims of the war were. Paradoxically, as the prospect of immediate victory receded and the toll of war became more obvious, the German desire for specific and far-reaching war aims rose inexorably. The underlying feeling was that such heavy sacrifices could only be justified if the threat to the security of the Reich was removed in perpetuity. But the Reich in the centre of Europe could only be secure if it wielded a continental hegemony, though how exactly this hegemony was to be exercised remained a subject of debate. It was never clearly realized by the vast majority of Germans that such a continental hegemony, however informally exercised, was precisely what had brought the great hostile coalition into the field against Germany. If a negotiated peace should become necessary it could not be obtained on that basis.

Bethmann Hollweg was a moderate on the war aims question, but it was precisely this moderation that undermined his position and was a major factor in his eventual downfall. In a famous preliminary memorandum, drawn up by his confidant Kurt Riezler on 9 September 1914, before the Battle of the Marne ended hopes of a decisive German victory, the chancellor envisaged minor territorial acquisitions in the west, but a satellite status for Belgium and virtually for France as well. In the east a belt of buffer states would throw Russia back to where she had been somewhere in the eighteenth century. Soon more far-reaching territorial annexations east and west were vociferously demanded, a kind of formal continental empire, with colonial appendages, as opposed to Bethmann's vision of an informal empire based on German economic predominance. Intellectuals, academics and initially a majority of Germany's artistic community were to the fore in promoting a vision of the superiority of German *Kultur*, which justified not only Germany's self-defence but her claim to hegemony. In October 1914 ninety-three leading academics, writers and artists published an appeal to their opposite numbers in the western democracies in which they identified themselves unreservedly with alleged German militarism, without which 'German culture would long ago have been extinguished'. It ended with the words: 'Rest assured that we will fight this fight to the finish, as a *Kulturvolk*, for whom the legacy of a Goethe, a Beethoven, a Kant is as sacred as its hearth and home.' This was the response to an equally self-righteous appeal from leading western intellectuals asking their German colleagues to distance themselves from atrocities committed by German militarism in Belgium and castigating in particular the destruction of the library at the University of Louvain and of the cathedral at Rheims.

The way in which the German intellectual and cultural élite was swept up in the euphoria of August 1914 went deeper than obstinate self-righteousness in face of foreign attacks. The alienation from the bourgeois world that many German intellectuals had experienced before 1914, which accounts for their fascination with the ideas of Nietzsche, the deep gulf between avant-garde and official art, made them welcome the war as a liberating event. Hermann Hesse, whose ethereal, atmospheric prose has made him in our own day a cult figure, volunteered from Switzerland for the German army and wrote: 'I put on the whole a high estimate on the moral values of the war. For many it is good to be torn from the stupid peace of capitalism, especially in Germany, and for a true artist it seems to me that a nation of real men, who have faced death and have learnt the immediacy and freshness of camping in the field, will be of greater value.' Thomas Mann, another major literary figure then still in his nationalist phase, became an eloquent and subtle advocate of the distinctiveness and superiority of German *Kultur* against the shallowness of western, enlightenment-based civilisation. German freedom was more duty than rights, democracy was individualism and materialism run riot, whereas the more authoritarian German state was orientated towards the common good. Two leading sociologists, Max Scheler and Werner Sombart, pilloried the free market and free trade as hypocritical generalizations from insular British experience, the philosophy of the 'trader' against the faith of the 'hero'. Germany, the Reich of the centre, was always under threat, needed a strong state, a strong army and a sphere of economic autarchy. These and other related notions became 'the ideas of 1914', the ideological underpinnings of the war in Germany and the justification for fighting it to total victory, when Germany's hegemonic position in Europe and status as a world power would be permanently secured. The ideas of 1914 had a clear domestic dimension, for if the semi-authoritarian German state was so superior and uniquely suitable for the country, then it had to be preserved against all attempts to make it more like the western democracies. Therefore those who were most in favour of annexations also tended to be most opposed to domestic change. In July 1915, as the sacrifices imposed by the war grew, 1347 intellectuals, including 352 professors, put forward a far-reaching annexationist programme, which in the east included proposals for settling annexed areas with German farmers. It was a mixture of pan-German and social-Darwinist ideas and its underlying supposition was that war was endemic between nations and Germany had to be ready for the next one. There was also a more moderate petition, which was nearer to the ideas entertained by the chancellor and his entourage.

Bethmann tried to prevent any official debate on war aims, for this was bound to break down the Burgfrieden. As with his policy of the diagonal before the war he sought to remain above the camps and to throw sops to all. He could not show his hand too openly, for any suggestion that moderate war aims might be necessary to leave the door open for a compromise peace would be damaging to morale and attacked as defeatism. The strength and high profile of the annexationist lobby forced the SPD leaders to become more vocal in defence of a peace without annexations, if only to maintain the cohesion of their party. As the war became more onerous, those on the left who had only reluctantly supported it or actually condemned it as imperialist, became stronger and more open in their opposition. In December 1915 the SPD brought an anti-annexation motion in the Reichstag, opposing any Belgian annexation; at the same time 44 SPD deputies opposed a further voting of war credits within the party caucus and twenty of these carried their opposition into the chamber. A major split in the party was foreshadowed. A small group of leftists and outright opponents of the 'imperialist' war around Karl Liebknecht and Rosa Luxemburg, the nucleus of the Spartakus group and later of the German Communist party, had organized themselves as the Group International in March 1915. Liebknecht had already voted against the war credits in December 1914 and was excluded from the party in January 1916. More moderate opponents of the war, which included the party chairman Hugo Haase as well as Bernstein and Kautsky, were coming into the open with criticism of the majority leadership. They constituted themselves the conscience of the party and sought to recall it to its mission to work for a peace without annexations. In the face of these pressures the leaders of the party and of the unions, who had staked everything on cooperation with the government in the hope that this would after the war be rewarded with major reforms, felt it necessary to prove their credentials. This they did by reinforcing their anti-annexationist attitude, but in the view of the left they were policing the Burgfrieden and the working classes on behalf of the ruling élites. Within a year of the outbreak of war the Burgfrieden had thus been replaced by something like the pre-war divisions of German politics, with war aims and annexations now the defining issue. Only the need to maintain morale and the survival, to an extent, of the official party truce in the Reichstag put a dampener on the open recrudescence of domestic conflict.

The strains of war at the front and at home

In 1915 an outright German military victory came no nearer. Turkey's declaration of war on the side of the Central Powers in November 1914 was counterbalanced by Italy's entry into the war on the side of the Allies in May 1915. There were some notable military successes for the Central Powers, big advances and territorial gains against Russia in the summer, the failure of the British Gallipoli campaign and of Italian attacks on their north-eastern front, the defeat of Serbia after the Bulgarian entry into the war on the side of the Central Powers. In the West, still the main front, big Allied attacks failed to achieve a breakthrough. Falkenhayn, with a glimmer of political realism unusual in German military men, had at the end of 1914 advocated seeking a separate peace with Russia, but instead the argument prevailed that only big military successes in the east and in the Balkans could prepare the ground for it. In the event even the successes of 1915 did not achieve it.

Austrian aspirations were a major obstacle to a Russian peace and the Germans could not simply set them aside.

A prolonged war, in which Germany would prove inherently the weaker combatant, loomed. The British blockade and German efforts to withstand it became crucial factors. Ironically the German fleet, the Kaiser's pride and joy, on which so much diplomatic capital had been expended, could do little about it, for it was a distant not a close blockade. Submarines, in the development of which the Germans had a lead, might have been more relevant, but at the outbreak of war only nine were available for long-distance operations. In February 1915, when sinking without warning in the waters around the British Isles became German policy, there were still only 21 submarines in the North Sea, of which only a third could be at sea at one time. Although the tonnage sunk by these boats was considerable, the repercussions particularly in stoking up American hostility, were enormous. Bethmann Hollweg was more than others in the German political élite aware that American entry into the war on the side of the Allies would prove fatal for Germany. He managed on several occasions, after the sinking of the *Lusitania* in May 1915, and again in September 1915 and in March 1916, to place restrictions on the ability of U-boat commanders to sink on sight. It was only a postponement of the confrontation with America. If submarines adhered to the so-called cruiser rules and gave warning of an intended attack, they were themselves left very vulnerable.

German inability to break the deadlock on land or sea put the capacity for endurance of the home front, *durchhalten* as it was called in German, under great strain. The blockade cut off Germany from some raw materials vital for the armaments industry such as nitrogen and rubber, for which the advanced German chemical industry managed to develop substitutes. Ironically two men, both of Jewish origin, who played leading roles in the organization of raw materials and in the invention of substitutes, the industrialist Walther Rathenau and the chemist Fritz Haber, later fell victim to German chauvinism turned racist. Rathenau was assassinated when foreign minister in 1922 by right-wing extremists, Haber had to leave Germany in 1933 in old age and died in Cambridge. It proved even more difficult to make good the shortfall in the German consumption of foodstuffs, about 20 per cent of which had been imported before the war, especially as it was aggravated by the loss of male agricultural workers conscripted into the army. Nothing did more to damage German morale than the shortage of food which became drastic by the winter of 1916/17, the so-called turnip winter, but as early as 1915 discontent became vocal in the food queues that formed in large cities, especially among women. The authorities were unable to run a fair rationing scheme and there was a great deal of black marketeering which favoured the rich. Attempts to manage farm production through offices set up to control specific scarce commodities such as grain, sugar, and finally through a war food office, had little success. The intrusion of officials and police into the countryside was resented by the farmers and their grossly overworked wives, who were trying to make up for the loss of labour from the countryside. Decline of support for the war in rural communities was one of the factors that undermined the will to fight on.

In the industrial centres and the armaments industries there was a huge influx of new labour, women and young men, to replace those who were serving in the army. Already by the end of 1914 a third of all industrial workers were serving in the army. It was again the army itself, through the commanders of the military districts with their draconian powers, and through the war ministry, that took the lead in the management of industrial manpower. They could do so only in collaboration with the trade unions, though many employers, particularly in the heavy industries, resented the role which the unions and their officials now assumed. They hoped that it would only be temporary for the duration of the war. It was, however, just this enhanced role which gave substance to the hopes of the union and political leaders of the labour movement that their cooperation would be rewarded by far-reaching reforms. They assumed that many of the changes brought about by the war, which amounted to a suspension of the market economy and of normal capitalism, were in any case irreversible. The policy considerations that impressed labour leaders did not mean much to the rank and file. Union membership, over two million on the eve of war, dropped to less than a million by the end of 1916, though it then rose again. What mattered for the rank and file were long hours, wages not keeping up with prices and food shortages. This gradually produced anti-war feeling and radicalization, the hope that the class society that the war was perpetuating and even intensifying, would end. Among the sentiments that had made so many among the educated élites welcome the war was the hope that 'war socialism' would lead to a permanent change in society in the direction of community and solidarity, but in practice the opposite happened.

Inflation was a phenomenon experienced in all countries in wartime and was difficult to understand for a generation brought up with stable money. In Germany inflation became established in the monetary system with particular virulence. The Reich taxation system had been inadequate ever since the time of Bismarck and attempts to remedy the situation decisively had failed. The obstacles to a cure persisted into wartime: the federal system, the disagreements over income and capital taxes versus consumption taxes aggravated by the Prussian three-tier election law. Consequently the war was financed mainly by loans. It is estimated that of the 155 billion marks which the war cost only nine billion were raised by actual taxes (see Appendix: Table 11). The consequent price rises engendered a sense of injustice, rich against poor, town against country, war profiteers, often mythical, against the rest. Those on fixed incomes, civil servants for example, previously privileged, did badly, so did white-collar employees and artisans; workers, unless in particularly favoured armaments industries, did not do well. The German middle classes patriotically subscribed to war loans, but these could only be repaid if Germany won the war and imposed heavy indemnities on her enemies. Much of the poison that vitiated the politics of Weimar and led to the rise of Hitler was incubating in the war years, hyperinflation, reparations, proletarianization of sections of the middle class. Even during the war the authorities characteristically tried to divert discontent onto the usual scapegoats, the Jews. Pandering to sentiment that Jews were profiteers and shirked military service, the Prussian minister of war in October 1916 ordered a 'Jew count' in the army. Its results were never published, as it failed to prove the anti-Semitic point.

At the end of 1915 Falkenhayn realized that hopes of a separate peace in the East were vain. In his view the western front had always been the decisive theatre and he now sought to achieve the defeat of France which had so far eluded the Germans. His plan was to bleed France dry until she could not continue by forcing her to commit all her remaining strength to the defence of the pivotal fortress of Verdun. If this fortress fell the damage to French morale would be fatal. Falkenhayn underestimated French powers of resistance and did not sufficiently allow for the fact that the rate of attrition for the German forces would almost equal that for the French. The big, mainly British, offensive on the Somme in July 1916, although not achieving a decisive breakthrough, took him by surprise in its ferocity. The fluctuating battle in the bone cruncher around Verdun, the ultimate in horror, in which probably around 700,000 died on both sides, impressed itself deeply on the consciousness of French and German soldiers and civilians. After Verdun there was nothing left of the euphoria of 1914, only the freemasonry of the trenches, a nihilistic camaraderie in the constant presence of death. Falkenhayn's strategy had failed and the entry of Rumania into the war against the Central Powers on 27 August 1916 provided the occasion for his departure. He continued to serve in major commands on the eastern front and his swift campaign against Rumania, which almost totally occupied that country in a few weeks, redeemed his reputation in German eyes.

Hindenburg and Ludendorff form the third *Oberste Heeresleitung*

Hindenburg and Ludendorff now moved into the supreme command and became known as 3 OHL. It was a decisive change, for on major matters of strategy, politics and personnel they could now always get their way. If they were opposed they threatened resignation and their position with the German public was such that this was a conclusive weapon. Ludendorff was not exactly the military dictator of Germany, but there was no one who wielded superior power. The Kaiser had long resisted the appointment of this duumvirate, because it would deprive him of almost all that remained of his power. Since August 1914 he had been segregated in his military headquarters behind the front and exercised largely ceremonial duties, though in matters of appointment he still retained the ultimate say. He and his entourage realized that the Hindenburg–Ludendorff duo would now largely draw to themselves the charismatic aura normally surrounding the monarch. The power of 3 OHL was circumscribed only by the fact that they needed to rely on the continued will to fight of the people and of the soldiers.

Strangely enough, Bethmann Hollweg believed that the arrival of 3 OHL would provide a cover for his own attempts at finding a negotiated way out of the war, a substitute as it were for the sidelined Kaiser. The weakness of Germany's non-parliamentary government stood more than ever revealed by the contrast with the rise of strong, politically legitimated personalities like Lloyd George and Clemenceau in the western democracies. The chancellor was able to announce a German offer to negotiate in the Reichstag in December 1916, but being entirely non-specific it made no impact. At the same time 3 OHL's determination to fight with no holds barred was demonstrated by two decisions, the enactment of the Auxiliary Labour Law, and the proclamation of an independent Kingdom of Poland under German aegis, which ended any hope of a separate peace with Russia and had annexationist implications. Poland was, besides Belgium, always a test case for any war aims programme. It was also a bone of contention between Germany and Austria and the satellite Poland proposed at this stage went against the aspirations of Vienna. The Auxiliary Labour Law imposed a labour obligation on all male Germans between seventeen and sixty and controlled their freedom to choose their place of work. Arbitration committees, equally composed of employers' and employees' representatives were established, and so were works councils in all enterprises employing more than fifty people. The concessions to the unions meant that the Reichstag passed this law with the support of the majority of the SPD. The law may not have had a great immediate practical effect, as German labour resources were already fully mobilized, but it marked a further advance of state socialism and signified that 3 OHL needed the help of the labour movement. Another aspect of this total resource mobilization was the Hindenburg programme, which set new and ambitious production targets. An armaments office, somewhat similar to the munitions ministry established under Lloyd George in 1915, was set up. General Groener, a non-Prussian desk general with great organizing gifts and good relations with the union leaders, became its head. He was still Ludendorff's man, but would eventually become his successor and play a political role in the Weimar Republic.

The most crucial step arising from 3 OHL's determination to fight a total war for total victory came with the decision to return to unrestricted submarine warfare. The pressure for it came not only from the new military supremos, but from public and parliamentary opinion and from the naval high command. The admirals were bound to welcome anything that would restore the prestige of their service. The high expectations which Tirpitz had built up for his ocean-going fleet as a deterrent proved illusory with British entry into the war and Tirpitz himself resigned in March 1916. Two months later there was the battle of Jutland, the only occasion when the German High Seas Fleet engaged the British. It could be presented as a German success, for British losses in tonnage and manpower were greater than the German losses. Strategically it changed nothing and the only achievement of the German fleet was that it prevented an attack on the German North Sea coast or an Allied incursion into the Baltic. German morale was boosted by the daring exploits of their commerce raiders, but these could not seriously dent the flow of Allied supplies. This left only the submarine and it was tempting to see it as the ultimate weapon, particularly as its full deployment had twice been reversed for political reasons. The admirals supplied what seemed like conclusive statistical justification for resuming sinkings on sight, but their figures turned out to be more wishful thinking than fact.

At the beginning of 1917 the German public thought that their reasonable offer to negotiate had been rejected, while specific Allied terms made public in January included items such as the return of Alsace-Lorraine to France which were totally unacceptable in Germany. Bethmann Hollweg was unable to resist any further the pressure to resume unrestricted submarine warfare, even though he knew full well that it was likely to lead to American entry into the war. Nothing is more striking than the arrogance with which German opinion from the élites downward underestimated the power of the United States. It was once more 'heroes against traders'. The American declaration of war was belittled as only making *de jure* an undeclared state of war. Wilson's intention 'to make the world safe for democracy' was dismissed as typical Anglo-Saxon hypocrisy. Britain would be on her knees within five months and by the time American power could make itself felt, Germany would have won the war. It was a fatal miscalculation. Unrestricted submarine warfare was reopened on 1 February 1917; by 6 April the USA had declared war. Initially the successes of the German submarines presented a formidable challenge to the British, but the convoy system and other measures gradually mastered the threat.

1917: the turning point

The American declaration of war rivalled the Russian revolution in making the year 1917 into a turning point. The Tsar fell in March, the Bolshevik take-over took place in November. Lenin's arrival in St Petersburg in April undoubtedly helped to undermine the Russian will and capacity to continue the war. He and his fellow-revolutionaries travelled from Switzerland through Germany in a sealed train, by courtesy of 3OHL. It was characteristic of Ludendorff's determination to fight total war regardless of all other considerations that he facilitated this journey. The revolutionary disintegration of Russia, while it might free Germany from the nightmare of a two-front war, would pose an obvious threat to the monarchical regimes in Berlin and Vienna, as well as changing the ideological basis of the war to Germany's disadvantage. By 1917 the social situation in Germany was in any case becoming more fragile. The SPD and union leaders stuck to their patriotic line, but their post-dated cheque for reforms no longer impressed the grass roots. In April 1917 there were big strikes, mainly provoked by discontent about reduced bread rations and the injustices of food distribution in general, but also connected with dissatisfaction about the slow progress of political reform. The outbreak of revolution in Russia was raising expectations of change and made the war look more like a war of conquest in the eyes of radicals. The strikes caught the unions unawares, for they had little contact with the newly recruited elements in the work force. In order to get a grip on the situation, unions and their organizers had to associate themselves with many local strike actions in the last two years of the war. This gave rise to the myth that they and the leaders of the SPD had deliberately undermined the home front and thus caused the German defeat, the vicious stab-in-the-back myth that did so much harm to Weimar democracy. It was a long way from the truth. The growing unrest arose spontaneously from the parlous condition into which the German home front had been allowed to drift by the authorities, but the unrest itself was never a major cause of Germany's collapse, but a symptom of the cumulative exhaustion of the population.

In the meantime the tensions over German war aims, the intractability of the

war itself and the growing hardship had caused a split in the SPD. The exclusion
of Liebknecht from the party was followed in March 1916 by the expulsion of
eighteen rebels, who had voted against an emergency budget. This group, which
included Hugo Haase, who now resigned the party chairmanship, constituted themselves the *Sozialdemokratische Arbeitsgemeinschaft* (Socialdemocratic Working
Group), but were not yet a separate party. There were increasingly bitter
recriminations between this group and the leaders of the party majority, with the
former calling the latter traitors to socialism, while the majority leaders accused the
anti-war group of splitting the party. There was a fierce battle over control of the
party press. When the SAG called a nationwide conference in January 1917, its
concern was as much to differentiate itself from the extreme left, the Spartakus
group, Liebknecht, Luxemburg and others, as to break away from the main party.
The SPD leadership now concluded that expulsion of the group was inevitable and
thus the group established itself as a separate party, the *Unabhängige Sozialdemokratische Partei Deutschlands* (USPD, Independent SPD), at a congress in
Gotha in April 1917. The USPD was never a very coherent party and not coter-
minous with the pre-war radical revolutionary Left, as is shown by the adherence of
Bernstein and Kautsky. It was an anti-war group, held together by a loathing of the
war, though not necessarily pacifist or even anti-national, by disgust with the policy
of cooperating with an annexationist, militarist establishment, by the way in which
this cooperation was enslaving, as they saw it, the workers, for example through the
Auxiliary Labour Law or the activities of the commanding generals in the military
districts. On the left of the USPD there was some sympathy with the radicals and
with imprisoned leaders like Liebknecht and Luxemburg. The radicals were by this
time trying to set up an international anti-war socialist movement and participated
in conferences like Zimmerwald in September 1915. Not that the USPD, and even
less the radical groups, which had to function largely underground, had popular
followings comparable to that of the Majority SPD, as it was now called. But the
huge new wartime labour force mostly had no traditional party ties. The activists
organizing strikes and protests received encouragement from the groups opposing
the official support for the war, while the Majority SPD and the unions found it
harder to maintain control of their followers. The domestic situation in 1917 as
well as the Russian Revolution forced them to emphasize that they were not
supporting a war of conquest or annexation.

In the spring of 1917 the course of the war, as well as domestic developments,
thus gave a new twist to the German political debate. Reform of the Prussian three-
tier law and even parliamentarization of the system were back on the agenda.
Bethmann Hollweg, who so often knew what needed to be done, but had neither
the power nor the will to bring it about, admitted in the Reichstag in March 1917
that there was need for far-reaching reform. The Reichstag itself had become more
assertive and had in the autumn of 1916 established, with the agreement of the
government, a permanent committee for consultation on matters of strategy and
foreign policy. In April 1917 a constitutional committee was set up to discuss
various issues of reform, not the Prussian three-tier law, which was not strictly a
Reich matter, but matters such as changes in the Reichstag electoral districts and

the eligibility of Reichstag deputies to become members of the Bundesrat. It was this separation between legislative and executive membership that was the barrier to ministerial responsibility in the German constitution. Stresemann, now the National Liberal leader, was an annexationist and a supporter of Ludendorff, but significantly he was now in favour of some of these changes designed to bridge the gap between political institutions and the popular will. Without national solidarity there could be no victory. For the moment these pressures produced little result. The Conservatives were adamantly opposed to an equal electoral law in Prussia and even the other parties had reservations. The manifold organizations of the right, 3 OHL and the Kaiser were against almost any change or concession. The Kaiser's Easter message contained a vague promise of the abolition of the three-tier electoral system, but said nothing about what was to take its place. Bethmann Hollweg's position was further weakened; he could not deliver reforms, but the right and 3 OHL saw him as a weakling both at home and abroad and were working for his removal.

The fall of Bethmann Hollweg and the Reichstag's peace resolution

Matters came to a head in July. America had entered the war, submarine warfare had failed to achieve decisive results, Russian developments and domestic unrest were piling on the pressure. The SPD, conscious of war weariness among its followers and of the rivalry of the USPD, threatened finally to end the *Burgfrieden* by voting against further war credits. The Centre Party joined the SPD and Progressives in demanding a clear resolution by the Reichstag in favour of a negotiated peace on the basis of the status quo. The National Liberals were drawn into these discussions, which led to the permanent creation of an Interparty Committee (*Interfraktioneller Ausschuss*), in which one can see, in embryonic form, the coalition on which the Weimar regime was based. Simultaneously the movement to get rid of the chancellor moved to a climax. Ludendorff and 3 OHL had worked towards his fall for some time, but the Kaiser had hitherto been unwilling to let him go. The Centre Party had moved towards the demand for a negotiated peace under the influence of Erzberger, the ubiquitous and energetic leader of its left wing. He had been a strong populist annexationist, but his excellent sources of information now told him that the situation was desperate. As a Catholic he knew well what was going on in Vienna and that the dual monarchy was on the verge of collapse and trying to obtain a separate peace. Stresemann, known as Ludendorff's young man, and Erzberger joined 3 OHL in demanding Bethmann's departure. They considered him too weak for the great decisions now impending and thought any peace resolution passed by the Reichstag would require a fresh face to give it credibility. The Kaiser was put under pressure to drop Bethmann by a threat of resignation from Hindenburg and Ludendorff. On this and subsequent occasions the two warlords did not scruple to take a line which amounted to insubordination to the Supreme Warlord. Their actions irreparably damaged the Hohenzollern kingship they were pledged to uphold. When the leading parliamentarians, and even sections of the SPD, no longer backed the chancellor, the monarch gave way and accepted Bethmann's resignation on 13 July.

It was a bizarre outcome: the one major figure who had shown some insight into the need for a negotiated peace and domestic reform, and had as a result incurred the bitter hostility of the military leaders and of the right, had been toppled with the help of the parliamentary leaders of the centre and the left, who wanted much the same things as the man whom they helped to bring down. Admittedly Bethmann was weak, far too conservative to give himself the necessary leverage by challenging the constitutional system in its foundations. But the Reichstag parties were themselves still stuck in the constitutional system and too disunited to demand real parliamentarization. They could help topple a chancellor, but they had no one to put in his place. The choice was still left to the Kaiser, who, in some embarrassment, appointed a colourless civil servant, Michaelis, an undersecretary of state who had worked as a food administrator. On 19 July the Reichstag passed a rather anodyne peace resolution, all that the fragile unity between the parties would permit. Its key sentence said that the Reichstag desired a peace of understanding and permanent reconciliation of nations and that annexations and imposed political, economic and financial conditions were incompatible with such a peace. Even this did not have the support of the National Liberals, who remained semi-detached from the Interparty Committee. Bethmann's reluctance to accept the peace resolution, which was presented to him as an accomplished fact, helped to bring him down. Michaelis accepted it, with the proviso 'as I understand it', and it ran into the sand. Ludendorff, the champion of total war, and 3 OHL had triumphed and retained the power of initiative. We will never know what would have happened if the parties of the Interparty Committee had formed a genuine coalition, had installed their candidate in the chancellorship and been united in working for a negotiated peace. The future could hardly have been worse than it turned out to be.

The fact was that a majority of the political leaders as well as of the population, including followers of the SPD, still had confidence in the military leaders and believed that a victory could still be secured by force of arms. The either-or mentality was widespread, which saw no alternative to victory other than decline, a word which hardly conveys in full the meaning of the German *Untergang*. The opponents of a negotiated peace, most of them also opponents of domestic reform, now founded, with the support of Ludendorff, the Fatherland Party, which soon boasted 2500 local chapters and 1.25 million members. It was not a party in the parliamentary sense but can be seen as the largest mobilization of German chauvinism before the Nazis. Tirpitz was its chairman and Kapp, its principal organizer, headed the first right-wing attempt to overthrow the Weimar Republic in March 1920. There was a weaker counter-organization, the *Volksbund für Freiheit und Vaterland* (Popular Association for Freedom and Fatherland), which made the case for domestic reform and peace by negotiation. Intransigence on both sides brought all efforts at a negotiated peace, such as those of the Pope, to naught in 1917, but in the event it was the Germans who could least afford to be uncompromising.

There were, however, by the second half of 1917 still sufficient positive factors in the war situation, from a German perspective, to enable the advocates of a *Siegfrieden* to prevail. On the western front the big offensive planned by the French Commander in Chief Nivelle achieved no breakthrough and led to mutinies in the French army, which his successor Pétain brought under control with difficulty. The great British offensive in Flanders, usually known as Passchendaele, achieved little and British casualties were probably higher than the German. In November the British used tanks for the first time on a major scale at Cambrai, broke the German line, but could not follow it up. In Britain there were also signs of exhaustion and discontent. Arthur Henderson, the one Labour representative in Lloyd George's war cabinet, resigned over his support for attendance at an international socialist conference in Stockholm, intended to promote peace. There was much pessimism even in the war cabinet, a realization that the defeat of Germany might be achieved only at the cost of Britain's own status as a world leader. The Austrian will to fight was to some extent restored by a big victory at Caporetto on the Italian front, achieved with German help, which moved the front from the mountains north of Trieste down to the river Piave not far from Venice in October 1917. But by far the biggest event that gave hope to the Germans of winning the war after all was the armistice with Russia, which was concluded in December 1917, little more than a month after the Bolshevik take-over.

The Russian collapse

The Germans had done their best to forward the progressive collapse of the Russian will to resist throughout the year 1917. Not only had they allowed Lenin and his fellow-revolutionaries to return from exile, they had also refrained from any offensive action that might have halted the disintegration of the Russian armies. They failed, however, to offer the Russians a peace without annexations, for 3 OHL had far-reaching aims of turning Eastern Europe into a German supply base in a future war. There was also a powerful Baltic German lobby, which pressed for retention of control over Courland, Livland, and later parts of Latvia and Estonia, and of Lithuania in order to safeguard the position of the German minority and German culture in these areas. A more moderate policy of creating genuinely independent buffer states could not gain the day, and differences with Austria remained over the status of Poland. When Lenin and his colleagues asked for an armistice immediate solutions were required. By this time the brief chancellorship of Michaelis had ended and his place had reluctantly been taken by Count Hertling, the seventy-four-year-old Bavarian prime minister. His appointment was made with a greater involvement of the Reichstag and the parties on the Interparty Committee but still did not amount to a parliamentarization of the system. The new Vice-Chancellor Friedrich von Payer, a Progressive, was the candidate of the parties, but he had to give up his Reichstag seat on joining the ministry. Richard von Kühlmann had become state secretary for foreign affairs in August 1917 and, backed by Hertling, was the chief advocate of a conciliatory approach to the peace negotiations with Russia. Kühlmann had a realistic sense of the limits of German power. Annexations were, at any rate in a formal sense, to be avoided. Some high ground was to be gained for any future negotiations with the Western Allies, at least for propaganda purposes, Austrian susceptibilities, particularly over Poland, had to be respected. and, even more importantly, regard had to be had for the anti-annexationists at home. The SPD leaders had now to be constantly looking over their shoulders at the growing anti-war feeling among their followers, while their continued support for the war remained essential to the government.

All this was of secondary importance to 3 OHL, who had in the meantime decided on a spring offensive on the western front. The German army, strengthened by troops freed from the eastern front, would achieve the breakthrough which had eluded them since 1914 and thereby a victorious end to the war. Apart from the role Eastern Europe might play as a German annex in a future conflict, Hindenburg and Ludendorff now wanted an immediate exploitation of this huge area to underpin their final push for total victory in the west. In the peace negotiations between Germany and Russia at Brest-Litovsk the demands of 3 OHL always shaped the German tactics in the final resort. A decisive moment was the signing of a separate peace treaty with the newly elected Ukrainian parliament, the Rada, on 9 February 1918. It was expansion under the cloak of self-determination. There was in any case little that the Russians could now do to avoid a German diktat. Trotsky's ploy of suspending the negotiations on 10 February while waiting for revolution to erupt behind the German delegation and even in Western Europe was a counsel of despair. Ludendorff pressed for an ultimatum and resumed the German advance. Lenin realized that the only chance of the Bolsheviks surviving in power was to give in and on 3 March the Treaty of Brest-Litovsk was signed. Russia lost control of about a third of the Tsarist empire's population and its agricultural land, 73 per cent of its iron-ore output and 89 per cent of its coal. It could be said that at the end of the twentieth century most of this area was again outside Russian control and that there was some superficial regard to the principle of self-determination. But it was a Carthaginian peace as far as Russia was concerned and undermined any remaining disposition in the West to seek a negotiated peace with Germany. Later on it made German complaints against the Treaty of Versailles ring somewhat hollow. The extent to which the German public still believed in ultimate victory may be gauged from the fact that the Reichstag passed the Brest-Litovsk treaty with only the USPD voting against it, while the SPD abstained, secure in the knowledge that the treaties would pass anyway. The other parties saw no incompatibility between Brest-Litovsk and the Reichstag's peace resolution of 1917. It was a further step towards parliamentarization that the treaty was submitted to the Reichstag at all, for the constitution did not require it. As far as the reaction of the German public was concerned Ludendorff's calculations therefore proved more correct than Kühlmann's, who had feared major protests and a SPD vote against war credits. Following Brest-Litovsk there was virtually no limit to the further expansion of German influence eastward, facilitated by the confusion of the Russian civil war. The Germans had, however, to maintain considerable forces in the east, though they were mainly second-line troops made up of older reservists. A peace treaty signed at Bucharest with

Rumania on 7 May gave Germany far-reaching control of the country's important economic resources, particularly oil.

Ludendorff's gamble of staking everything on victory in the west was risky. In January 1918 Wilson made public his Fourteen Points, a clear manifesto against annexation, for self-determination and for an international order no longer based on a balance of power. At the end of the month there was the biggest wave of strikes yet, involving about a million workers across Germany, between one hundred and three hundred thousand in Berlin alone. The leaders of the Majority SPD had to join the organization of the strikes to maintain any control. This exposed them to bitter attacks from the right and endangered the cohesion of the Interparty Committee. The strikes were suppressed by the proclamation of an aggravated state of siege around Berlin and by drafting some of the ringleaders into the army, but the organization of revolutionary shop stewards survived in Berlin to play a role in the revolution of November. The strikes were partly a protest against hardship and hunger and against the oppressive regime of the military district commanders, but the strikers now had clear political demands, a peace without annexations as demanded by the Russian delegation at Brest-Litovsk and internally the immediate introduction of electoral equality in Prussia. After barely a week the strikes crumbled, but they showed that the social cohesion and the powers of endurance of the German population were weakening.

The German army crumbles

The Treaty of Brest-Litovsk was ratified by the Reichstag on 22 March 1918, the day after the great German offensive in the west, code-named Michael, opened. It was aimed at the southern end of the British front and with the capture of Amiens to separate the British from the French. For the first time since 1914 the Germans had, on paper, a larger number of divisions than the Allies. Seventy of the German divisions were specially equipped for the attack and the German advance was greater than anything seen on the western front since 1914. The British Fifth Army was almost completely smashed and at Westminster Lloyd George was engulfed by a severe political crisis. But a conclusive victory again eluded the Germans. Their mobility was insufficient, artillery and supplies could not keep pace with the advancing infantry. Tank development had been neglected and the Allies were superior in the air. Ludendorff tried to follow up with a number of other attacks, one of them in June bringing Paris within range of the German big guns and producing a crisis for the Clemenceau government. By July the German offensive capability was all but exhausted. On 18 July a big French counter-offensive on the Marne forced a German retreat and signalled that the initiative had passed to the Allies. Three weeks later, on 8 August, a massive British tank attack near Amiens forced the German to surrender all the gains they had made in the spring. It was the 'black day' of the German army. Loss of morale and disease, an influenza epidemic, were now seriously reducing the strength of the German formations, sometimes by as much as half. There were many prisoners, many deserters and many who went absent when on leave. The German line was forced back relentlessly, though it did not actually break. The situation of Germany's three allies, Austria, Turkey and Bulgaria, was even more serious and their collapse merely a matter of time.

By August 1918 any chance the Germans might still have had earlier in the year to break the Allied will to win had clearly gone. While the German armies were melting away, one hundred thousand fresh American troops were arriving monthly in France and the pace of new arrivals was quickening. Yet Ludendorff and the inner circle of the German leadership were unwilling to acknowledge that defeat was staring them in the face. When in June Kühlmann spoke cautiously in the Reichstag of the need for an exchange of views on peace negotiations with Britain, he was fiercely attacked from the right. Hindenburg and Ludendorff, who had never liked him, demanded his dismissal and he went on 9 July. On 14 August a crown council at GHQ under the chairmanship of the Kaiser agreed, according to the minutes taken by Admiral von Hintze, Kühlmann's successor as foreign secretary, that it was no longer possible to break the enemy's will to fight militarily, but that it was still feasible to paralyse it gradually by a 'strategic defensive'. This would require resolute measures to prevent the disintegration of the home front. These lame conclusions showed the extent to which the German leaders, Ludendorff in particular, had lost all sense of reality. With the German military situation deteriorating by the day the chances of bringing the Allies to negotiate on anything like the status quo was remote.

With a sense of realism so much lacking among the inner circle of leaders it is not surprising that a routine meeting, a week later on 21 August, between Hintze, Payer and some other officials and the Reichstag party leaders, lacked all sense of urgency. There was of course talk of the need to make moves towards negotiation, but then there had been for at least the past year. An official offer of peace was, however, not opportune, said Hintze, because it would be a German admission of weakness, an argument that had been made at intervals throughout the war. Moreover, all defeatist talk on the home front must be vigorously suppressed. This totally unrealistic approach to the situation continued to mark the discussions and deliberations of the German political élite for nearly another six weeks. There were discussions in the Interparty Committee, which the National Liberals rejoined after an absence since January, about forming a parliamentary cabinet. This would entail the replacement of Hertling, but such a cabinet would be in a stronger position in peace negotiations. There was, however, still no agreement on parliamentarization. The Centre Party wished to keep Hertling in office, which meant no parliamentarization and no change in the incompatibility between holding office and retaining a seat in the Reichstag. The SPD now wanted parliamentarization and a new chancellor, prepared to implement it. Time was wasted on further treaties with the Lenin government, all of which, including Brest-Litovsk, would shortly be rendered irrelevant by Germany's collapse. There was still talk about the claims of various German dynasties, including the Wittelsbachs, to thrones that might become available in Eastern Europe, grotesque when the fall of all German dynasties was only weeks away.

The catalyst in tearing apart the miasma of illusion that paralysed the German leadership was the collapse of Bulgaria, which became apparent on 25 September.

By the evening of 28 September Hindenburg and Ludendorff had reached the conclusion that an immediate armistice was required and that to secure it the government had to be reconstructed on a parliamentary basis. This conclusion was endorsed by a crown council the next day, at which the Kaiser, the Crown Prince, Hertling, Hintze, Hindenburg and Ludendorff were present. This sudden volte-face after so much procrastination is sometimes attributed to a nervous collapse on the part of Ludendorff, sometimes to a cynical calculation by him to put the responsibility for defeat on to the shoulders of the Reichstag politicians. There had to be a hasty revolution from above to forestall a revolution from below. The cynicism of Ludendorff's calculations is borne out by the often quoted remarks he made to his staff the next morning, when the full implications of what had been decided hit them: 'I have advised his Majesty to bring those groups into the government whom we have in the main to thank for the fact that matters have reached this pass. We will now therefore see these gentlemen move into the ministries. Let them now conclude the peace that has to be negotiated. Let them eat the broth they have cooked for us.'

Ludendorff's pressure for an armistice without delay was due to the fear that at any moment the German lines might break and that a demoralized, Bolshevized army would flood back into Germany. These fears proved for the moment somewhat excessive, for the Allied commanders were cautious about launching another offensive prematurely. But if 3 OHL thought that the request for an armistice meant anything other than an admission of defeat and that somehow the fight could be resumed at a moment of their choosing, they were deluding themselves. The only bargaining counter left to the Germans was the fear on the Allied side that chaos in Germany might enable the Bolshevik revolution to spread westward. It could not be in the Allied interest to allow all vestiges of authority to vanish in Germany.

The first consequence of the decisions taken on 29 September was that Hertling had to go. Now that 3 OHL insisted on immediate parliamentarization, Hertling's stand against it was undermined. Even now the Reichstag parties could not find a candidate of their own to replace him and this left it open once more to the Kaiser to choose Hertling's successor. He was Prince Max of Baden, heir to the most liberal throne in Germany. He had been talked about as a possible chancellor for some time and his advisers, among them Dr Kurt Hahn, later the founder of Gordonstoun School, and the banker Max Warburg, had made him palatable among Ludendorff's entourage and with the Quartermaster General himself. Prince Max might have made a good figurehead for a carefully choreographed transition to parliamentary democracy in quiet times, but he was not the man for this supremely critical moment, when earth-shaking events followed each other precipitately. He initially resisted the call for an immediate armistice made by Ludendorff, realizing that this would set his government on a slippery slope from the start and would foreclose most options. Ludendorff insisted on the immediate despatch of the armistice request to President Wilson and it went off late on 3 October. Wilson replied on 8 October and with two further notes on 14 and 23 October; there were German responses on 12, 20 and 27 October. Wilson's demands gradually increased: he required assurances that full parliamentary democracy would be introduced in Germany, that the military authorities would in future be under the control of the civilian government, that unrestricted submarine warfare would cease. It became clear that in the west Germany would have to surrender not only all occupied territory, but also Alsace-Lorraine. In the east the settlement imposed by Germany at Brest-Litovsk and in the treaty with Rumania would become invalid. The Fourteen Points specifically demanded an independent Poland with access to the sea. Wilson's third note of 23 October was widely interpreted in Germany as requiring the abdication of the Kaiser and even the abolition of the monarchy, though all it did was to express the view that the change from the military–monarchical system had still not been clearly made. Wilson was still committed to the concept of a just peace based on self-determination enshrined in his Fourteen Points, but he could not disregard his European allies, nor his own public opinion, much of which wanted no punches pulled in ramming home the German defeat. It was inevitable that the armistice conditions must be framed to prevent the Germans from resuming the conflict.

The Wilson notes hit a German public opinion which was in a state of severe shock. It was only on 2 October that a confidential briefing of all the party leaders by an officer from OHL revealed the full extent of the military débâcle that had led to the request for an immediate armistice. When the news percolated to the general public the effect was devastating. Some advocated a last desperate resistance. Rathenau, strangely, was one of them, suggesting a *levée en masse* in a newspaper article on 7 October. The great mass of the people, however, now wanted nothing but the immediate end of the war and would brook no delay. Anything that stood in the way, be it Kaiser, monarchy or the generals, lost what authority and legitimacy they still possessed. What had up to this point motivated a radical minority, albeit a growing one, became general property. The accusations about militarism and autocracy reflected in the Wilson notes now found a ready audience in Germany. Against this powerful trend last minute changes in the system, a kind of deathbed repentance, could achieve little and were indeed hardly noticed. The government of Prince Max was a semi-parliamentary one, in which such notable parliamentary personalities as Erzberger from the Centre Party and Scheidemann from the SPD held office. The system under which censorship and the state of siege was administered by the military authorities was reformed and subjected to civilian control. Imprisoned opponents of the war, including Karl Liebknecht, were released. Most important of all, under laws which went into force on 28 October, the chancellor and his ministers were made responsible to the Reichstag and could be removed by a vote of no confidence. Reichstag deputies who became ministers did not have to give up their seats.

The revolution begins

All last-minute change and reform availed little against the perception among the masses that the old system, which had subjected them to so much hardship and indignity and yet failed them so abysmally, was still hanging on. The Kaiser was the most obvious symbol of it and the pressure for his abdication was rising by the day. It was fuelled by the obvious fact that within the military and naval commands defeat was still not acknowledged. There the hope was cherished that the struggle could be continued and that the government's efforts to make peace could still be thwarted, but this was a prospect no longer acceptable to the German public. After the third Wilson note of 23 October Hindenburg and Ludendorff publicly reversed their position, declaring that the terms were unacceptable and that the fight had to be resumed. Their advice was militarily entirely unrealistic. A core of frontline troops and their officers in the west were still holding their positions well to the east of the previous battle areas, but still clear of the German borders. They had so far carried out a controlled retreat, but their final defeat could only be a matter of time. Meanwhile the remaining German allies, Turkey and Austria, had collapsed and were negotiating separate ceasefires. Germany's flanks lay wide open. Neither the chancellor and his government nor the Kaiser were prepared to accept the advice of the military leaders and on 26 October Ludendorff was dismissed, while Hindenburg decided to stay. It was not to be the last crucial occasion when the Field Marshal, the symbol of steadfastness to the German people, decided to throw to the wolves a subordinate to whom he owed a great deal. Groener became Ludendorff's successor, but the continuing power of the military was illustrated by the fact that these decisions were still taken by the Kaiser and not by the government. Groener was a much greater political realist than his predecessor, but his actions were designed to safeguard what remained of the authority of OHL and in the next few crucial weeks largely succeeded in doing so.

The refusal of the naval command to accept defeat was even more flagrant and finally precipitated revolution. The naval high command wanted to use the fleet, which had spent most of the war in harbour, in an attack on the British navy in the Thames estuary and the Channel. The attack was to help the German land forces in Flanders, but like Ludendorff's advice to go on fighting, was dictated by an anachronistic sense of honour rather than a realistic strategic appreciation. Morale in the navy was low, conditions on board ship caused tension between officers and men and there had been a mutiny in 1917, which had led to two executions. There had been some contact between the mutineers and the USPD, later expanded into the myth that socialists had encouraged the mutiny. The sailors interpreted the decision to seek battle as suicidal and as a revolt of the admirals against the government, which had just agreed to the Wilson note of 23 October, and the crews of several ships extinguished the fire under the boilers of their vessels on the night of 29 October. The mutiny could not be contained and spread inland from the German coast. The sailors made contact with sympathetic workers in many major German cities, and workers' and soldiers' councils were established. The revolution spread like wildfire, officers had their epaulettes torn down, the forces of law and order were paralysed. A separate revolutionary outbreak occurred in Munich. In the surrounding countryside the farming community had become increasingly disaffected by the attempts of the authorities to control agricultural production and distribute its produce. The old anti-Prussian sentiment, which had faded away after 1870, revived. In the cities there was the war industry, where workers, many of them women and youths who had not previously worked in factories, were alienated by excessive hours and exhaustion. There was also in Munich a community of intellectuals and artists, among whom anti-war sentiment was strong. The collapse of the Habsburg monarchy had left Bavaria open to invasion from the south. A resolute USPD leader, Kurt Eisner, was able, against virtually no resistance, to overthrow the monarchy on 7 November. Thus the Wittelsbachs, one of the oldest and most deeply rooted of German ruling families, was the first to fall, 'not with a bang but a whimper'.

Meanwhile in Berlin, where the radicals, the left wing of the USPD, the revolutionary shop stewards and the Spartakus group had one of their strongholds the revolutionary pressure was rising. The Kaiser had removed himself to GHQ at Spa on 29 October, in order to escape the pressure for his abdication. It was yet another signal that the military influence was still powerful and spurred on the revolutionaries. The Majority SPD made last-minute attempts to ward off insurrection by demanding the Kaiser's immediate abdication, but Groener, who had gone to Berlin on 5 November to represent the views of OHL, turned down the demand out of hand. It may well have been the last chance to save the monarchy. The radical forces in the capital were mobilizing for an uprising. By 9 November, a Saturday, the city was on the move, workers were leaving their factories and streaming into the government quarter. There were no longer any reliable troops available to oppose the revolution. Prince Max announced the abdication of Kaiser and Crown Prince even before he had obtained consent from Spa. William was still toying with the idea of returning at the head of the army to quash the revolution, but it finally fell to Groener to tell him that the army was no longer willing to follow him. He and Hindenburg advised him to seek refuge in Holland and he went there on 10 November. In the meantime Prince Max had handed the chancellorship to Ebert, and Scheidemann had proclaimed a republic from a window of the Reichstag. The Kaiser's abdication had come too late to save the monarchy and Imperial Germany was no more. The question that remained open was to what extent and in what shape Germany as a nation would survive.

Conclusion

The hope that the twentieth century would be the German century was shattered irrevocably in 1918. The German *Sonderweg*, which had occasioned so much pride and in the defence of which the Germans fought in 1914, had proved a source of weakness. The strong German state, constitutional, but neither parliamentary nor democratic, was at the core of the Sonderweg and much of the blame for Imperial Germany's failure is attributed to it. The inability of the German political system to cope with modernity became most evident during the war. Thorsten Veblen in 1915 described Germany as a technocracy unwilling to pay the democratic price for modernity, and this explanatory model retains validity. Bismarck facilitated the survival of the pre-industrial, military feudal Prussian state, and social groups like the Junkers used these facilities to ensure their grip on power and privilege long after this had become an anachronism. Political movements which did represent sections of the rapidly developing mass society, the Centre party, the SPD, even the Conservatives with their *Bund der Landwirte,* blocked each other and con-tented themselves with remaining in the antechamber of power. They were as up to date as anything to be found elsewhere in Europe or North America in the techniques of mass mobilization, but they did not use this leverage to reform the system. They believed in the German Sonderweg, that the Reich in the centre of Europe had to be a *Machtstaat* and should not be weakened by the disunity endemic to democracy.

The roots of the Sonderweg went deeper than politics. Inwardness, soul, spirit were seen by the German middle classes as the source of true *Kultur,* while institutions, organizations, the distribution of power, were regarded as being played out on a lower plane. The educated German, the *Bildungsbürger,* sought 'high culture', but did not dirty his hands with politics. He searched for the organic, the vital, the truth beyond reason; he despised the pragmatic, the commonsensical; he feared the masses. He averted his eyes from the conflict of sectional interests and parties and from the grasping greed of the market place. He sat back waiting for the charismatic leader, the hero who could make it all chime together. Such attitudes were not unique to Germany, but for the Germans they invested their semi-autocratic system, regarded in the west as retrograde, with unique value. It was a mentality that fostered dislike of modernity, with its concomitant values of equality, individualism and democracy. The German middle classes in the imperial era were torn to an exceptional degree between anti-modernism and the mainly materialist belief in the manifest destiny of their nation. Modernity was an exceptional problem in Germany in any case, for it came so quickly. The losers were nostalgic, backward-looking, an easy prey to anti-liberal ideologies. Both the seekers after 'high culture' and the resentful losers were paranoid in looking for enemies, socialists, Jews, the perverters of the race. Insecurity about nationhood only recently achieved required enemies, *Reichsfeinde*, to cement it. A whole cluster of mentalities thus provides some explanation for the lack of realism about their country's situation that pervaded large sections of the German public. After Bismarck there was no one who could provide an adequate check and even the Iron Chancellor had found it increasingly difficult in his latter years.

It is therefore doubtful if a change in the political system itself, such as seemed sometimes imminent in the decade before 1914, would have preserved Germany from disaster. When in the 1960s the German historian Fritz Fischer wrote about the extent of German chauvinism and annexationism around 1914 his critics often pointed out that German official policy was more sober and realistic, defensive rather than offensive. But even before the outbreak of war German hegemonic aspirations had wide support, had seeped into most of the political parties and were well represented in the Reichstag. If the SPD had been positively rather than negatively integrated, through a parliamentarized political system, it would not necessarily have proved an effective barrier to the pursuit of *Weltpolitik*. The hold which such ideas had was made evident in the war aims debate after 1914 and with the emergence of Hindenburg and Ludendorff they became official policy. These leaders retained the confidence of most of the German public as late as the summer of 1918. Even the Bethmann Hollweg concept, informal hegemony through industrial pre-eminence, would have been in its practical execution, as outlined in his programme of September 1914, too threatening to Germany's neighbours to be acceptable. Germany was not strong enough for hegemony or even semi-hegemony. In power-political terms she would have needed to impose upon herself a kind of self-denying ordinance, akin to Bismarck's notion of a satisfied power. No such self-denying ordinance was forthcoming from the other major European powers either, but they were in possession, Germany was the newcomer. It is easy to see with hindsight that Germany should, as she became a major industrial and economic power, have seen herself as a trading nation operating in an open international system. It required two world wars to convert the Germans to that view, which had few historical roots in the German experience. *Weltmacht oder Niedergang* was an unreal and unnecessary dilemma.

Appendix: Tables

Table 1 Completed railway lines (in km)

Year	Germany	Great Britain
1850	5,856	9,797
1871	21,471	21,558
1891	43,424	27,902
1913	63,378	32,623

Table 2 Employment by sectors (in thousands)

	1867		1913		Growth
Primary (agriculture, forestry, fisheries)	8,333	51.5%	10,701	34.5%	28.4%
Secondary (industry, mining, crafts)	4,380	27.1%	11,720	37.8%	167.6%
Tertiary (services, transport, etc.)	3,458	21.4%	8,547	27.6%	147.2%

Table 3 Population (in thousands)

Land	1849	1875	1910
Prussia	20,431	25,742	40,165
Bavaria	4,485	5,022	6,887
Saxony	1,894	2,761	4,807
Württemberg	1,745	1,882	2,437
Baden	1,363	1,507	2,143
Hessen	812	884	1,282
Hamburg	221	389	1,015
Alsace-Lorraine	1,569	1,532	1,874
German Reich (as in 1910)	35,128	42,727	64,926

Table 4 Population growth of major cities (in thousands)

	1850	1880	1900	1910
Berlin	419	1,122	1,889	3,730
Hamburg	132	290	706	932
Munich	110	230	500	595
Leipzig	63	149	456	588
Dresden	97	221	396	547
Cologne	97	145	373	516
Breslau	114	273	423	512
Frankfurt a.M.	65	137	289	415
Düsseldorf	27	95	214	358

Table 5 Electoral participation in Prussia in the three Classes 1849–1913 in per cent

Year	Class I	Class II	Class III	Total
1849	55.4	44.7	28.6	31.9
1855	39.6	27.2	37.1	16.1
1858	50.2	37.1	18.5	22.6
1861	55.8	42.4	23.0	27.2
1862	61.0	48.0	30.5	34.3
1863	57.0	44.0	27.3	30.9
1866	60.4	47.5	27.6	30.4
1867	41.2	28.3	14.8	17.6
1893	48.13	32.05	15.21	18.40
1898	46.22	30.65	15.67	18.36
1903	49.24	34.27	21.08	23.62
1908	53.48	42.89	30.18	32.84
1913	51.42	41.85	29.90	32.74

No reliable figures are available for elections held between 1867 and 1893.

Table 6 Parties in the Prussian Chamber of Deputies (the lower house of the Landtag) 1870–1913

Year	Total	Conservative	Free Conservative	National Liberal	Progressive	Centre	SPD	Others
1870	432	114	41	134	49	58	–	36
1873	432	30	35	177	68	88	–	34
1876	433	41	35	169	63	89	–	36
1879	433	110	51	104	38	97	–	33
1882	433	122	57	66	53	99	–	36
1885	433	133	62	72	40	98	–	28
1888	433	129	64	86	29	98	–	27
1893	433	144	65	84	20	95	–	25
1898	433	145	59	71	35	100	–	23
1903	433	143	60	79	33	97	–	21
1908	443	152	60	65	36	104	7	19
1913	443	148	54	73	40	–	10	15

Table 7 Index of wages and cost of living 1871–1913 (1895 = 100)

Year	Nominal wages	Cost of living	Real wages
1871	70	106	66
1875	98	113	87
1880	82	104	79
1885	87	99	88
1890	98	102	96
1895	100	100	100
1900	118	106	111
1905	128	112	114
1910	147	124	119
1913	163	130	125

Table 8 German industrial growth 1870–1913 (1913 = 100)

Year	Metals	Coal	Transport	Construction	Textiles	Total industry	Total production
1870	7.5	13.9	8.9	20.1	31.9	18.8	29.2
1880	13.9	24.7	16.1	29.0	40.1	26.1	36.5
1890	23.8	36.9	27.9	45.6	65.0	39.9	48.7
1900	47.5	57.5	50.1	67.0	72.8	61.4	68.4
1913	100.0	100.0	100.0	100.0	100.0	100.0	100.0

Table 9 Results of Reichstag elections 1871–1912

	1871		1874		1877		1878		1881		1884		1887	
	%	Seats	%	Seats	%	Seats	%	Seats	%	Seats	%	Seats	%	Seats
Conservative	14.1	57	6.9	22	9.7	40	13.0	59	16.3	50	15.2	78	15.2	80
Free Conservative	8.9	37	7.2	33	7.9	38	13.6	57	7.4	28	6.9	28	9.8	41
National Liberals	30.1	125	29.7	155	27.2	128	23.1	99	23.1	93	17.6	51	22.3	99
Progressives	9.3	47	9.0	50	8.5	39	7.7	29	14.7	69	19.3	74	14.1	32
Centre	18.6	63	27.9	91	24.8	93	23.1	94	23.2	100	22.6	99	20.1	98
SPD	3.2	2	6.8	9	9.1	12	7.6	9	6.1	12	9.7	24	10.1	11
Others	15.8	51	7.9	22	8.9	32	8.6	35	6.1	30	5.6	28	5.3	21
Alsace			4.5	15	3.7	15	3.1	15	3.0	15	2.9	15	3.1	15
Voting/seats	51	382	61.2	397	60.6	397	63.4	397	56.3	397	60.6	397	77.5	397

Table 9 (continued)

	1890		1893		1898		1903		1907		1912	
	%	Seats	%	Seats	%	Seats	%	Seats	%	Seats	%	Seats
Conservative	12.4	73	13.5	72	11.1	56	10.0	54	9.4	60	9.2	43
Free Conser- vative	6.7	20	5.7	28	4.4	23	3.5	21	4.2	24	3.0	14
National Liberal	16.3	42	13.0	53	12.5	46	13.9	51	14.5	54	13.6	45
Progressives	18.0	76	14.8	48	11.1	49	9.3	36	10.9	49	12.3	42
Centre	18.6	106	19.1	96	18.8	102	19.8	100	19.4	105	16.4	91
SPD	19.7	35	23.3	44	27.2	56	31.7	81	28.9	43	34.8	110
Others	6.9	45	9.7	48	12.9	55	10.7	45	11.8	55	9.3	43
Alsace	1.4	10	1.5	8	1.4	10	1.1	9	0.9	7	1.3	9
Voting/Seats	71.6	397	72.5	397	68.1	397	76.1	397	84.7	397	84.9	397

Progressives includes all left liberals as well as the German People's Party (Deutsche Volkspartei) throughout. The Secessionists are included with the National Liberals for the only election they fought independently, 1881. Others includes Poles, Guelphs, Danes and Anti-Semites. Up to 1878 it also includes independent liberals.

The figures show the percentage of votes cast and the number of seats obtained by each party. The final row shows the proportion of voters who participated and the number of seats in the Reichstag.

Table 10 Some comparisons between Great Britain and Germany

	GDP per man-hour (1970 US$)		Coal production (million tons)		Steel production (million tons)	
	1870	1913	1890	1913	1890	1913
Great Britain	0.80	1.35	184,000	292,000	2,195	6,903
Germany	0.43	0.95	70,200	191,500	3,579	18,654

Table 11 State indebtedness and inflation during the First World War

		1914	1915	1916	1917	1918	1914–18
Germany (billion mk)	Expenditure	8.8	25.8	27.8	52.2	44.4	159.0
	Revenue	2.5	1.8	2.1	8.0	7.4	21.8
	Deficit	6.3	24.0	25.7	44.2	37.0	137.2
France (billion fr)	Expenditure	10.4	22.1	36.8	44.7	56.6	170.6
	Revenue	4.2	4.1	4.9	6.2	6.8	26.2
	Deficit	6.2	18.0	31.9	38.5	49.8	144.4
Great Britain (million £)	Expenditure	560	1,560	2,200	2,700	2,580	9,600
	Revenue	230	340	570	710	890	2,740
	Deficit	330	1,220	1,630	1,990	1,690	6,860

Suggestions for further reading

A large literature in English is available on the unification of Germany and on Imperial Germany. American and British historians have made original contributions to the subject and some of these titles are cited below.

General

There are two relevant volumes in the *Oxford History of Modern Europe*, J. J. Sheehan, *German History, 1770–1866* (1989) and G. A. Craig, *Germany, 1866–1945* (1978). Others include V. R. Berghahn, *Imperial Germany, 1871–1914: Economy, Society, Culture and Politics* (1994), and D. Blackbourn, *Germany in the 19th Century* (1994) and *The Fontana History of Germany 1780–1918. The Long Nineteenth Century* (1997). W. J. Mommsen, *Imperial Germany, 1867–1918* (1995) covers the subjects in a series of essays.

The Historiographical Debate

The classic statement of the post-1945, largely negative view of Imperial Germany was H.-U. Wehler, *The German Empire 1871–1918* (English translation, 1984). Important contributions to the Sonderweg debate are: G. Eley and D. Blackbourn, *The Peculiarities of German History: Bourgeois Society and Politics in Nineteenth-Century Germany* (1984); R. J. Evans, *Rethinking German History* (1987); G. Eley, *From Unification to Nazism. Reinterpreting the German Past* (1992); J. Kocka, 'German history before Hitler. The debate about the German "Sonderweg"', *J. Contemp. Hist.*, 23 (1988), 3–18. A valuable overview is provided by R. Chickering (ed.), *Imperial Germany: A Historiographical Companion* (1996).

The Unification Process

The important older works by T. S. Hamerow, *Restoration, Revolution, Reaction. Economics and Politics in Germany, 1815–1871* (1958) and *The Social Foundations of German Unification, 1858–1871*, 2 vols (1969, 1972) remain very useful. J. J. Sheehan, *German Liberalism in the Nineteenth Century* (1978) is a standard work. Of Otto Pflanze's three volumes on *Bismarck and the Development of Germany*, the first volume *The Period of Unification, 1815–71* (2nd edn, 1990) is indispensable. J. Breuilly, *The Formation of the First German Nation State, 1800–1871* (1996) is an excellent survey. D. E. Barclay, *Frederick William IV and the Prussian Monarchy, 1840–1861* (1995) gives an insight into Prussian politics before Bismarck. The international aspect of German unification is well dealt with in W. Carr,

The Origins of the Wars of German Unification (1991), and W. E. Mosse, *The European Powers and the German Question, 1848–1871* (1958) remains important, as does M. Howard, *The Franco-Prussian War* (1961). D. G. Williamson, *Bismarck and Germany 1862–1890* (2nd edn, 1998) provides a succinct summary with documents. Essential documentation, particularly on foreign policy, is also to be found in W. N. Medlicott and D. Coveney (eds), *Bismarck and Europe* (1971). There is a large literature on nationalism and the emergence of the German identity, for example H. Schulze, *The Course of German Nationalism – From Frederick the Great to Bismarck 1763–1867* (1990), or H. James, *A German Identity 1770– 1990* (1989). A German classic, Meinecke's *Weltbürgertum und Nationalstaat*, first published in 1907, which analyses the emergence of German nationalism in the nineteenth century, is available in an English translation, F. Meinecke, *Cosmopolitanism and the National State* (1970). For an introduction to the economic background to unification, see M. Kitchen, *The Political Economy of Germany 1815–1914* (1978), W. O. Henderson, *The Zollverein* (1959) and *The Rise of German Industrial Power 1834–1914* (1975).

Bismarck

Recent biographies available in English include L. Gall, *Bismarck. The White Revolutionary*, vol. I: 1815–71, vol. II: 1871–98 (1986), an English translation of the standard modern German biography. E. Crankshaw, *Bismarck* (1981) and A. Palmer, *Bismarck* (1976) are readable biographies, G. O. Kent, *Bismarck and His Times* (1978) is valuable, and B. Waller, *Bismarck* (1985) provides a short survey in the Historical Association series. Among older books A. J. P. Taylor, *Bismarck* (1955) and E. Eyck, *Bismarck and the German Empire* (English trs., 1950) remain the most interesting. The two later volumes of O. Pflanze's *Bismarck and the Development of Germany*, vol. II: *The Period of Consolidation*, and vol. III: *The Period of Fortification* (1990) are standard works. The role played by Bismarck's banker Bleichröder in the personal and public activities of the chancellor were brought to light by F. Stern in *Gold and Iron: Bismarck, Bleichröder, and the Building of the German Empire* (1977).

The Empire in the Bismarck Era

In addition to the titles cited above, especially the relevant chapters in W. J. Mommsen, *Imperial Germany*, the constitutional structure is discussed in W. Carr, *A History of Germany 1815–1985* (3rd edn, 1987) and H. W. Koch, *A Constitutional History of Germany in the Nineteenth and Twentieth Centuries* (1984). G. Martel (ed.), *Modern Germany Reconsidered* (1992) is a useful collection of essays. A great deal is available in English on elections and parties: K. Rohe, *Elections, Parties and Political Traditions. Social Foundations of German Parties and Party Systems 1867–1987* (1990); L. E. Jones and J. Retallack (eds), *Elections, Mass Politics and Social Change in Modern Germany: New Perspectives* (1992). On specific parties: D. S. White, *The Splintered Party: National Liberalism in Hessen and the Reich, 1867–1918* (1976); S. Zucker, *Ludwig Bamberger* (1975); M. L. Anderson, *Windthorst. A Political Biography* (1981); E. L. Evans, *The German Center Party 1870–1933. A Study in Political Catholicism* (1981); J. N. Retallack, *Notables of the Right. The Conservative Party and Political Mobilization in Germany, 1876–1918* (1988); L. E. Jones and J. Retallack (eds), *Between Reform, Reaction and Resistance. Studies in the History of German Conservatism* (1993); H. Grebing, *The History of the German Labour Movement* (rev. edn, 1985); W. L. Guttsman, *The German Social Democratic Party, 1875–1933: From Ghetto to Government* (1981); V. L. Lidtke, *The Outlawed Party. Social Democracy in Germany, 1878–1890*

(1966); J. A. Moses, *German Trade Unionism from Bismarck to Hitler*, vol. I (1982); R. J. Evans, *Proletarians and Politics. Socialism, Protest and the Working Class in Germany* (1990). Other aspects are covered in: W. J. Mommsen (ed.), *The Emergence of the Welfare State in Britain and Germany* (1981); P. Hennock, *British Social Policy and German Precedents* (1987); I. N. Lambi, *Free Trade and Protection in Germany, 1868–1879* (1963). On foreign policy I. Geiss, *German Foreign Policy, 1871–1914* (1976), G. F. Kennan, *The Decline of Bismarck's European Order* (1979) and P. M. Kennedy, *The Rise of the Anglo-German Antagonism, 1860–1914* (1980) provide overviews for this period. On the beginnings of German colonialism, see S. Förster, W. J. Mommsen, R. Robinson (eds), *Bismarck, Europe, and Africa. The Berlin Conference 1884–1885 and the Onset of Partition* (1988).

Social and Cultural Issues

There is a wealth of literature on many aspects: L. Abrams, *Workers' Culture in Imperial Germany* (1991); V. L. Lidtke, *The Alternative Culture. The Socialist Labor movement in Imperial Germany* (1985); R. J. Evans, *Death in Hamburg: Society and Politics in the Cholera Years, 1830–1910* (1987); M. Lamberti, *State, Society and the Elementary School in Imperial Germany* (1989); S. Volkov, *The Rise of Popular Antimodernism in Germany: The Urban Master Artisans 1873–1896* (1978); C. E. McClelland, *The German Experience of Professionalization: Learned Professions and their Organization from the early 19th Century to the Hitler Era* (1991); D. Blackbourn and R. J. Evans (eds), *The German Bourgeoisie. Essays on the Social History of the German Middle Class from the Late Eighteenth to the Early Twentieth Century* (1991); J. R. Dukes and J. Remak (eds), *Another Germany: A Reconsideration of the Imperial Era* (1988); W. E. Mosse, *Jews in the German Economy. The German-Jewish Economic Elite 1820–1935* (1987); M. A. Kaplan, *The Making of the Jewish Middle Class in Imperial Germany* (1991); P. J. Pulzer, *The Rise of Political Anti-Semitism in Germany and Austria* (1964); G. Iggers, *The German Conception of History: The National Tradition of Historical Thought from Herder to the Present* (1968); and, significant on modernism in art, P. Paret, *The Berlin Secession* (1980).

Wilhelmine Germany

William II has attracted much attention from historians, including J. G. C. Röhl and N. Sombart (eds) *Kaiser Wilhelm II: New Interpretations* (1982), I. Hull, *The Entourage of Kaiser Wilhelm II* (1982), M. Balfour, *The Kaiser and his Times* (1964), J. G. C. Röhl, *Young Wilhelm. The Kaiser's Early Life, 1859–1888* (1998) and L. Cecil, *William II: Emperor and Exile* (1996). On the chancellors, see K. A. Lerman, *The Chancellor as Courtier. Bernhard von Bülow and the Governance of Germany, 1900–1909* (1990) and K. H. Jarausch, *The Enigmatic Chancellor. Bethmann Hollweg and the Hubris of Imperial Germany* (1973). On politics generally: J. G. C. Röhl, *Germany without Bismarck: The Crisis in Government in the Second Reich 1890–1900* (1967); G. Eley, *Reshaping the German Right: Radical Nationalism and Political Change after Bismarck* (1980) showed that organized chauvinism was a force not wholly amenable to manipulation by the political establishment; R. Chickering, *We Men Who Feel Most German* (1984) is the standard work on the Pan-German League; see also P. M. Kennedy and A. J. Nicholls (eds), *Nationalist and Racialist Movements in Britain and Germany before 1914* (1981); B. Heckart, *From Bassermann to Bebel* (1974) over-estimates the solidity of this alignment; C. E. Schorske, *German Social Democracy, 1905–1917: The Development of the Great Schism* (1955) remains valuable, see also J. P. Nettle, *Rosa Luxemburg*, 2 vols (1966), and S. Pierson, *Marxist Intellectuals and the Working Class*

Mentality in Germany 1887–1902 (1993). For the Centre party D. Blackbourn, *Class, Religion and Local Politics in Wilhelmine Germany. The Centre party in Württemberg before 1914* (1980) is essential; see also R. J. Ross, *Beleaguered Tower. The Dilemma of Political Catholicism in Wilhelmine Germany* (1976). On the anti-Semitic parties there is R. S. Levy, *The Downfall of the Anti-Semitic Political Parties in Imperial Germany* (1975). Other political issues are discussed in W. W. Hagen, *Germans, Poles and Jews. The Nationality Conflict in the Prussian East, 1772–1914* (1980); R. Blanke, *Prussian Poland in the German Empire 1871–1900* (1981); D. P. Silverman, *Reluctant Union. Alsace-Lorraine and Imperial Germany 1871–1918* (1972); and D. Schoenbaum, *Zabern 1913: Consensus Politics in Imperial Germany* (1982).

Social and Cultural Issues After 1890

R. J. Evans (ed.), *Society and Politics in Wilhelmine Germany* (1978) is a very valuable collection of essays. On the theme of cultural pessimism and the mood of those who felt themselves to be losers in the process of modernization, there is an ample literature, amongst others: F. Stern, *The Politics of Cultural Despair* (1961); R. H. Thomas, *Nietzsche in German Politics and Society, 1890–1918* (1983); R. Gellately, *The Politics of Economic Despair. Shopkeepers and German Politics 1890–1914* (1974). Other specific aspects are covered in: R. J. Evans, *The Feminist Movement in Germany, 1894–1933* (1976); W. Z. Laqueur, *Young Germany* (1962) and P. D. Stachura, *The German Youth Movement 1900–45* (1981); F. K. Ringer, *The Decline of the German Mandarins: The German Academic Community 1890–1933* (1969).

Foreign Policy, Military and Naval Affairs

German foreign policy after Bismarck and the causes of the First World War have attracted more attention from historians than almost anything else. In the inter-war period the energies of the German historical profession were concentrated on rebutting the charge of German war guilt. A great challenge to orthodox German opinion arose with the publication of Fritz Fischer's *Griff nach der Weltmacht* in 1961, translated into English as *Germany's Aims in the First World War* (1967). The historiographical debate is discussed in J. A. Moses, *The Politics of Illusion: The Fischer Controversy in German Historiography* (1975). Fischer published a further book *War of Illusions: German Policies from 1911 to 1914* (1975). Here are a few among many titles: L. L. Farrar Jr., *Arrogance and Anxiety. The Ambivalence of German Power, 1848–1914* (1981); J. Lowe, *The Great Powers, Imperialism and the German Problem, 1865–1925* (1994); P. M. Kennedy (ed.), *The War Plans of the Great Powers, 1880–1914* (1979); G. Barraclough, *From Agadir to Armageddon. Anatomy of a Crisis* (1982); G. Schöllgen (ed.), *Escape into War?* (1990); V. R. Berghahn, *Germany and the Approach of War in 1914* (1974); K. Wilson (ed.), *Decisions for War, 1914* (1995); D. G. Herrmann, *The Arming of Europe and the Making of the First World War* (1996); D. Stevenson, *Armaments and the Coming of War in Europe* (1996). Books dealing with the army and navy and the political influence of their leaders include: W. Deist (ed.), *The German Military in the Age of Total War* (1985); M. Kitchen, *The German Officer Corps 1890–1914* (1968); J. Steinberg, *Yesterday's Deterrent. Tirpitz and the Birth of the German Battle Fleet* (1965); H. H. Herwig, *'Luxury' Fleet. The Imperial German Navy 1888–1918* (1984).

The First World War

There are two good recent overviews, R. Chickering, *Imperial Germany and the Great War, 1914–1918* (1998) and H. H. Herwig, *The First World War: Germany and Austria-Hungary, 1914–1918* (1997). Some of the military and strategic issues are discussed in A. Buchholz, *Moltke, Schlieffen and Prussian War Planning* (1991); G. Ritter, *The Schlieffen Plan* (1958); J. Snyder, *The Ideology of the Offensive* (1984); L. L. Farrar, *The Short-War Illusion: German Policy, Strategy, and Domestic Affairs, August–December 1914* (1973); N. Stone, *The Eastern Front, 1914–1917* (1975); D. Showalter, *Tannenberg: Clash of Empires* (1991). On the commanders: C. Barnett, *The Sword-Bearers: Supreme Command in the First World War* (1963); R. B. Asprey, *The German High Command at War: Hindenburg and Ludendorff and the First World War* (1991). On politics, in addition to titles cited above: M. Kitchen, *The Silent Dictatorship. The Politics of the German High Command under Hindenburg and Ludendorff 1916–1918* (1976); K. Epstein, *Matthias Erzberger and the Dilemma of German Democracy* (1959); D. Morgan, *The Socialist Left and the German Revolution: A History of the German Independent Social Democratic Party, 1917–1922* (1975); A. J. Ryder, *The German Revolution of 1918: A Study of German Socialism in War and Revolt* (1967); E. J. Feuchtwanger, *From Weimar to Hitler: Germany 1918–33* (2nd edn, 1995). On society and economy: J. Kocka, *Facing Total War: German Society, 1914–1918* (1984); G. Feldman, *Army, Industry and Labor in Germany, 1914–1918* (1966) and, more recently, *The Great Disorder: Politics, Economics and Society in the German Inflation, 1914–1924* (1993); W. J. Mommsen, 'German Artists, Writers and Intellectuals and the Meaning of War, 1914–1918', in J. Horne (ed.), *State, Society and Mobilization in Europe during the First World War* (1997).

Index

Note: Bold page numbers refer to the Appendix tables (pp. 199–202).